Everyday and Prophetic

Everyday and Prophetic

The Poetry of Lowell, Ammons, Merrill, and Rich

Nick Halpern

THE UNIVERSITY OF WISCONSIN PRESS

The University of Wisconsin Press
1930 Monroe Street
Madison, Wisconsin 53711

www.wisc.edu/wisconsinpress/

3 Henrietta Street
London WC2E 8LU, England

Printed in the United States of America

Library of Congress Cataloging-in-Publication Data

Halpern, Nick.
   Everyday and prophetic : the poetry of Lowell, Ammons, Merrill, and
   Rich / Nick Halpern.
   p. cm.
   Includes bibliographical references and index.
   ISBN 0-299-17340-2 (alk. paper)
   1. American poetry—20th century—History and criticism. 2. Lowell, Robert,
1917–1977—Themes, motives. 3. Ammons, A. R., 1926—Themes, motives. 4. Merrill,
James Ingram—Themes, motives. 5. Rich, Adrienne Cecile—Themes, motives.
6. Prophecies in literature. 7. Self in literature. I. Title.
PS323.5 .H35   2002
811'.509384—dc21   2002153278

Permissions to reprint the poetry in this book will be found on page 294,
which is to be considered as an extension of this copyright page.

Publication of this book has been made possible in part by the generous support
of the Anonymous Fund of the University of Wisconsin–Madison.

Contents

Acknowledgments

I am profoundly grateful for Helen Vendler's advice and support during every phase of the writing of this book. Her generosity and encouragement have been a tremendous help to me, and I cannot thank her enough. I would also like to acknowledge the enormous benefit I derived from Elaine Scarry's extensive comments and suggestions.

For their help and encouragement I would also like to thank Tom Reinert, Joyce Van Dyke, Leo Damrosch, John Burt, Laura Quinney, Billy Flesch, MaryJo Marks, Rei Terada, Jenny Weil, Scott Stevens, Willard Spiegelman, Jane Hedley, Seamus Heaney, Denis Donoghue, Allen Grossman, A. R. Ammons, Vernon Shetley, Stephen Burt, Kristen Poole, Martin Brückner, Bud Kliment, Elaine Orr, Tom Hester, Linda Holley, Jon Thompson, Allen Stein, Eyal Amiran, Mike Grimwood, Matthew Vollmer, Kelly Pender, Ella Quinn Long, Haven Kimmel, Julie Cooper, Amy Eisner, Wynn Thomas, Hugh Mason, Cal Mason, Chuck Stigliano, Stephanie Mahon Stigliano, Tamar Udovitch, Linda Quasebarth, Tracy Grayson, Stefanie von Clemm, Alan Fitch, David Wondrich, Kyoko Miyabe, Emily Kunreuther, Daphne Rosenblitt, Betsy Halpern, Jeff Halpern, Tamara Halpern, Tia Halpern, Josh Halpern, and Manfred Halpern. Maile Meloy was indispensible. I would like to thank the audiences at the MLA conventions in Washington, D.C., and San Francisco for responding to earlier versions of the arguments made in these pages. I am grateful to the audience at the National Poetry Foundation conference on American Poets of the 1950s in Orono, Maine. I would also like to thank the *Centennial Review* for publishing an earlier version of the chapter on Robert Lowell. I am grateful to Blythe Woolston for the index. The two anonymous readers for the University of Wisconsin Press made very helpful suggestions. I am grateful for the help of David Bethea, Sheila Moermond, Janneke van de Stadt, and Adam Mehring at the University of Wisconsin Press.

William Halpern and Paula Halpern have my deepest gratitude and love.

Finally, I would like to express my gratitude to Elizabeth Kunreuther for our conversations and for her constant encouragement. The extraordinary quickness of her mind and the depth of her insights have made this a better book. The book is dedicated to her.

Everyday and Prophetic

Introduction

This is a book about the tension between the prophetic voice and the everyday voice in postwar and contemporary American poetry. The relationship between these voices is, as the prophetic poet Allen Grossman writes, "a problem which I do not believe to be the problem merely of people who write poems."[1] This tension is, in other words, likely to be already present in readers of poetry, something that they recognize. Most people want to have access to plausible versions of both voices. We want a version of an elevated voice that feels authentic, memorable, and persuasive rather than pretentious, forgettable, and impossible to believe. Similarly, no reader is likely to be drawn toward every voice that offers itself as an everyday voice. Some versions we may find sentimental, derivative, bullying, possible to believe but impossible to remember, and difficult to care about. Everyday voices and prophetic voices must be convincing in poems: it is crucial, as Louise Glück puts it, "to get the poem right, to get it memorable."[2] The disappointment we feel when either voice goes wrong is particularly sharp. We have a stake in both of them.

Readers may also feel that such voices ought not to be mutually exclusive in a poet's repertoire, that something crucial is missing in a poet's career if one of these voices is missing. Why shouldn't a poet be fluent in both? The voices, however, cannot simply be thrown into the poem and left to fend for themselves: anthologies are full of poems in which no one part of the poem seems to know much about any other. I said that when either voice goes wrong the reader may experience a feeling of disappointment. It is as if there is a resource—of feeling, of thought, of language—about which the poet pretends to know nothing. The reader is abandoned to the old guides. At the same time, a tremendous excitement gathers in poems in which the prophetic and everyday voices work together. It is difficult to imagine another problem related to voice in poetry that is more urgent to contemporary poets and readers of contemporary poetry. This book is about efforts to do justice to both voices, and it is itself an attempt to do justice to the intricacies of the relationship.

The Prophetic Voice

By prophetic I do not mean an ability to see the future. Twentieth-century prophetic poets may communicate a sense of vague dread about the future, but they certainly claim no special ability to predict it. Joseph Wittreich writes that "the prophet, often thought to foretell the future, more exactly attempts to fashion it."[3] It may help to define what I mean by the prophetic voice if I say at once that, among twentieth-century poets, Rainer Maria Rilke, William Butler Yeats, Ezra Pound, T. S. Eliot, H.D., Conrad Aiken, Hart Crane, Robinson Jeffers, Robert Penn Warren, Allen Ginsberg, Geoffrey Hill, Audre Lorde, and Allen Grossman have written much of their poetry in the prophetic voice.

To refer to the prophetic voice is to evoke related poetic enterprises: the "mystic," "visionary," and "bardic" voices. It is important to remark that this is a situation where, to borrow Ludwig Wittgenstein's language in *Philosophical Investigations*, "similarities crop up and disappear." Wittgenstein writes about a "complicated network of similarities overlapping and criss-crossing: sometimes overall similarities, sometimes similarities of detail." The term he uses for this "network of similarities" is "family resemblance," by which he means "the various resemblances between members of a family: build, features, colour of eyes, gait, temperament, etc. etc. [that] overlap and criss-cross in the same way."[4] I invoke Wittgenstein here to emphasize that I do not think of the prophetic, mystical, visionary, and bardic voices as interchangeable, as if they all named one sort of poetry that a reader could then dismiss or endorse. There are poets who are compelled to write mystical poetry, for example, just as there are poets who must write prophetic poetry.

My major emphasis in this book is on the relationship between the prophetic and the everyday, not between other sorts of elevated voices and the everyday voice. Why should the prophetic be the central term rather than the mystic or the visionary? The prophetic is my focus because of the peculiar urgency of its relationship to the everyday.

Prophetic poets in our own time no longer have the relationship with God that their predecessors had and may not even have a belief in God. They still, nevertheless, have a mission, and that mission feels assigned to them simply by their consciousness of the *sound* of the prophetic voice. Helen Sword writes that "prophetic discourse" refers to "any mode of speech or writing that lays claim to prophetic authority by echoing traditionally prophetic cadences or appropriating prophetic language and imagery."[5] The prophetic poet of our time may echo the biblical prophets and may make use of the vocabulary and images we associate with them.[6] But prophetic poetry is, in our own time, chiefly about its relationship to the everyday. The everyday is what the prophetic poets focus on, that is what fills them with rage, that is what they want to transform. The prophetic poets tell us that we must give up our reliance on the everyday, with its life lessons and consolation prizes. In Rainer Maria Rilke's poem "Archaic Torso of Apollo," the statue seems to say to us, "You must change your life."[7] This is what the prophetic poets, in a continual rage (which may distract them from anxiety about the source of their authority), want to say to us: "You must change your life." Rilke's poem ends with those words, as if they were unanswerable. The everyday has its own poets, though, and they have their own way of talking about how change happens in a life. James Merrill, in a late poem, "Bronze," wittily suggests a possible response to Rilke's archaic speaker.

> Expect no
> Epiphany such as the torso
> In Paris provided for Rilke. Quit
> Dreaming of change. It is happening
> Whether you like it or not,
> So get on with your lives.[8]

Two kinds of speech, two "speech genres."

Speech Genres

When I discuss the prophetic and the everyday, I refer to something I variously call voice, tone, rhetoric, discourse, speech genre. The term *speech genre* is taken from Mikhail Bakhtin, who writes, "We learn to cast our speech in generic forms and, when hearing others' speech, we guess its genre from the very first words; we predict a certain length (that is, the approximate length of the speech whole) and a certain compositional structure; we foresee the end; that is, from the very beginning we have a sense of the speech whole." To think about prophetic speech and everyday speech as speech genres is to be conscious that every prophetic or everyday poem is in relationship to previous versions of its speech genre and that every poet already has, in some sense, a version of such language in his or her head. Bakhtin writes, "When we construct our speech, we are always aware of the whole of our utterance. . . . We do not string words together smoothly and we do not proceed from word to word; rather, it is as though we fill in the whole with the necessary words."9 There is a tension between the poets' own sense that they are proceeding from word to word and the sense that they are simultaneously aware of a "whole" that they are going to fill with words. In this tension lies the possibility of flexibility. The prophetic poets may acknowledge that they speak in a prophetic voice; they are not likely to acknowledge (in their poetry) that they are *using* the prophetic voice. To recognize the existence of speech genres is to get just enough distance from the project to be able to reflect on it and describe it without imperiling it. The possibility of play is introduced without undermining the possibility of authority. Without such recognitions by the poet, large areas of experience will be missing, and it will be left to readers to acknowledge this absence; such readers, grateful but dissatisfied, will feel that they know something the poet unaccountably does not.

There is a variety of other speech genres prevalent in contemporary poetry. Love poets and political poets, for example, use other speech genres, though, of course, all of them are connected in various ways. There is meditative speech as well, which is the speech genre to which Stevens and Ashbery are drawn. Some readers may feel that Stevens ought to be included here as an example of a poet who combines everyday and prophetic voices. I see him instead as a poet who meditates endlessly and often passionately about the relationship between them but will rarely go very far in either direction.

Mystical, Visionary, and Bardic Voices

Abraham Heschel, in his study of the prophets of the Hebrew Bible, stresses the importance of trying, at least, to imagine what was going on inside a prophet's consciousness. He stresses the importance of attempting to understand "what it means to think, feel, respond, and act as a prophet" and adds, "We must think as if we were inside their minds."10 The injunction seems to me valuable and productive in reading the prophetic poets of our time. In my discussion of the mystical, visionary, and bardic voices, I attempt to describe them as they appear in relation to the prophetic poets.

What are the important differences between the mystical poets and the prophetic poets? William James offers certain terms by which to define the mystical state. One of them is *ineffability*. The mystical poets celebrate the experience of oneness with a version of transcendence, and the experience will offer a feeling of truth, though that truth will defy expression. James writes, "The subject of it immediately says that it defies expression, that no adequate report of its contents can be given in words. It follows from this that its quality must be directly experienced; it cannot be imparted or transferred to others."[11] The prophetic poets, on the other hand, do not experience feelings of union. Furthermore, they must give "adequate report," and they must give it in words. Sword writes, "Mystical experience . . . takes place, by definition, outside of language; thus, although mystics do frequently attempt verbal descriptions of their experiences . . . the mystical mode is ultimately antithetical to the poet's craft."[12] Mystical experience does not require expression in language. Prophets, by contrast, are nothing if they do not speak. The mystical poets are often turned away from us, while the prophetic poets are focused on us. There are other differences. The mystical poets may be playful. The prophetic poets' playfulness, if it appears, is likely to seem more estranging to us even than their rage. The mystical poets will find analogies for their experience in sexual intercourse, while prophetic poets who can write about sexuality without disgust are rare. (Walt Whitman and D. H. Lawrence can do it because the divisions between the prophetic and the mystic are fluid in their work. They become mystical when they write about sex and prophetic when they turn again to us.) Isolation represents another difference. The isolation of the mystical poets is comfortable, and they are likely to be content with it. James quotes Saint John of the Cross: "The soul . . . feels as if placed in a vast and profound solitude, to which no created thing has access, in an immense and boundless desert, desert the more delicious the more solitary it is" (444). The prophetic poets' solitude is not delicious. They are voices crying in the wilderness. Intellectually, the mystical poem may be as abstruse as any prophetic poem, but emotionally, it can seem like a welcoming ocean. It is more inviting than the prophetic poem, which is likely to be full of turbulent feeling (rage, incredulity, bitterness). The prophetic and the mystic will seem very close to each other when we think of poets such as Whitman or William Blake, who were able to cross back and forth. But the differences between the two voices are important to bear in mind as well and will become more vivid when we think of two not very gifted versions of each: the prophetic Unabomber, say, and the mystical Kahlil Gibran.

What about the relationship to the everyday? The prophetic poets feel threatened by the everyday but need it. It is their whole reason for being. The prophetic poets' relationship to the everyday may take the form of a kind of call and (inadequate) response; theirs is a voice of ungratified desire. The mystical poets do not need the everyday. They may occupy it, demonstrate (in a bravado display of versatility) their ability to feel at home in it. They can search it for metaphors. But in general, they are not threatened by it. The mystical poets often know how to "perform" everydayness and understand the ways in which self-demystification can deepen the mystery surrounding them. Their sociability makes us marvel and makes their unworldliness seem more formidable by preventing us from seeing it plainly. To the extent that they desire everydayness, their desires are gratified. Prophetic poets, in general, have the opposite of *sprezzatura;* they never make anything look easier than it is. There is little room to maneuver: anything that happens in the poem that is not prophetic endangers the poem. Consider, finally, the relationship to silence. The mystical poets are comfortable with silence. Silence is recurrent, temporary, full of lessons for the mystical poets' readers. If silence descends on the prophetic figure, it is likely to be the kind that descended on John Ruskin and Ezra Pound in their last years.

The term *visionary* can be used in a variety of ways. It can be used to describe the kind of poet who sees visions. There is certainly a "family resemblance" between this kind of visionary poet and the prophetic poet. An important difference is the prophetic poets' sense of what their mission feels like. The prophetic poets may have had visions, and they may write about these visions in their poetry, but they probably do not see it as their lifelong task to write about them. Their speech finds its source in something harder to define and less reliable than a vision. Visions, if modern prophetic poets have had them, will do little to alleviate the sense that *language* is all they have.

Another kind of visionary poetry (more common, probably, in our time) is based on what might be called visionary perception. "If one looks long enough at almost anything," May Sarton writes in her journal, "looks with absolute attention at a flower, a stone, the bark of a tree, grass, snow, a cloud, something like revelation takes place."[13] What is interesting here is the relationship between this kind of visionary perception and the everyday world. Attempts to find "revelation" or "transcendental vision" within the everyday tend to work: everyday objects, as readers of visionary poetry know, are ready, in general, to cooperate in the visionary poets' plans for them. On those occasions when the flower, stone, or tree does not cooperate, poets may take a tone of cheerful haplessness. Charles Altieri refers to the kind of poem that consists of "six perceptions in search of a transcendental vision."[14] Visionaries are not uncomfortable with each other: one can speak of a visionary (but not a prophetic) company.

Another important difference can be found in the relationship to readers. Contemporary mystical and visionary poets tease readers with the sense that they could join the poets' company. What would readers need to do but concentrate very hard on everyday objects? The word "everyday" appears in certain kinds of self-help books nearly as often as it does in works of cultural criticism: we are often being urged to discover the extraordinary in the ordinary, the magical in the commonplace, the transcendent in the everyday. The mystical experience, too, is available to us, to some degree. Raymond Nelson writes, "Students of mysticism generally agree that while mystics are geniuses in applying it, the substance of the mystical experience is common to everyone."[15] What the prophetic poets want is usually not that readers become prophetic poets (although some prophetic poets do want that) but that readers keep themselves in a state of intense attention, sometimes a state of moral or psychological preparedness. What happens next will be moral and not perceptual. Meanwhile, we must stay awake.

Having to stay awake may be less monotonous to some readers than having to be enchanted. Those attracted to prophetic poetry may find mystical and visionary poetry too predictable, too sure of what its success will consist in and of how to achieve that success. For such readers, visionary perception is more likely to be compelling on the rare occasions when they cannot be sure where it will end. "I can look at a knot in a piece of wood," Blake writes, "til I am frightened by it."[16] Many visionary poets look at the knot in the piece of wood until they feel visionary, which is what they understand by happiness. Such happiness is central to both the visionary and the mystic. If the prophetic poets experience happiness, it is not a happiness others will know how to share. It is not likely to be appealing or contagious. The mystic and the visionary experience and communicate a near-childlike happiness. Think of Robert Duncan, of Robert Bly. If visionary and mystic poets are like children, what are prophetic poets like? It is difficult to

say. One version of the prophet—in some ways the most formidable—
is of someone who was a prophet in the womb, who has never lived in
the world except as a prophet. Jeremiah could be offered as an example. There are prophetic poets in our time whose sense of themselves
corresponds to the model suggested by Jeremiah. Other prophets in
the Bible were called upon to become prophets, and their sense of election erases any sense of a childhood. If the prophetic poets were
never—or feel themselves never to have been—children, is it possible
to call them adults? Prophetic poets do not, in general, write about
life's stages and seem not to care much about them. "THE GREAT
SCRIBES EXIST OUT OF TIME IN RADIANCE," one of James Merrill's spirits
tells him in *The Changing Light at Sandover*.[17] The prophetic poets exist
not just outside historical time but personal time as well. The prophetic poets do not generally acknowledge aging or acknowledge that
there once were younger and will soon be older versions of themselves. This is not an evasion; that is, the prophetic poets are not afraid
of growing old or dying. If they can be connected to any stage of life, it
is probably old age. Prophetic poets may take the tones of old men or
women who would like to die; they may sound like Eliot's Sibyl or
Tennyson's Tithonus.

Finally, I want to suggest some differences between the prophetic
poets and the bardic poets. The bards have a following, a tribe. Jeffrey
Walker says of the bardic poet that "his literary tribe encircles him, a
cordon sanitaire between himself and the world his high ambition wants
to change."[18] The prophetic poets, on the other hand, are not conscious
of literary tribes encircling them, nor are they conscious of encouragement or sponsorship; in general, there is nobody to protect or interpret
them, no exegetes or critics or disciples. Here is Allen Grossman on
Hart Crane: "Crane's style requires of his uneasy readers tolerance of
proximity to undefended authenticity and the ability to endure the absurdity of imaginary states of language without ironizing them by a
meaning or dismissing them by a judgment."[19] Readers with the stamina to withstand Crane's "hurricane poetics," his primitive intensity
and harshness, would still have to be able to tolerate his absurdity, that
is, the absurdity of a poet trying, in the absence of God, to be a "prophetic poet." The prophetic poets demand of their readers that they neither interpret (translate into their own language) nor say whether the
prophetic poetry is good or bad, coherent or incoherent. The poets'
readers must simply acknowledge the poetry as authentic and try to
survive in its proximity.

You must change your life, the prophetic poet says. Willing recipients of such commands will probably not be part of a tribe but instead isolated and uneasy, with little invested in the everyday world anyway, people who have lives they *want* to change. Such readers—we might call them prophetic readers—will resemble the prophetic poet in being marginalized, eccentric, lacking access to social resources and recompenses. What the prophets will offer such readers is access to eloquence and seriousness. If nothing else, the prophets can make the readers' outcast state seem literary. Prophetic readers will not be likely to be as surprised by the oddness of the request that they change their lives as other readers might be. Other readers might expect those who tell them to change their lives (therapists, for example) to rely heavily on the rhetoric of the everyday, and they expect to be told to make their lives a little bit more like everyday lives. This is not what the prophetic poets ask their readers to do. When we are told, in everyday life, to change our lives, we expect to hear some compassion or tenderness in the request. The prophetic poets offer nothing like this. Their detachment is not professional or clinical. They will do nothing to win readers, nothing to keep them. They have no interest in a tribe but desire the ear of *all* readers, the complacent readers especially. (They want even the people who read everyday poets, though they have no way to attract them.)

The bardic poets do not tell readers to change their lives. For Terrence Des Pres, the bards speak on behalf of the "real." The bards insist that "the real is unavoidable" and that all readers must be made to feel "the press of the real."[20] This is not the same, necessarily, as changing your life. Generally, it involves collective political action rather than a kind of solitary transformation. Walker judges the failure of his bardic poets by the failure of their rhetoric. He writes that they "seek an extraordinary power over the public consciousness" and that the bardic poets' desire is "ultimately to alter and direct the national will" (5, xi). When the bards say "you" they are often thinking of a people, a nation, and when they talk of change they are thinking of great political and cultural changes. The prophetic poets may write profoundly political poems: the prophetic voice in poetry has, of course, a long and fascinating connection with the political voice.[21] They are unlikely, though, to engage in political argument. The bardic poets may not stoop to argue, but they do enter what might be called political space. They want to persuade. The prophetic poets may cry out, chant, announce, command, explain, or accuse, but they do not try to persuade. The bards think in terms of a tribe and a nation; they want to try to persuade first one group, then the other. Walker writes that passages of the bardic Whitman work only "if the reader already has a sensibility so transcendental that the poet's declarations can pass for truism— or unless the commanding self-assurance of Whitman's tone is in itself a sufficient bluff" (21). The prophet's chief concerns, on the other hand, tend to be linguistic ones. Achieving a "commanding self-assurance of tone" can feel as if it were almost the whole battle. The prophetic poets are, as I said, not conscious of followers. There is no tribe. Certain prophetic poets—Pound is an example—may have access to a version of the bardic voice at times, may address a tribe. Pound may have been motivated by a desire to escape prophetic isolation. One senses, though, that the prophetic and not the bardic was his real vocation. Pound shows the differences as well as the similarities between the bardic and the prophetic. Both share a kind of obsessiveness with "the real" or "the everyday" as well as a kind of obliviousness to it. In both, the refusal to argue can be seen as a refusal of conversation, a refusal to engage in language that is not bardic or prophetic. Prophets do not speak any language but their own, and one senses that they cannot hear any other language. The prophetic poets, for example, often present themselves as able to hear only their own voices and unable to hear what people are saying in everyday life. Like Lowell, they may hear only the flies of Babylon buzzing in their eardrums. They do not know what an argument is; they would not be able to hear one. Where we might hear persuasion, the offering up of evidence, the making of claims, the prophetic poets will hear only an intensification of the hum of everyday speech.

Examples of the Prophetic Voice

I have represented the prophetic poet as someone who refuses the energies associated with the mystic, the visionary, and the bardic. At the same time, I have pointed out that the prophetic poet has no easy or conventional access to or use for everyday language. The prophetic poet is "worldpoor" (to use Heidegger's term) and knows it and is trying to make the best of it.[22] "The world has starved to a single peak," writes A. R. Ammons, "you and what you know alone."[23] The prophetic poets will not refuse recompenses from their own worldview, though that worldview is sparing with them. At the same time, as I said, they are trying to do without the pleasures offered by mystical delight or visionary concentration or bardic ambition. Again, William James quotes Saint John of the Cross on mystical experience: "A single one of these intoxicating consolations may reward [the soul] for all the labors undergone in its life—even were they numberless" (451). The prophetic poets refuse, as well, the consolations enjoyed by other poets who use highly elevated language—love poets, for example, or epic poets. Prophetic figures may seem to be running on empty in a world of abundance, and all their "doing without" may seem pointless or even cowardly to some readers. Like Melville's Bartleby or Kafka's hunger artist, they may appear to be perverse, recalcitrant, giving up a life for a life of allegory. They are "looking for what was, where it used to be," and they are not going to find it.[24] If they do find it, both the poem and the poet are in danger of seeming "foredefeated" (to use a word from a Robinson Jeffers poem) or tiresomely anachronistic or "quaint." In *The Changing Light at Sandover* Merrill asks,

> What at this late date
> Can be done with the quaint idiom that slips
> From nowhere to my tongue—or from the parchment
> Of some old scribe of the apocalypse—
>
> (*CLS*, 274)

Yet most readers, even if they think of prophetic poetry as too much, too late, will acknowledge that the prophetic voice in our time has astonishing energy:

> What are the roots that clutch, what branches grow
> Out of this stony rubbish? Son of man,
> You cannot say, or guess, for you know only
> A heap of broken images, where the sun beats
> And the dead tree gives no shelter, the cricket no relief,
> And the dry stone no sound of water.

> O Thou steeled Cognizance whose leap commits
> The agile precincts of the lark's return;
> Within whose lariat sweep encinctured sing
> In single chrysalis the many twain,—
> Of stars Thou art the stitch and stallion glow
> And like an organ, Thou, with sound of doom—
> Sight, sound and flesh Thou leadest from time's realm
> As love strikes clear direction for the helm.

Still the walls do not fall,
I do not know why;

there is zrr-hiss,
lightning in a not-known,

unregistered dimension;
we are powerless,

dust and powder fill our lungs
our bodies blunder

through doors twisted on hinges,
and the lintels slant

cross-wise;
we walk continually

on thin air
that thickens to a blind fog,

then step swiftly aside,
for even the air

is independable,
thick where it should be fine

and tenuous
where wings separate and open,

and the ether
is heavier than the floor,

and the floor sags
like a ship floundering;

we know no rule
of procedure,

we are voyagers, discoverers
of the not-known,

the unrecorded;
we have no map;

possibly we will reach haven,
heaven.

Not picnics or pageants or the improbable
Powers of air whose tongues exclaim dominion
And gull the great man to follow his terrible
Star, suffice; not the window-box, or the bird on

The ledge, which mean so much to the invalid,
Nor the joy you leaned after, as by the tracks the grass
In the emptiness after the lighted Pullmans fled,
Suffices; nor faces, which, like distraction, pass
Under the street-lamps, teasing to faith or pleasure,
Suffice you, born to no adequate definition of terror.

who sat in boxes breathing in the darkness under the bridge, and rose
        up to build harpsichords in their lofts,
who coughed on the sixth floor of Harlem crowned with flame under the
        tubercular sky surrounded by orange crates of theology,
who scribbled all night rocking and rolling over lofty incantations
        which in the yellow morning were stanzas of gibberish

The flies, the flies, the flies of Babylon
Buzz in my ear-drums while the devil's long
Dirge of the people detonates the hour
For floating cities where his golden tongue
Enchants the masons of the Babel Tower
To raise tomorrow's city to the sun
That never sets upon these hell-fire streets
Of Boston, where the sunlight is a sword
Striking at the withholder of the Lord:
Flies, flies are on the plane tree, on the streets.

I have been standing all my life in the
direct path of a battery of signals
the most accurately transmitted most
untranslatable language in the universe
I am a galactic cloud so deep   so invo-
luted that a light wave could take 15
years to travel through me   And has
taken   I am an instrument in the shape
of a woman trying to translate pulsations
into images   for the relief of the body
and the reconstruction of the mind.

Now in my observatory withdrawn
I am given up the sky, and strain my eyes across the spaces between;
On cloudy nights I sit in the lower room dreaming,
And listening to the tick of the heart, until the wind rises

And the clouds turn and turn and depart, and I climb
To the unroofed upper room once more, and adjust my instrument
Praising the wind.

I am not entirely human,

writing in
Stony wind, and watry fire,

In these lines from Eliot, Crane, H.D., Warren, Ginsberg, Lowell, Rich, and Grossman, the prophetic voices variously warn, celebrate, protest, rave, give an account of their own practices, are defiant.[25] Many of them find their prophetic space difficult to move around in. They pick their way among stony rubbish. Doors are twisted on hinges. Even the air is "independable." But their space is preferable to ours simply because it is *not* everyday space. Picnics and pageants are not enough, they do not suffice—but not because the comfort they offer is insufficient. In fact, they do not offer comfort, they are terrifying. They are insufficient because they are not adequate objective correlatives of the terror the prophets feel. There is no relief, except in prophetic speech. There is no shelter, unless in a box under a bridge. The prophetic poets want to be steeled like the bridge, to feel a sense of clear direction. The space in some prophetic poems does, in fact, become habitable. The prophetic poets show that they can live there. The sunlight may be a sword, the sky may be tubercular, but the poets give themselves up to them. The wind may be stony, but they praise it. There is a battery of signals, and the poets stand in its direct path on our behalf. They adjust their instruments. If they can live here, so can readers. The landscape may be made beautiful in the future, but first it must be acknowledged. The everyday world must be seen as the prophetic space it is.

The prophetic voice does not seem to be fading away in our time, either in individual poems or as a tradition. It is important to note that to respond with excitement to such voices is to have agreed to nothing, is simply to have allowed into our consciousness—in a sense, to engineer a return of—a version of something we might resist in other forms. Grossman says of Crane's poems that "they are both unforgettable (like an obligation that cannot be extinguished) and forever unacceptable by mind."[26]

Prophetic poetry may have the force of obligation, but that is not the only kind of force it has. The prophetic poets are not playful, but they are often seductive. They take pleasure in writing the way they do, and readers, noticing this pleasure, may experience a version of it themselves. Readers sometimes forget that poets write this kind of poetry not only because, like Yeats, they "have a marvellous thing to say" but also because they want to hear themselves saying "beautiful, lofty," and disturbing things. The prophetic poets know that they are engaging in a kind of wild excess. They have ways of justifying the excess, but they also have ways of enjoying it. Readers can participate in this excess. Readers who recognize that prophetic voices in our time are various and powerful and offer pleasure will be more responsive to elements of prophetic poetry that will not be so vivid to completely unsympathetic readers. Prophetic poets write poetry and not simply "prophecy," and this fact gives them an intimacy with certain readers that the poets cannot fully acknowledge. Readers themselves, however, can acknowledge it.

The space of prophetic poetry is very much a world of unacknowledgable intimacies. The prophetic poets have a kind of intimate relationship, for example, with their own voice. Nobody may be listening to this voice, but the prophetic poet is listening. Poets have to encourage, sponsor, protect, interpret themselves. The poem may enact some of these gestures. The prophetic poets, that is, may allow us to see them making life-or-death adjustments on their life support system. It is as if there *were* somebody to witness and adjust.

> Pull down thy vanity, it is not man
> Made courage, or made order, or made grace,
>   Pull down thy vanity, I say pull down.
> Learn of the green world what can be thy place
> In scaled invention or true artistry[27]

Although the prophetic poets may often wish to see themselves as a "Cognizance" steeled against anything that might distract or undermine them, in this passage from Ezra Pound we can hear the prophetic poet giving himself instructions, trying to educate himself about scale. Pound remains a prophetic poet; he is simply, here, adjusting his instrument. But there is a limit to the flexibility of the prophetic poets. Left to their own devices, they can write "lofty incantations," but sometimes those devices must seem scary or useless. In "the yellow morning" they seem "stanzas of gibberish." Here are excerpts from poems that show us the prophetic voice panicking:

> The bells I say, the bells break down their tower;
> And swing I know not where.

> are these the thoughts you want me to think I said but
> > the wind was gone and there was no more knowledge then.

> Place a man in the center, and he becomes
> The man who has prepared for a lifetime
> To answer, and now is ready.[28]

Near the end of the poem just quoted, Allen Grossman's "The Lecture," we are told:

> After a long time, the voice of the man
> Stops. It was good to talk on and on.
> He rises. And the sea or forest becomes
> A level way reaching to night and the thunder.

It may be that everything is going to be okay for the prophetic figure who has prepared a lifetime. "But, in fact, there is no night. There is / No thunder." These are the lines with which the poem ends. For another poet, such a poem would constitute a kind of farewell to prophetic poetry. We are told that there is no center from which to speak, that

> the center is some eccentric region
> Of a bed or a room, and the question
> Is the half-demented glance of a child,
> Or the blurred silence on the telephone,
> For which the man who has prepared a lifetime
> Is ready.

Still, no epiphany, however unsettling, can stop prophetic poets for long. Allen Grossman, though he ended an early book of poems with "The Lecture," has continued to write prophetic poems in the years since.

Part of my aim here is simply to call attention to the strength and power of prophetic poetry in an age that is not sympathetic to it. But I also want to ask the kinds of questions that champions of prophetic poetry (and visionary and mystical poetry) do not often ask. Once prophetic poets begin writing this way, are they bound to write this way until death? What happens when this kind of voice becomes not discredited but monotonous to the poets? All ways of writing can become monotonous, but not all ways of writing demand this kind of allegiance from the poets who use them. What possibilities are there for more than minor adjustments? The prophetic poets might, as I suggested earlier, experiment with the visionary or the bardic in order to borrow additional sources of energy. They might use parody. The prophetic poets might simply reinvent themselves as an everyday poet, turn their backs on a strange past. They might find religion like Eliot or lapse into silence like Pound or choose an early death like Crane. But suppose they wanted to write at this level of intensity and authority and awareness and freshness for a lifetime; what if they refused to abandon or renounce the prophetic voice? "I would give up nothing if I had my way," writes Ammons. Some prophetic poets will turn and consider the voice most immediately threatening and most deeply challenging to them, the everyday voice.

The Voice of the Everyday

Powerful poets of the everyday—in the twentieth century, William Carlos Williams, Langston Hughes, Stevie Smith, the later Auden, Frank O'Hara, Randall Jarrell, Marianne Moore, Elizabeth Bishop, and John Ashbery work almost entirely in this voice—can make readers feel that unelevated voices are more exciting than elevated voices. Here again they are encouraged by Wallace Stevens, who called the everyday "the one / Discovery still possible to make."[29] There is a sense of adventurousness, of possible heroism, what Milton called "things unattempted yet." At the same time there is a kind of subversive humor. The prophetic voice might say, "O Thou steeled Cognizance." The everyday voice says, "Blouaugh!" (And then a later everyday poet will write, "Puaagh. Vomit. Puaaaaagh. More Vomit.") The everyday voice talks about "groping to bed after a piss" and says that "just reeling off the names [of lakes] is ever so comfy." The everyday voice has its own grand rhetorical questions: "Who shall say I am not / the happy genius of my household?"[30] The everyday voice is often exuberant, wanting to do justice to, in a sense to *advertise* the abundance it has taught itself to find in the everyday world. Such exuberance may come to feel necessary to the everyday poets; without it, their voices may seem complacent and trivial. Exuberance, though, can sometimes seem relentless, automatic, pious about its habits. "I don't know exactly what a prayer is," writes a contemporary poet. "I do know how to pay attention, how to kneel down in the grass."[31] (The prophetic poet sees a world of happy geniuses getting comfy in the grass and feels more isolated.)

Here are some passages from poems that offer versions of the voice of the everyday:

When I was younger
it was plain to me
I must make something of myself.
Older now
I walk back streets
admiring the houses
of the very poor:
roof out of line with sides
the yards cluttered
with old chicken wire, ashes

I am twenty-two, colored, born in Winston-Salem.
I went to school there, then Durham, then here
to this college on the hill above Harlem.
I am the only colored student in my class.
The steps from the hill lead down into Harlem,
through a park, then I cross St. Nicholas,
Eighth Avenue, Seventh, and I come to the Y,
the Harlem Branch Y, where I take the elevator
up to my room, sit down, and write this page:

I'm not going to cry all the time
nor shall I laugh all the time,
I don't prefer one "strain" to another.
I'd have the immediacy of a bad movie,
not just a sleeper, but also the big,
overproduced first-run kind. I want to be
at least as alive as the vulgar.

The little black dog runs in his yard.
His owner's voice arises, stern,
"You ought to be ashamed!"
What has he done?
He bounces cheerfully up and down:
he rushes in circles in the fallen leaves.

Obviously, he has no sense of shame.
He and the bird know everything is answered,
all taken care of,
no need to ask again.
—Yesterday brought to today so lightly!
(A yesterday I find almost impossible to lift.)

> I am afraid, this morning, of my face.
> It looks at me
> From the rear-view mirror, with the eyes I hate,
> The smile I hate. Its plain, lined look
> Of gray discovery
> Repeats to me: "You're old." That's all, I'm old.

And then there always came a time when
Happy Hooligan in his rusted green automobile
Came plowing down the course, just to make sure that everything was O.K.,
Only by that time we were in another chapter and confused
About how to receive this latest piece of information.
Was it information? Weren't we rather acting this out
For someone else's benefit, thoughts in a mind
With room enough and to spare for our little problems (so they began to seem)
Our daily quandary about food and the rent and bills to be paid?
To reduce all this to a small variant,
To step free at last, minuscule on the gigantic plateau—
This was our ambition: to be small and clear and free.

These quotations give only a preliminary sense of the variety to be found in the voice of the everyday.[32] The everyday poet can do much that the prophetic poet cannot. The everyday poet can say, "When I was younger . . ." The poets of the everyday can walk happily away from the notion of having to make something of themselves (though, as we will see, the everyday poets, too, have a mission). As a poet of the everyday, Williams can walk through a landscape somewhat like the landscape H.D. describes, but her landscape is one of the Blitz, his one of poverty. Like H.D., Williams admires the fortitude of the people who manage to survive in these conditions, but H.D. takes a prophetic tone, and Williams does not. We can see what is "everyday" about Williams's poem even more clearly if we imagine what Eliot would have done with these back streets. The Eliot of "Preludes" and "Rhapsody on a Windy Night" is not so very far from the Williams of "Pastoral." Eliot is simply much more melancholy than Williams. By the time of *The Waste Land*, though, Eliot would have to ask, What is this chicken wire, this furniture gone wrong, what fences and outhouses grow out of this stony rubbish? Both the prophetic poet and the poet of the everyday go for walks looking for heaps of broken images, but one goes to deplore them, and the other to enjoy them.

The everyday poet may, like the prophetic poet, take on a variety of tonalities. Some everyday poets admire the houses of the very poor, others live in those houses. Streets that are major thoroughfares ("St. Nicholas / Eighth Avenue, Seventh") are seen by the nation as "back streets." Some poets of the everyday tend to be sad, others happy. Others do not see why they should have to be one or the other "all the time." Some of them see their lives as a movie: both Williams and Hughes seem (after we have read Frank O'Hara) to be highly conscious of themselves walking through their neighborhoods, almost as if they are appearing in a serious black-and-white documentary. O'Hara says straight out that he sometimes feels as if he is in a movie, but it is not always the same movie. Sometimes he feels as if he is in an "overproduced first-run kind." "I want to be / at least as alive as the vulgar," he says, and the reader immediately feels that what he is saying resembles what Williams is saying in his poem. Reading Bishop after O'Hara, the reader feels that O'Hara is like the little dog in her poem. "He bounces cheerfully up and down: / he rushes in circles in the fallen leaves." And the woman in the poem by Randall Jarrell says what the woman in the Bishop poem would never say.[33] Meanwhile, the last four lines of Ashbery's poem are wonderfully characteristic of another aspect of the everyday voice. He writes about the desire "to step free at last," but although he finds himself on a "gigantic plateau," the everyday poet has not changed his life in the way the prophetic poet wants him to change it. He is not a prophet, lofty, difficult to understand, enslaved to his sense of obligation. Instead, he is "small and clear and free"—free not of the burden of speaking momentous and serious utterances but free, simply, of the "daily quandary about food and the rent and bills to be paid." His gigantic plateau feels more like a vacation spot than a prophetic space.

I have chosen the everyday as the other central term in this book in part because it poses the greatest challenge to the prophetic poet. The everyday wants to trap the prophetic poet in time—not in some grand or tragic version of time, not in fallen time, but simply in everyday time. Everyday time is not just uncongenial to the prophetic poets but potentially fatal. Once they step into everyday time, the prophetic poets fear they will have to change their way of writing. The tones of stalwart forbearance, cheerful stoicism, guarded optimism, all of them will have to be theirs; the prophetic poets will have to use the quaint idiom of everydayness, knowing how false it will sound coming from them. Another day another dollar, tomorrow is another day, every day in every way I am getting better and better. If there is happiness in the everyday world, there is also much unhappiness. It is Freud's ordinary unhappiness, though, and the proper response to it is to shrug or chuckle. The poems quoted above steer clear of all these clichés—at least they seem to most readers to do so. Still, many prophetic readers, reading Williams or O'Hara, will be certain they are being advised to live life day by day.

If everyday poets are drawn to gentle humor, prophetic poets are drawn to sharp wit. Wit can be useful in resisting the advances of the everyday into our lives. Many prophetic poets adopt a posture of increased sureness. Blake says that God "does a Human Form Display / To those who Dwell in Realms of day."[34] Everyday people (who do not dwell in realms of any sort and certainly not in "Realms of day") temporarily feel not at home in their own world. Blake tells them how much they are missing in the very space they call their own. Other poets have other strategies of subversion of the everyday. Jorie Graham does not feel vulnerable in the context of everydayness. Instead, it is everydayness that is made to feel vulnerable in her work. It is always about to be interrupted, and what she feels is suspense, referring, in an interview, to "the light of day with its terrible raised expectations."[35] Terrible raised expectations? The point for an everyday poet is to lower expectations. Noneveryday imaginations love to take revenge on the everyday. Apocalyptic imaginations offer representations of the Day of Judgment that feature rush-hour commuters being taken up to rapture. Other prophetic poets mock the notion that everyday life could be a blessing. For Eliot it's a punishment. James Merrill refers to himself cheerfully as someone who is "condemned to write about real things," but Eliot seems really to feel himself condemned.[36]

> Under the brown fog of a winter dawn,
> A crowd flowed over London Bridge, so many,
> I had not thought death had undone so many.
> Sighs, short and infrequent, were exhaled,
> And each man fixed his eyes before his feet.[37]

If Eliot invokes Dante to write about people walking to their office jobs, whom could he invoke to represent those people sitting down at their desks? Meanwhile, the crowd scene above is about to be interrupted by a cry of prophetic disgust, the voice of someone trapped in the everyday who refuses to adapt to it, who insists on being himself the interruption to it. Heschel, writing about the prophets of the Hebrew Bible, asks, "Who could bear living in a state of disgust day and night?"[38] To which the prophetic poet answers, who could bear to live in the everyday world every day? The workaday world is not so bad, the everyday poet might respond, referring us, perhaps, to Brad Leithauser's poem "Two Summer Jobs" or to the comic strip *Dilbert*.[39]

I mentioned raised expectations. Political theorists may also feel them. In their introduction to a recent issue of *Yale French Studies* called "Everyday Life," Alice Kaplan and Kristin Ross write, "The Political, like the purloined letter, is hidden in the everyday, exactly where it is most obvious: in the contradictions of lived experience, in the most banal and repetitive gestures of everyday life—the commute, the errand, the appointment. It is in the midst of the utterly ordinary, in the space where the dominant relations of production are tirelessly and relentlessly reproduced, that we must look for utopian and political aspirations to crystallize."[40] The everyday is, for some theorists, something that is *always about to be* interrupted by utopian political action. Meanwhile (a central word in the vocabulary of poets of the everyday), the everyday is not usually (another crucial word) interrupted, and it usually returns after interruption.

The utopian thinker, the millenarian dreamer, and the prophetic poet are all wrong about the everyday. The everyday poet knows this but is sympathetic and recasts all their hopes as "human." Randall Jarrell, for example, calls one of his poems "Next Day." The next day will be just like today and the day before, according to Jarrell. The proper response, though, is not prophetic rage but rueful whimsy. The reality of the everyday, it turns out (over and over), is the only reality one can trust. Poets of the everyday feel a kind of wary, bemused gratitude for this fact, not because they do not feel larger appetites but because they are tired of or feel betrayed by those appetites. It is important to remember that the everyday poets do not necessarily relish the everyday. They understand its difficulty. May Sarton writes, "It may be that I set my sights too high and so repeatedly end a day in depression. Not easy to find the balance, for if one does not have wild dreams of achievement there is no spur even to get the dishes washed. One must think like a hero to behave like a merely decent human being."[41] One must think like a hero or heroine. If one thinks like a prophet, all hope of decency is gone.

The everyday too has a set of terms that gather around it, and a family resemblance operates here as well. These terms are the *human*, the *domestic,* and the *ordinary.* Poets who emphasize these aspects of the everyday are "adepts," as are mystical and visionary poets, but on another terrain. It should be said that these terms are closer to each other, resemble each other more closely than do the terms that gather around the prophetic. But there are important differences between the everyday and the human and the domestic and the ordinary, and I hope to suggest some of those differences. My descriptions in this introduction are meant to be preliminary, however, and I hope the implications of these terms and the differences between them will be at once made clearer and more complicated in the chapters to follow. Here it should be emphasized that every poet, every person, will have a different relationship to each of these terms. James Merrill, for example, was a poet who did not have much access to the ordinary. (What he had instead of the ordinary—what kept him from access to the ordinary—was a certain kind of wit.) What he did have was access to the everyday, the domestic, and the human. His poetry registers, after a certain point, his sense of this as a kind of good fortune. Merrill was conscious throughout his career of wanting to avoid "reduced circumstances."[42] There are poets who do write in reduced circumstances. A poet can be domestic without seeming fully human, although this was more common in the nineteenth century in poems written about, or by, "the angel in the house." (In our own time, magazines like *Martha Stewart Living* offer help.) A poet can write poems in an everyday voice without having any access to a domestic voice. John Ashbery seems to live much of his everyday life under the sky. One can be human without a sense of either the everyday or the domestic. Wallace Stevens offers examples of this kind of poem.

It is crucial that readers remember that these are not hoops for poets to jump through. Poets who are equally adept or fluent in all these voices are not "better" poets because of this fluency, but they will be more versatile and therefore more unpredictable, and their poems may have a kind of greater richness, the result of diversified investments.

The Voice of the Ordinary

The family resemblance between the everyday and the ordinary is, of course, very great, and the terms are often used synonymously. I include the ordinary as a separate category because of the special resonance the term often seems to have in certain discussions. To use the term *ordinary* is to exert a few degrees more pressure on the everyday;

those drawn to the term are interested in trying to see if they can get to the heart of everyday experience. To evoke the everyday is to evoke a certain mode of being in the world, a mode that depends on never having more consciousness of the everyday experience than such experience seems to require. The ordinary, on the other hand, suggests (to my ears) an experience of being deeper inside the everyday, occupying a space within the everyday where it might be possible to think about where one is. The difficulty here, as I will suggest, is that the ordinary (like the everyday) requires a light touch—a lighter touch, it sometimes seems, than anybody possesses. This is tantalizing, of course. As with the everyday, an atmosphere of excitement gathers around the project of ordinariness (in whatever form it is conceived) and makes it seem like something worth exploring.

The ordinary seems harder of access than the everyday, though it is (almost) always everywhere around us. Ordinary language, in particular, has tremendous prestige in our time. It is the language we want to, or are tempted to, or feel obliged to translate other languages into. Ordinary language is, in any event, a language we hesitate to translate out of: Michel de Certeau observes that "the usual ways of speaking do not have any equivalent in philosophical discourse and they cannot be translated into it because they are richer and more varied than it is."[43] What interests me about ordinary language (whether, as they write, poets think of Wittgenstein or the way their grandmother spoke or both) is the scenario in which poets suddenly find themselves in a state of panic that is intriguingly analogous to the panic of the prophetic poets. The anxiety may be based on two contradictory realizations. No reader can be interested in so much ordinariness, such poets might suspect, feeling at the same time *forsaken* by ordinariness, since it seems now to be nowhere in their work. (There are various avant-gardes within contemporary poetry where such poets may find rest.)

The first realization has to do with the difficulty of writing the ordinary and writing poetry at the same time. Readers may indeed wonder why poets would want an ordinary voice. Do very young poets dream, One day I'll say human things in ordinary speech about my household arrangements? Essays by prophetic poets are full of an understandable incredulity. Pound writes, "There are few fallacies more common than the opinion that poetry should mimic the daily speech."[44] Why, Pound wonders, would anyone want to mimic daily speech in poetry? Why not simply speak? Or write prose? Why write *poems*? Frank O'Hara tells his readers, "While I was writing [a poem] I was realizing that if I wanted to I could use the telephone instead of writing the poem."[45] Allen Grossman asks such poets to say why they want to write *poems* at all. Addressing the poet Mark Halliday in one of their "Winter Conversations," he says, "It strikes me, you have not yet accounted for the motive of speaking in verse."[46]

The second realization has to do with the possibility that ordinariness is impossible to achieve. I said that visionary attempts to find the transcendent within the everyday tend to work. Writing poetry about ordinariness is much more difficult. The ordinary no longer seems ordinary when it has been written down. One reason has to do with style. Richard Poirier discusses the "stylistic imbalance that becomes especially evident when the writer's rhetorical claim to ordinariness is coupled, as it so often is, with rhetorical practices that give every indication of individual, eccentric and unique mastery."[47] The ordinary seems to resists inclusion in *any* art form. Norman Bryson writes that still-life painting "can experience extraordinary difficulty in registering the everydayness of the everyday—what it is actually like to inhabit 'low plane reality,' without departing from that into a re-assertion of painting's own powers and ambitions, or into an overfocused and obsessional vision that ends by making everyday life seem unreal and hyper-real at the same time."[48] How can poets bring the ordinary into poetry so that it stays ordinary? How, to put it another way, can poets keep the ordinary innocent, how can they protect it from their own designs on it? The problem of how to keep the ordinary ordinary has to be worked out by each poet word by word, line by line, object by object, detail by detail. Many prophetic poets, of course, will think of such work with impatience.

I choose the everyday as my central term because it is closer in its tonalities to the tonalities of the poems I compare with the prophetic. The ordinary suggests a world of difficulties. The everyday, like the human and the domestic, suggests a world of difficulties solved, and that is what is most provocative to the prophetic poets.

The Voice of the Human

I said earlier that the everyday poets tend to recast, sympathetically, if pityingly, all overweening hopes as human. *Human* is likely to be a term that evokes diminishment. Poets are being human, we feel, when they instruct readers to be patient, to learn to live with contradiction, to learn to live with less. It is a word that can be made to refer to abundance, but it is generally abundance *in spite of* loss, the abundance of counted blessings. To be human is to be an expert on diminishment, on damage control. The poets who use the human voice are experts on their own status, know always exactly what has been lost and what remains. Like Bishop's speaker in "One Art," such poets have mastered the art of losing and are always prepared to lose more. The poets of the human have given up whole vocabularies. In rejecting religion, the human voice rejected the vocabulary of the soul; in rejecting humanism, it rejected the old vocabularies of the self. The human voice in our time can mean the range of tonalities available to someone in the act of jettisoning. To be a poet of the human, though, is to feel, *no matter what,* that enough remains.

Such poets are, at the same time, capable of coming up with new versions of the human. Often this can mean writing about people who have not been written about before. When new versions of the human come into poetry, they tend to seem inevitable or at least prepared for; genealogies are quickly discovered for them. But these voices in poetry have many obstacles in their way—and there are always new obstacles. One of them is itself cultural: new voices keep breaking into poetry at just the moment when *voice* and *presence* are (in some places) terms under erasure. Donna Haraway writes, "Nonfeminist poststructuralist theory in the human sciences has tended to identify the breakup of 'coherent' or masterful subjectivity as the 'death of the subject.' Many feminists resist this formulation of the project and question its emergence at just the moment when raced/sexed/colonized speakers begin 'for the first time' to claim, that is, with an originary authority, to represent themselves in institutionalized publishing practices and other kinds of self-constituting practice."[49] Some prophetic poets will be sympathetic to attempts by women and minorities to represent themselves in poetry but may lose interest as soon as the urgency has left the project. What are prophetic poets likely to think of "the death of the subject"? Some might feel they have died already as subjects and might observe (with mixed feelings?) that theorists are hastening the transformation of everyday speakers into something more like prophetic speakers. To the extent that everyday language is revealed as play, though, it becomes even harder for prophetic poets to convert readers to the fundamentally harsh and difficult language of prophecy. In addition, contemporary theory might be seen as a destruction of the everyday world such that the prophetic poet no longer has any access to it, so that there is no place any longer to be addressed. It is true that literary theorists have stolen some of the energy of prophetic poetry. But prophetic poets, who need to think of the human as complacent, easygoing, and myopic, may feel grateful that theorists have left so many readers untransformed.

The Voice of Domesticity

There are many different versions of the domestic voice in postwar and contemporary poetry. Readers may respond differently to different versions, and some of these responses will be connected to gender. Women's treatment of the domestic, for example, has been praised and patronized; men's treatment of the domestic has been praised as an exciting negotiation with ideas of limitation.

Both male and female poets may sometimes write about the versions of domesticity that were imposed on them and sometimes about the versions they have chosen. Some poets write about houses they might have chosen—the cryptodream house. When Elizabeth Bishop in her poem "The End of March" begins to describe her dream house she immediately adds, "Many things about this place are dubious."[50]

Many things about all versions of domesticity are dubious now, in part because of their relation to the nondomestic. The relationship between the domestic and the prophetic is unpredictable. The domestic might be, in one poet's imagination, a kind of protection against another poet's prophetic mode. Elizabeth Bishop praised the early installments of Merrill's *The Changing Light at Sandover* but cautioned Merrill that the poem was "much too big" to write about on "a morning when I have to start cleaning house."[51] Another poet might simply take the domestic and move it, all of it, out of the world. Robert Duncan in an essay writes, "And then (I am not domestic by nature) the home is the sheerest product of my imagination, a triumph of soul—at every point magically imaginary."[52]

What can domesticity represent to the prophetic poet? Some prophetic poets can turn any home into a house. "Who will make the dinner, then, for the man of stone?" Grossman's speaker asks in a recent poem, with the implication that the speaker will continue to be a man of stone during and after that dinner.[53] The prophetic poets may make a separate or temporary peace with the domestic. Prophetic poets are sometimes married with children, though these rarely appear in their poems. Domesticity does not necessarily present a particular challenge to the prophetic poets, though it might be something they try movingly to leave unaffected by the atmosphere of their minds. The prophetic poets may try to experience the domestic as a comfort while rejecting its agenda. What can domesticity offer the prophetic poets? One thinks of the popular books *Chicken Soup for the . . . Soul*, with their implication that what our souls, with their supposed Promethean or Faustian longings, have turned out really to be longing for is chicken soup.

Rich and Merrill and Lowell are three poets who are particularly involved in writing about and rethinking what is evoked and enforced by the idea of domesticity, and I will reserve further discussion of domesticity to my chapters on those poets.

The Prophetic Voice and the Everyday Voice

I hope it is clear by now that neither the prophetic nor the everyday voice stands alone. Each exists in relation to versions of itself, with which it shares a family resemblance. I have raised into view some of the tensions between the prophetic and the mystical, the visionary, the bardic. I have also suggested some of the various ways in which the everyday, the human, the domestic, and the ordinary will alter the poem that has tried to accommodate them.

What about the relationship *between* the prophetic and the everyday? The differences between these voices have been a site of enormous anxiety for centuries. For a long time decorum demanded that these discourses be kept apart: the anxiety manifested itself as a "separation of styles." The ancient Greeks and Romans believed, according to Erich Auerbach, that "everyday practical reality could find a place only within the frame of a low or intermediate kind of style, that is to say, as either grotesquely comic or pleasant, light, colorful and elegant entertainment." There were limits to the ways in which such reality could be represented. Auerbach points out that "in antique theory, the sublime and elevated style was called *sermo gravis* or *sublimis*; the low style was *sermo remissus* or *humilis*; the two had to be kept strictly separated." But the two discourses were, of course, mixed by the Bible. In the stories of the Hebrew Bible, Auerbach writes, "the sublime, the tragic and the problematic take shape precisely in the domestic and commonplace." In these stories "the two realms of the sublime and the everyday are not actually unseparated but inseparable." And the New Testament brought these two styles together once again. The church fathers (Gregory of Tours, for example) continued to mix these styles, and so did Dante. "The themes which the Comedy introduces represent a mixture of sublimity and triviality which, measured by the standards of antiquity, is monstrous."[54]

When the Renaissance humanists, in their rediscovery of antiquity, brought back the separation of styles, this separation began once again to exert tremendous force. Seventeenth- and eighteenth-century theorists of decorum tried to show why certain mixtures could not be permitted—and this mixture was one of them. Although the vocabulary of Christian thought made it easier for imaginations working within it to bring the discourses together, the desire to combine them was not always able to contain itself within scriptural models. George Herbert, for example, managed to mix the styles in a way that seems surprising and fresh and not predetermined by Scripture. By reimagining what the merging of the two voices might sound like, poets like Herbert would be useful to poets who came later.

But the sense of decorum that demands that the voices be kept apart is still with us. It presents itself to us most often as a sense that when we have certain kinds of things to say we use one voice, and when we have other kinds of things to say we use another voice. Wallace Stevens writes, "To say more than human things with human voice, / That cannot be; to say human things with more / Than human voice, that, also, cannot be."[55] Along with this decorum goes the sense that the voices do not go well together, that the presence of the human voice, say, will make the more-than-human voice seem empty, not poetry, and that the presence of the more-than-human voice will make the human voice seem empty, not poetry. Many poets accept this as a rule and feel they must choose one and not both of the voices. One way of speaking might contaminate the other. William Butler Yeats, who used his wife as a medium for messages from the spirit world, writes, "I have heard my wife in the broken speech of some quite ordinary dream use tricks of speech characteristic of the philosophic voices. Sometimes the philosophic voices themselves have become vague and trivial or have in some other way reminded me of dreams."[56] Theodore Roethke, to offer another example, writes in his notebook, "Diction: one of the problems of diction, in certain kinds of poems, is to get all the words within a certain range of feeling; all elemental, all household, etc., etc. Often a very good figure from another level or range will jar."[57] But too much attention to decorum may give to the poetry a sense of energies excluded: Robert Duncan writes, "I have 'selected' my works, weeded out the poetry which is not all of a tone." Then he adds, "But resurrect everything: and one will discover my true book—no pleasure for aesthetes. A composite

indecisive literature, attempting the rhapsodic, the austere, the mysterious, the sophisticated, the spontaneous, higglety-pigglety."[58] Other
poets too make gestures toward what they may feel sometimes is their
"true book." Marianne Moore, according to Robert Pinsky, writes "sentences that tease and yearn toward idiomatic speech, then away from
it." In her *Paris Review* interview, Moore says, "The accuracy of the vernacular! That's the kind of thing I'm interested in, am always taking
down little local expressions and accents. I think I should be in some
philological operation or enterprise, am really much interested in dialect and intonations. I scarcely think any of that comes into my so-called
poems at all."[59] She is always taking such material down, but she cannot imagine it in her poems or in *anyone's* poems but instead in some
"philological operation or enterprise." There are poets whose emphasis
on scrupulous observation and common sense, say, may take on some
of the characteristics of the prophetic, may seem as insistent, as sealed
off, as emotionally unreadable.

There are, of course, poets in our time who have tried to use a human
voice *and* a more-than-human voice within the course of a career, of a
poem, of a part of a poem—but poets who are *persuasive* in both voices
are rare. Such poets seem able to bring the two voices into a complex and
intimate relationship with each other and to do it in a way that carries
conviction. They have tried to develop not just one "answerable style"
but a style in which these two voices can be answerable to each other.

Poets will read back into the past to see what has worked, but there
are not many postreligious poets who can show the way. Lowell writes,
"I felt my guides no longer carried me."[60] There are *some* guides to a
successful mixing of the two voices, though (Whitman, for example),
and it is one purpose of this book to show that the number of guides is
increasing. And poets can always read back into the past to see what
hasn't worked. It seems not to work, for example, when the prophetic
poet tries to use the lexicon of the everyday poet or the everyday poet
tries to use the vocabulary of the prophetic poet. The desire to shift to a
new lexicon is understandable: either voice may elicit in the reader
what John Berryman calls a "counter-mutter"—an appetite for what
might be thought of as its antidote or (more sympathetically) as the
completion of its partialness.[61] It is true that writing about prophetic
material in the voice of the everyday or everyday material in a prophetic voice *can* be productive of interesting effects. Some poems are
momentarily (in a sense, temporarily) prophetic or everyday. Sometimes
it can be a matter of the relationship between the title of a poem and its

first word. Stevens, for example, begins a short poem called "Negation" with the word "Hi!"[62] Still, though a poet might change vocabularies in the hope that the new one will check and balance the old, a change of vocabulary is not inevitably a change of voice. And some of the undeniable strangeness of the prophetic voice is revealed when the prophetic poets try to talk about the everyday using everyday terms. When Rilke, for example, wonders if "perhaps we are *here* in order to say: house, / bridge, fountain, gate, pitcher, fruit-tree, window—/ at most, column, tower," he is using the vocabulary of the everyday but not its voice.[63] Some readers may hear in this passage Rilke's incredulity at the idea that we really could be here only to say such everyday words and may detect an attempt at the end to smuggle in two more gratifying words. Simply to shift lexicons, then, will not always bring about a deeper shift. And there are many opportunities for embarrassment. Robert Duncan, for example, begins a poem called "The Quotidian" with the bathetic words, "There is no way that daily I have not been / initiate. / The admission is all." Or again: "O daily actual life, I am deep in your thrall."[64] Here is Stevens's "Large Red Man Reading":

> There were ghosts that returned to earth to hear his phrases,
> As he sat there reading, aloud, the great blue tabulae.
> They were those from the wilderness of stars that had expected more.
>
> There were those that returned to hear him read from the poem of life,
> Of the pans above the stove, the pots on the table, the tulips among them.
> They were those that would have wept to step barefoot into reality,
>
> That would have wept and been happy, have shivered in the frost
> And cried out to feel it again, have run fingers over leaves
> And against the most coiled thorn, have seized on what was ugly
>
> And laughed, as he sat there reading, from out of the purple tabulae,
> The outlines of being and its expressings, the syllables of its law:
> *Poesis, poesis,* the literal characters, the vatic lines,
>
> Which in those ears and in those thin, those spended hearts,
> Took on color, took on shape and the size of things as they are
> And spoke the feeling for them, which was what they had lacked.[65]

The pans above the stove, the pots on the table do not seem very much like everyday objects, do not, in these "vatic lines," have the color, shape, and size of things as they are. Those (here, for example, the dead) who are starved for the real will not find it in these "phrases." Stevens's poem, though, is about how the prophetic voice can invoke the real for readers who have lost all access to it, about how such readers may feel a crazed and disoriented gratitude for such access. The pathos of the poem is in its suggestion that we could get so far away from the everyday that we could be thankful for any evocation of it. The poem is also haunting in its suggestion that ghosts yearn "to step barefoot into reality" and that the everyday may itself be surprised and grateful to be worthy of such "great blue tabulae."

The relationship between the poetry of the everyday and prophetic poetry is complex and unpredictable, taking paths it is not always easy to trace. Imagine the prophetic as a space, as Ammons does. The prophetic space is the space farthest from the everyday from which the everyday is still visible, audible. The prophetic and the everyday, I have been suggesting, could not be more different from each other. But readers, looking at poems of both kinds, may start to think of similarities. Readers looking at poems that are neither everyday nor prophetic, poems that may not be intimately involved in the tensions I have been describing because they are poems of psychological trauma or surrealistic or "deep image" poems or mythological poems, may find themselves thinking more and more of these similarities, may start to imagine the everyday and the prophetic as one space.

To acknowledge and exploit these similarities is (borrowing Merrill's words) to complicate things irretrievably.

The Similarities between the Voices

What kinds of similarities can be noted? Everyday poets, like prophetic poets, are, on their good days, true believers. All these poets have a mission. (This sense of mission can affect, in obvious and subtle ways, the ways their poems conduct themselves. It may, for example, make either kind of poet overly conscious of his or her own dignity, and the poem may then be an attempt to conceal or chasten that consciousness.) Helping to make palatable this true belief in a mission may be a kind of sincerity or at least a last-ditch rhetoric. Both everyday and prophetic poets are capable of intimating that they may have written in a variety of voices in the past, but this, frankly, is the end of the line for them. They can't write any other kind of poetry *now*.

What other similarities are there? Both everyday and prophetic poets have in common the indefinability of what inspires them. That is, neither kind of poet can define exactly what makes him or her write poetry. There is something larger than the poet: for prophetic poets it is the force that compels them to speak, and for everyday poets it is everydayness itself (experienced, too, as a force that compels). To say that both everyday and prophetic poets feel "compelled" seems inadequate, though the reader can, of course, leave it at that and feel genial and broadminded like William James. But what does compel the prophetic poets or the poets of the everyday? Why would poets take it upon themselves to write poem after poem about the day, capitalized or lowercase? Both sorts of poet can seem just hypnotized, one by momentousness and the other by moment to momentness. But none of our objections can make the poets' relationship to what compels them any less absorbing to them and therefore, perhaps, absorbing to us.

There are more similarities to notice. Both kinds of poets feel the source of their inspiration as not simply absorbing but all-consuming. The source of their inspiration seems to them inescapable. Norman Bryson writes that "no one can escape the conditions of creaturality, of eating and drinking and domestic life," that no one can escape "the everyday world of routine and repetition . . . [the] level of existence where events are not at all the large-scale, momentous events of History, but the small-scale, trivial, forgettable acts of bodily survival and self maintenance."[66] No one can escape the everyday world. Prophetic poets, too, imagine their condition—and therefore ours, whoever we are—as inescapable. The inescapability of the force that inspires them may act as a kind of guarantee—against madness, for example, or the possibility of running out of things to say. At the same time, prophetic poets and everyday poets feel safe enough to *lose* themselves in the prophetic poem or in the poem of dailiness. The everyday version of this absorption is expressed by Bishop in a letter to Anne Stevenson. "What one seems to want in art, in experiencing it, is the same thing that is necessary for its creation, a self-forgetful, perfectly useless concentration."[67] The prophetic version is, perhaps, expressed in Lawrence's cry, "Not I, not I, but the wind that blows through me!"[68]

Extreme—we could say pure—versions of the prophetic and the everyday are versions in which the prophetic or everyday voice seem to be produced without mediation by the poets. Both everyday and prophetic poets, that is, share an odd pleasing dream of disappearing as poets but allowing the voice to continue. Both kinds of poets may feel that the more passive they are the more authentic will be the material that appears in their poetry. The danger is that the language that comes when they try to stop "interfering" with it will not seem prophetic or everyday but simply inadequate. The closest they can come to this dream is to refuse to revise—or to claim to have refused to revise.[69]

Both kinds of poets, perhaps because their work takes them into realms of experience that resist language, have invented new poetic languages and new forms to accommodate them. Critics will sometimes insist that the result is not poetry. The everyday poets may write in a way that is too much like the way they speak, and many readers are exasperated by this kind of poem. (Stanley Cavell's dramatization of impatience with ordinary language philosophy, its "stubbornly resting within its relentless superficiality," is an eloquent version of the scorn we sometimes feel for poems that are too everyday. Cavell talks of the philosopher's insistence on "going over stupidly familiar words that we are every bit as much the master of as they.")[70] There is clearly an analogy here with certain kinds of poems. As I said earlier in the introduction, readers (and not just prophetic poets) demand to know in what sense poets can be said to be writing poetry. "Location" by Mark Halliday is an example of an everyday poem that is provocative in its ordinariness. Here is how the poem starts:

> You could begin by saying, "This summer in Philadelphia . . ."
> But then you might instantly feel a gush of weariness
> and think No, no—something else—not
> "this summer," not "Philadelphia" . . .
> The thousands of men in sleeveless shirts
> who never bother to disturb your suspicion that
> they are all awesomely stupid.
> The teenage girls chewing green gum outside pizza joints.[71]

Writing about a poem by Frank Bidart, Robert Pinsky observes that "there is an initial shock at reading a poem which bases itself so genuinely on the writer's way of speaking."[72] Here, too, there is an initial shock, though there are not many surprises to follow. The poet shows how difficult it is to capture "this summer in Philadelphia" in poetry. He evokes it a little, in language the "thousands of men" and "the teenage girls" would understand though not be moved or changed by. "Not this," the poet continues. "But what?" The prophetic poet would have suggestions. Dante might suggest that he imagine the heat clotted on the skin of the baseball fans as a foretaste of the fires of hell. Robinson Jeffers would advise him to do more with the relationship between the City of Brotherly Love and the poet's disgust for the "awesomely stupid" men in sleeveless shirts. Whitman might say, Imagine the thousands of men as *sleepers*. Halliday moves the poem to Chicago. "Winter? In Chicago?—You could work that up." Although he tries to write about Chicago, he soon returns the poem to Philadelphia, which is "the mess on hand."

"The mess on hand" has power to compel here, and, like the power that compels the prophetic poet, "the mess on hand" does not care if what the poet writes is "poetry." Both kinds of poets speak, can only speak, from and about the space in which they find themselves. (Halliday's poem is called "Location.") Other kinds of spaces are glanced at and turned away from. Halliday's version of everyday poetry moves between summer in Philadelphia and winter in Chicago, "awesomely stupid" men and figures like Saul Bellow. In the next to last verse paragraph, he rejects the idea of writing poems that take place in Europe. It is as if he imagines everyday poetry as American and prophetic poetry as European. Here is the last verse paragraph of the poem:

> This summer in Philadelphia
> people on their front stoops glanced up at a jet
> droning toward the airport (one more thing beyond their control)
> and bent down to grasp today's thumb-smudging *Inquirer.*

Everyday poetry is people on their front stoops, while prophetic poetry is the jet they glance up at. The jet drones, and Halliday, whatever he has done, has not droned. A prophetic poet, too, may write poetry that seems more interested in establishing its space than in making music. It is one more thing the two kinds of poets have in common: the desire to represent the prophetic and the everyday can override the desire to write poetry.

I am trying to suggest that the particularly charged atmosphere of the relationship between the two voices comes as much from the similarities between them as from the differences. The differences suggest that the poet has to choose one or the other, that a poet cannot serve two masters, that trying to write in both voices would be fatally to split one's identity as a poet. The similarities suggest that the voices are already linked and that poets cannot put themselves in relation to one voice without putting themselves in relation to the other. I hope to develop the implications of that hypothesis in the rest of my book. First, I want to discuss the ways in which critics of postwar and contemporary poetry have written about the relationship between these voices and then, finally, to introduce the poets whose adventures in the speech genres of the prophetic and the everyday are the subject of my book.

Critics as Poets of the Prophetic and the Everyday

The difficulties of doing justice to the prophetic voice and the everyday voice can be shown not only by reading contemporary poetry but by reading critics of contemporary poetry. There are critics who are drawn to each of the voices I have been describing and who write in a version of that voice.

Critics of visionary poetry are particularly susceptible to a certain kind of rhetoric. Here is one example.

> The poetic world is rooted in the concrete particularity of lived experience; and poetic art, in its deepest aspect, is a way of loving the concrete, the particular, the individual. But, of course, to love is to enter the dimension of what the French philosopher Gabriel Marcel called *presence:* it is to approach a given reality out of a sense of its having the character of a *Thou,* whether that reality be "Fountains, Meadows, Hills and Groves" or some "Attic shape . . . with brede / Of marble men and maidens over-wrought" or a father who "moved through dooms of love." The intensity of its love for the quiddities and haecceities of experience conditions the poetic imagination, in other words, to view whatever it contemplates as ignited by the capacity for exchange, for reciprocity: it has the dimension of presence.

The critic continues, later: "True, the poet is also an adept in the art of supervising language, but his literary craftsmanship is wholly dedicated to the disclosure of the things and creatures of this world in their sheer specificity, 'in the starkness and strangeness of their being what they are.'"[73]

Readers have varying levels of tolerance for this sort of thing; some have an appetite for it. "Rooted," "concrete particularity," "lived experience," "loving the concrete," "the particular," "creatures," "sheer specificity": this is not the real everyday, other readers might be tempted to say. This is abstraction—and it isn't even real abstraction. Abstraction implies ideas to which anything can happen. Only one thing is going to happen to something once it has been called "specificity" or "sheer specificity." It is going to be taken with utmost seriousness and honored. Such readers might feel that there is something perverse about loving the concrete so much, lingering over it as if the world were a kind of petting zoo. The language presents itself as a language of happiness, of healthy-mindedness; it has no way to talk about its own piousness and coerciveness. There is a kind of hypocrisy too, I think, in its appeal to utmost seriousness. The everyday world is not being taken seriously at all. Neither the visionary poet nor the visionary critic is interested in things for what they are (whatever that might be) but only in what they can do for the poet. The visionary poet is going to perform an operation on things, and it can seem as if the visionary language is intended to ready the speaker, the reader, and (some readers almost imagine) the objects themselves for this operation. Saying over to ourselves words like "the particular," "the individual," "the concrete," we are made to feel tough-minded, pragmatic, while all the while we are being softened up for words like "dimension," "presence," "Thou," "quiddities," "haecceities," "the starkness and strangeness of their being what they are." In a moment the things we were honoring will start to glow. But what about the real everyday, all the things that seem not to be described or addressed or accounted for *at all* by words like "thisness" and "itness"? What about real strangeness, which cannot be evoked by the critic in parsonical tones or the poet in the tones of an "enamord mage"?[74]

Visionary critics will deplore such questions. Readers who resist these critics' rhetoric must not have "an attitude of simple enthrallment before the various givens of the earth," must lack a sense of wonderment and humility, must be impatient of or oblivious to sheer specificity, must not love the concrete enough, must hate Hopkins and Buber.

If some critics see their criticism as a continuation of visionary poetry by other means, other critics see visionary poetry as a continuation of their criticism by other means. Hyatt Waggoner describes the visionary poet as "one who sees better or farther, deeper or more truly than we." He wants more visionary poems to be written because "it would be a cause for hope in a time when reasons for hope are not easy to come by. For visionary poems can help us to see better, in greater depth, and in more humanly meaningful patterns of order."[75] The visionary reader who can see better, in greater depth, begins to seem like a combination of Hardy's Thrush and a New Critic.

There are prophetic critics as well. These critics want to champion prophetic poetry and to be the continuation of it by other means. Because prophetic poetry is socially more vulnerable than visionary or mystic poetry, prophetic critics are likely to want also to protect it. They may do this by occupying the same space as the prophetic poets while at the same time defending or protecting that space. Harold Bloom will do as an example. Prophetic critics may make the space seem more attractive to readers by, for example, speaking in the same elevated voice as the poets but offering a greater liveliness of tone, a wider range of reference, or sharper wit. At the same time, the prophetic critics might enact the role of the ravished reader in whom the prophetic poets could never believe. At the same time, prophetic critics might offer a more formidable defense of the project than the prophetic poets were able to produce. (Allen Grossman's writing on Crane is an example.)

Grossman writes, in fact, a particularly resourceful version of prophetic criticism. Although he writes his criticism in a prophetic voice, he imagines the prophetic voice *in conversation* with the voice of the everyday. That is, he uses his criticism to enact what does not often take place in his poetry. In his book *The Sighted Singer: Two Works on Poetry for Readers and Writers*, he uses the younger poet Mark Halliday to represent the voice of the everyday. The two poets engage in two dialogues, "The Winter Conversation (1981)" and "The Summer Conversation (1990)."[76] Their conversations are indispensable to anyone interested in the tensions that are the subject of this book. The relationship between the prophetic and the everyday is at every moment being redefined, renegotiated. Halliday tries to draw Grossman into his world, and Grossman tries to draw Halliday into his. Grossman is elegant and formal, while Halliday is warm and outgoing. Concessions are made and lines are drawn. For example, Grossman remarks to Halliday, "I have admired over and over again the capacity of your language to be in repose at the point of ordinary experience" (41). Although Grossman is incredulous that any poet could be in repose at such a place, he is forced to admit if not the reality of ordinary experience then at least the reality of another poet's repose at the point of it. We also get a vivid sense from these conversations that the prophetic poet may see himself as someone who irritates people—and, more interestingly perhaps, as someone to whom others behave tactfully. (We rarely find in other gadfly figures the consciousness that others are being tactful with them.) Grossman tells Halliday, "I think you have been as irritated as you will allow yourself to be at my unwillingness to allow language to rest in the ordinary experience, which you regard as so precious" (41). The everyday poet expresses not irritation at his differences with the prophetic poet but quiet wonder and expresses it in the language we reserve for mild insight. Halliday says, "I'm struck with a sense that I would never have written this stanza, Allen" (58). Yet he is aware of similarities—both are aware of them. Each seems sometimes to long to say what the other would say, as if the other's sheer proximity were potentially transformative. At one moment Grossman says, "The poems [of mine] I value most are the poems which conserve the names and to some extent the words of lost friends, poems such as 'The Department,'" and Halliday replies, "Allen, I am puzzled by that because it sounds like what I would have said" (77). There is an exciting sense in these conversations that the prophetic and everyday speech genres are free floating, available to all.

Part of Halliday's job is to carry on as if he were having a regular conversation, while Grossman is, at all times, having a "Winter Conversation." Grossman says, "I am, as you have not yet had the boldness to remark, to some degree an invented man. My sense of myself is similar to other men's sense of an artifact" (60). (There is much in these conversations that is reminiscent of Merrill's *The Changing Light at Sandover*, and one sometimes expects Grossman to speak in capital letters and to say, for example, MYND YOUR WEORK.) Readers may sometimes wonder what would happen to the balance of power if Halliday were to become bold and irritated and heap scorn on Grossman. Would the prophetic poet flee? (The original name for the first set of conversations was "Against Our Vanishing.") Grossman is afraid (he uses the word "nightmare") of two things: that his poetry will be unintelligible and at the same time that it will misrepresent him. In fact, Grossman expresses a variety of fears on behalf of prophetic poets (impossible as it is to imagine prophetic poets as a group or as a group that would ever allow itself to have a *spokesperson*, of all things). He tells Halliday, "This is a terror that I feel about myself: an inability to allow myself to rest in the space that lies open to us in the world of ordinary gratifications" (72). The prophet as analysand, like the mobster as analysand, is intrinsically comic, but the remarks have a kind of pathos, in part because of our sense that the prophetic poet is trying to move as freely as possible around what space he has. Grossman tells Halliday, "I am, however, profoundly uncertain about the relationship between my voice as a poet and my social voice. The voice that I utter as a reader of poetry frightens me, because it reminds me that I do not know what the appropriateness of these tonalities might be to this particular audience or to any audience" (81). Halliday, perhaps encouraged by remarks like this, takes an upbeat approach. "Your poems have changed. There is a texture of diversity and a kind of discursive hopefulness in many of your new poems, along with more frequent comic elements" (173). Grossman, as if to disabuse readers of any suggestion that he has turned into Robert Pinsky, remarks in sepulchral tones. "The new poetry is a comic poetry, a summer poetry. It enters into the abundance of things" (177). Some readers might suspect that the abundance of things will immediately sense that something alien has entered.

Halliday, too, expresses frustration with his own project. The space of the everyday is not always a congenial one for him. Although Grossman has been implying throughout their conversations that the space of the everyday must be a constricted one, for Halliday it often feels too big. The abundance of things (always to be called abundance by the everyday poet and not excess) is one that poets of the everyday must take seriously: it is what they have pledged themselves to respond to or at least record. (The abundance of things is always to be spoken of by the everyday poet with gratitude and not with fear.) Still, Halliday too begins to use the language of nightmare (one suspects, in part, out of a social impulse):

> There's a kind of nightmare version of my poetry project, and that of other poets who are in this respect like me—what you might call the nightmare of endless linear narrative—in which my job would be to write billions of poems. You know, there would be a poem for every trip to the supermarket, about the pathos and beauty of the particular young woman at the checkout counter; and frankly, sometimes I can feel excited by the prospect of living for another twenty or thirty years and writing lots of such poems. However, I do at other times sense that there's something increasingly frustrated and frustrating about that project conceived in that way, because there are too many supermarkets, with too many cashiers. (186)

At this point one or the other poet could have quoted Neil Hertz, who reminds us that

> there is, according to Kant, a sense of the sublime—he calls it the mathematical sublime—arising out of sheer cognitive exhaustion, the mind blocked not by the threat of an overwhelming force, but by the fear of losing count or of being reduced to nothing but counting—this and this and this—with no hope of bringing a long series or a vast scattering under some sort of conceptual unity. Kant describes a painful pause—"a momentary checking of the vital powers" followed by a compensatory positive movement, the mind's exaltation in its own rational faculties, in its ability to think a totality that cannot be taken in through the senses.[77]

Halliday seems close to Grossman in his suggestion that the everyday is a totality that cannot be taken in through the senses. The conversation continues, though, and they move to other topics. The everyday, in its more benign aspects, reasserts itself. And Grossman responds with his own benign and arctic observations. The two poets reveal a great deal about the relationships between their projects, but what they reveal most, perhaps, is the tremendous interest of both projects when considered in conjunction and the eccentricity of each when imagined separately.

Some critics are neither obviously prophetic nor everyday but are interested in both. Such critics tend, though, to be more alert to the dangers than to the possibilities of these voices. Charles Altieri writes about the failure of poetic attempts to write in these voices and about what poets do, as it were, instead of writing in such voices. He identifies, for example, one poet's "self consciously anti-bardic voice" or another poet's "antidomestic ferocity." He sees the everyday and the prophetic as a Scylla and Charybdis between which poets try to sail. He writes of certain poets who use the scenic mode that they are "engaged in negotiating a difficult passage between two destructive forces, on one side lies the interminable self consciousness that cripples so much of contemporary writing and on the other . . . vacuous prophecy."[78] The "scenic style," he argues, offers a watered-down, inoffensive version of both voices.

This notion of sailing between "two destructive forces" is appealing to a variety of critics. Robert Pinsky, for example, calls for a discursive poetry, which he describes this way: "It is speech, organized by its meaning, avoiding the distances and complications of irony on one side, and the ecstatic fusion of speaker, meaning and subject on the other. The idea is to have all of the virtues of prose, in addition to those qualities and degrees of precision which can be called poetic."[79] There are many advantages to this kind of writing, though not all of them seem to be advantages for poetry. What interests me is the way the discursive takes on some of the aspects of the two voices it is meant to remedy. Pinsky promises his readers that "such discourse does not absolutely exclude irony or ecstasy; rather it subordinates them to the idea of 'making your mind known.' Both wittiness and revelation, in such writing, may be sacrificed in the interest of that more literal, plainer, and perhaps larger ambition" (136). The discursive seems sometimes to move into the larger space left empty by the prophetic. And what the discursive does to the ordinary is what the prophetic or mystical poet might do: "I have in mind," Pinsky writes, "a range of passages in which the dull plains of description or the exactions of the 'image' are not abandoned, but transcended" (145). For some readers, discursive poetry, like a vegetarian meal, is always going to be about what is missing. Furthermore, readers for whom wittiness and revelation are almost everything they like in poetry will be unable to imagine an adequate replacement for irony and ecstasy. "Rather than a turn of wit or an impressively deep metaphor," Pinsky writes, "we are offered something more like the effort at truth of an earnest conversation, an essay or a letter on the same topic" (138). Why can't we have turns of wit, impressively deep metaphors, *and* earnest conversation in a poem? Discursive poetry may sacrifice much that some readers look for in poetry, but it does offer an escape from both Grossman's *and* Halliday's terror.

Some critics champion everyday poetry, and some have championed the prophetic. Some critics are deeply suspicious of both. It is hard to find critics who have written about the everyday and the prophetic with equal sympathy for both.

This Project

In this book I discuss four poets in whose work the relationships between the prophetic and the everyday are most acutely manifested. My first chapter is on the poetry of Robert Lowell. He begins by seeing himself, without irony, as a Jeremiah-like prophetic figure. His early work is ferociously prophetic. What interests me in the context of this book is that he began gradually to think of prophetic speech as a speech genre. He did something prophetic poets do not do. He reread his own poems.

What can it be like for prophetic poets to reread their own poetry? Such poets might become conscious of readers' expectations of which they were not fully conscious at the time of writing. Poets and theorists have explored the ways poets raise readers' expectations that a poem will conduct itself in certain ways and not others. Bakhtin, in his essay on speech genres, observes that

> when we select words in the process of constructing an utterance, we by no means always take them from the system of language in their neutral, *dictionary* form. We usually take them from *other utterances*, and mainly from utterances that are kindred to ours in genre, that is, in theme, composition, or style. . . . A speech genre is not a form of language, but a typical form of utterance; as such the genre also includes a certain typical kind of expression that inheres in it. (87)

William Wordsworth, in his Preface to *Lyrical Ballads*, is alert to what is excluded in this process of selection. Wordsworth reminds us that the poet "makes a formal engagement that he will gratify certain known habits of association; that he not only thus apprizes the Reader that certain classes of ideas and expressions will be found in his book, but that others will be carefully excluded."[80]

We may think of exclusions as necessary, as natural. Stevens writes,

> A poet writes of twilight because he shrinks from noon-day. He writes about the country because he dislikes the city, and he likes the one and dislikes the other because of some trait of mind or nerves; that is to say, because of something in himself that influences his thinking and feeling. . . . There are stresses that he invites; there are stresses that he avoids. There are colors that have the blandest effect on him; there are others with which he can do nothing but find fault. In music he likes the strings. But the horn shocks him. A flat landscape extending in all directions to immense distances placates him. But he shrugs his shoulders at mountains.[81]

For some readers, though, the noon-day shrunk from, the city disliked, the stresses avoided, the mountains shrugged at may silently become ghost-presences in some of the poems, which may be haunted by what Pinsky calls "the avoided possibility."[82] Lowell may have felt the "careful exclusion," then, not as craft but as incapacity, at least as an avoided possibility. Why avoid any possibilities? Rereading his early poems, Lowell became a more demanding, a more surprising reader than any he was likely to win with those poems. Wordsworth's remarks suggest that there is one "Reader" for one style and another for the excluded styles. Lowell is remarkable not simply in his ability to become a reader of his own prophetic poetry but in his refusal to see himself as a reader who wants only "one style."

What could he do about this excluded and excluding style? Robert von Hallberg, glossing the passage in Wordsworth, observes, "Especially because words carry with them known habits of association a poet's diction is a sure sign of how a poet imagines his audience. Poetic diction consists not only of terms that are frequently used but, more important, of words employed in such a way as to show that their habits of association are so well known that they can be taken for granted."[83] It is as if a class of ideas and expressions, once introduced, will follow habits of association as if they were laws. Another style, hitherto carefully excluded, can then enter only as an interruption— frequently as a preemption or usurpation. This would seem to suggest a kind of violence—a kind that is different from the sort of "bumping" Pinsky describes in Hardy: "Above all, Hardy's poems convey, repeatedly, a sense of collision: colloquial language banging against formal or archaic language." It is different, as well, from the "collisions and

mismarriages of language" Pinsky describes in Berryman.[84] The violence in early Lowell seems different, perhaps because he is not so sure
as Hardy or Berryman about where he is going. Lowell's early poems
seem to *suffer* the violence more; they seem not to know that the poet is
simply experimenting with effects. It may be that the sense of unpre-
dictability attracted Lowell toward changing his early style. He may
have sensed that a poet who can do anything is more powerful than a
poet who can simply do "powerful" poetry well.

But Lowell began to see that violence, the violence of mere alternation and interruption, was not interesting enough. What would be
more interesting? This question led him ultimately into the increasingly
experimental poetry of the later books. I focus mainly on the later books
of blank verse sonnets—*Notebook, History, For Lizzie and Harriet, The
Dolphin,* and *Day by Day*—because they have received less critical attention than they deserve and because it is in these poems that Lowell
most explicitly explores his desire to be everyday and prophetic at once.
He shows us that the prophetic voice is, in fact, a voice that people use
in everyday life and explores its possibilities in that new and revealing
light. In addition, he develops a sense that the political can be, for him,
a hybrid speech genre, allowing him to be prophetic and everyday at
once. James Longenbach has written, "Today, Lowell more often appears as a minor, catalyzing figure in critical narratives about Bishop's
career."[85] I hope to suggest that Lowell is a major poet and one who can
still be important as a catalyzing figure to many kinds of poets.

My second chapter is about the poetry of A. R. Ammons. I describe
the stages by which Ammons came to his position of confidence and
freedom. Ammons interrupts one of his own long poems to say, "this is
one possible kind / of song / and has one kind of veracity." He does not
like to rule out any possible kind of song, trying instead to remain open
to what he calls, in *Tape for the Turn of the Year,* his "countermotions."[86]
Two of these countermotions—the everyday voice and the prophetic
voice—are, I argue, crucial to Ammons's longevity and success as a
poet. He explores, in poem after poem, the unpredictable ways these
voices behave in each other's proximity. (Ammons is, like the other
poets in this study, drawn to representation of conversation.) His
understanding of the prophetic and the everyday accounts, I will argue,
for the shape not only of his career but of many of his individual poems.

Ammons is constantly searching for ways he can, in his poetry, be
prophetic and everyday at once. His "folksy" voice offers one way. A
more successful way arises in his scientific voice. He is particularly

interested in the role that scientific language plays in the relationship between the prophetic and the domestic. The scientific voice sometimes acts as another "countermotion" and sometimes as a voice that incorporates both the prophetic and the everyday voice. Ammons, in a late poem, wrote, "I would give up nothing if I had my way." His poetry is, like Lowell's, remarkable for its recuperation of the prophetic voice as well as for its demonstration of the extraordinary variety of tones of which an everyday voice is capable.

Randall Jarrell writes about those readers who want a contemporary poem's greatness "to be exactly the same as, only somehow entirely different from, the *Divine Comedy*."[87] My third chapter is on the work of James Merrill and concentrates on *The Changing Light at Sandover*. James Merrill and his companion, David Jackson, had, over the course of two decades, been consulting a Ouija board. The messages they received from the board and their own responses to those messages make up much of the poem. As one critic puts it, "Even if the two did make all of it up unconsciously, an experience has befallen them scarcely less amazing and wonderful than if, like the prophets of old, they had heard God's voice address them aloud."[88] The supernatural is Merrill's version of the prophetic voice. (The supernatural figures often speak in voices readers recognize as prophetic in tone and intent.) Merrill is extraordinarily resourceful at bringing the prophetic into relation with the everyday and at dramatizing the enormous variety of possible relationships between these voices. The voices flirt, threaten, instruct, ignore, and encourage each other. They also give each other pleasure, make each other laugh.

The human has often been seen as preliminary in relation to the "more than human" (to use Stevens's phrase). In Merrill's trilogy it is reimagined as collaborative. Like Grossman and Halliday, Merrill wants to imagine what the voices could learn from each other in their conversations. What if conversation could make the one voice weightier, the other lighter? What if each voice could grant the other a kind of innocence by association? Merrill is particularly interested in the role wit plays in the relationship between the supernatural and the domestic. Wit is an act of finding the similarity in dissimilarity; for Merrill, it is a way of bringing the two voices together. Wit is Merrill's hybrid speech genre; it does the work the political and the scientific do for the other poets in this study.

Adrienne Rich, the subject of my fourth chapter, also puts the everyday and the prophetic at the center of her poetry, and, like Lowell,

Ammons, and Merrill, she struggles to find a workable relationship between them. Questions of gender that are largely unexplored by the other three poets are central to Rich's work. Homosexuality is also, as it is for Merrill, central to her redefinition of domesticity. There is little that is playful or witty, though, about Rich's work. Like Lowell, she brings the prophetic and the everyday together in the political, but her motives are different from his: she brings them together in order to have a lever and a place to stand. To have access to both the everyday and the prophetic is to be able to change the world. It is crucial, then, that she avoid false versions of them. She moves back and forth with constant vigilance between the everyday and the prophetic, making sure they are accountable and answerable to each other.

Her poetry has had, so far, three phases. The poetry of the first phase (the poetry of the fifties) is technically accomplished but not always memorable. Many of the poems in her first two books are about the intuition that the world she knows is going to explode. In the poetry of the second phase (the poetry of the sixties and seventies) that world *has* exploded. How can her poetry do justice to the way the world now appears to her? The poetry of her first phase was prophetic but only in the sense that it prophesied the end of the world. Her later poetry becomes prophetic in a wider and more interesting sense while it remains prophetic in that limited sense. That is, she still sees into the future, but now she does so to predict beginnings rather than endings. In this phase, too, she learns to make constant adjustments in her poetry. Her new domestic space begins to seem too large, too impersonal, in a sense inhuman. She does not want the domestic to become indistinguishable from the prophetic, and she adjusts both the prophetic and the domestic by turning to her childhood and remembering the sources of both dictions in her early life. In the poetry of the third phase, then (the poetry of the eighties and nineties), she begins to explore the sources of her own authority. She gains a deeper sense of her own commitment to the idea of community and begins to explore an explicitly biblical voice.

These four poets illustrate my central argument more precisely and more powerfully than other poets could. They have put the relationship between the everyday and the prophetic at the center of their poetry and have been most successful in combining the two voices. Though they have already been critically discussed, their work has not been given precisely the emphasis I give it. I hope that the kinds of readings I offer here will be useful in reading other poets. I have limited myself, unwillingly, to American poetry for the simple reason that the idea of the prophetic and the everyday, different for each poet, would become distractingly various if I were to bring in poets from other countries. In my conclusion, I write about two younger American poets and show how they are responding to this particular inheritance.

I do not, in this book, intend to imply that there are compositional strategies that, applied to the task of bringing the prophetic and the everyday into relation, will bring success. One can imagine a different sort of book in which strategies are named and some of them (covertly) recommended. What I hope to do is simply to watch what certain post-war poets did in bringing the prophetic and the everyday together and try to describe their work in terms that are not too far distant from those they might have used. Readers cannot know how these strategies may be adapted by other poets until they have seen it done.

I would like to add a note here about an interpretive strategy in the chapters to follow. Because I believe that the most illuminating perspective on one poet's work is often the work of another poet, I use, more than is customary, the device of quoting a poem (or a comment by a poet) in the discussion of a poem by another poet. I do this in an effort to reconstruct the kind of literary and cognitive space in which I imagine the poem was conceived and asks to be read.

1

"I felt my guides no longer carried me"

Robert Lowell

In 1943 T. S. Eliot wrote, in a language both prophetic and nonprophetic:

> What is the late November doing
> With the disturbance of the spring
> And creatures of the summer heat,
> And snowdrops writhing under feet
> And hollyhocks that aim too high
> Red into grey and tumble down
> Late roses filled with early snow?
> Thunder rolled by the rolling stars
> Simulates triumphal cars
> Deployed in constellated wars
> Scorpion fights against the Sun
> Until the Sun and Moon go down
> Comets weep and Leonids fly
> Hunt the heavens and the plains
> Whirled in a vortex that shall bring
> The world to that destructive fire
> Which burns before the ice-cap reigns.
>
> That was a way of putting it—not very satisfactory:
> A periphrastic study in a worn-out poetical fashion,
> Leaving one still with the intolerable wrestle
> With words and meanings.[1]

None of the prophets in the Hebrew Bible says, "That was a way of putting it—not very satisfactory." Although Eliot wants the authority of prophetic speech, he cannot have it without problematizing it. And everyday speech, the language of "that was a way of putting it," is equally problematic for Eliot. It is difficult to sustain, and it too is, after all, only "a way of putting it." Robert Lowell, publishing his first book of poems three years after Eliot's *Four Quartets*, tried to write prophetic poetry—poetry about "rolling stars" and "destructive fire"—that would sound like not one way of putting it but the only way. Lowell's first two books, *Land of Unlikeness* (1946) and *Lord Weary's Castle* (1948), contained many of the poems readers think of when they think of the postwar prophetic voice. It is a voice pitched for the end of history. When history let the poetry down, the poet began to find the prophetic voice "not very satisfactory." Lowell began, gradually, to think of prophetic speech as something someone might say:

> The flies, the flies, the flies of Babylon
> Buzz in my ear-drums while the devil's long
> Dirge of the people detonates the hour
> For floating cities where his golden tongue
> Enchants the masons of the Babel Tower
> To raise tomorrow's city to the sun
> That never sets upon these hell-fire streets
> Of Boston, where the sunlight is a sword
> Striking at the withholder of the Lord:
> Flies, flies are on the plane tree, on the streets.[2]

What sort of person would want to speak that way—and why? What would such a speaker think later about having spoken that way? What would others—the speaker's family, for example—think of that speech? How do other people speak? Nobody can ask these questions and remain a purely prophetic poet.

Prophetic speech began to seem to Lowell to be a speech genre. In addition, he had to face the temptations and dangers of mad speech and see that kind of speech as a speech genre as well. Then he had to take on the difficulties of representing the everyday. The most charged aspect of the everyday for Lowell was to be the domestic aspect. Once he had accomplished the extraordinary feat of turning himself into a poet who could write plausibly and powerfully about domesticity, other kinds of everyday subjects, though still deeply challenging, would be open to him. What was particularly valuable about Lowell's example was his determination not to leave the prophetic voice behind. What uses did he find for the prophetic voice in his later poetry? Extraordinarily resourceful uses for it were found, I argue, in dozens of later poems, but the most surprising and moving use he made of it was in his political poetry. Robert von Hallberg is right to say that "of all the poets who have tried their hand at political poetry in the last thirty-five years, Lowell is the most accomplished and surely the most ambitious."[3] Political speech was for Lowell the most trustworthy, the most reliable way of speaking in prophetic and everyday voices at once.

Elizabeth Bishop wrote to Lowell in 1949, "I've always felt I've written poetry more by *not* writing it than by writing it."[4] Lowell believed, at that time, that the way to write poetry was to *write* it. Whereas Ammons slowly found his way to a more everyday voice because his prophetic poems weren't working as poems, Lowell's prophetic poems do work as poems—certainly as the kind of poem the New Critics, Lowell's friends and mentors, were calling for. Lowell's early poems are certainly "well wrought," yet they also communicate, in every line, restlessness, impatience. The enjambment is relentless: neither the end of the line nor the end of the stanza can impede the poetic line. Neither can any reservation, emotional or intellectual: if the poet feels hesitations or second thoughts, they find no place in the poem. Poems like "A Quaker Graveyard at Nantucket" are so turbulent, so joltingly expressive that a reader is relieved to find, in the "Our Lady of Walsingham" section of that poem, that the statue of Our Lady is "expressionless" (*LWC*, 19). Even boredom is, for Lowell, another spur to action, another motive for metaphor. In "Dora Markus," his version of the Montale poem, he writes that "even your ennui is a whirlwind, / circling invisibly—/ the let-ups non-existent" (*Imitations*, 107). The sense of "circling" is everywhere: the poems are dense with allusions, and tracking their many allusions leads the reader to writers—Melville, for example—who offer an analogous excitement. There really is no let-up.

Readers associate freshness with variety, with an openness to the world. Lowell's early poems are closed to the world; the poems repeat themselves, repeat each other—nevertheless, they feel fresh. They are persuasive in the reading, implausible in the memory, and persuasive again in the rereading. They feel fresh and persuasive even when (intellectually) they are moving in iron grooves.

Prophetic poems do not have to be religious poems. Lowell's are, even if the religion is hard to pin down. Raised an Episcopalian, he converted temporarily to Catholicism, though his Catholicism seems, in the early poems, to have much in common with Calvinism. The religious context does not help much to contextualize the work. Marius

Bewley has a good account of the oddity of Lowell's Catholic poetry. He argues that Lowell's sensibility

> is never at its ease in Catholic images. The very structure of his sensibility is centred in considerations that were of overwhelming importance to the early New Englanders, but which are alien to Catholic feeling—ideas of innate depravity, the utter corruption of human nature and creation, regeneration, damnation of the non-Elect, and a habit of tortuous introspection to test the validity of grace in the soul. All these doctrines have in Lowell's poetry professedly undergone conversion to Rome, but on the face of it they still look very much their old Protestant selves.[5]

The poems are dogmatic, but there is an uneasiness, as Bewley suggests, at the heart of their dogma. The uneasiness is all for the reader, though. Lowell converts it, converts all of his feelings, into a kind of undifferentiated prophetic turbulence.

Poets, especially poets in the fifties, did not generally start their careers speaking at top volume. Nor do many poets, starting out, worry so little about their right to speak or seem so unconcerned about where they are speaking from. Lowell assumes, from the start, a position of loftiness. Adrienne Rich would soon write, "Poetry never stood a chance / of standing outside history."[6] Lowell, in the forties, would have taken this not as a criticism but as a dare. In the introduction I referred to the moment in James Merrill's *The Changing Light at Sandover*, when one of his spirits tells him that "THE GREAT SCRIBES EXIST OUT OF TIME IN RADIANCE."[7] Substitute darkness for radiance, and that is the effect Lowell is trying for. He is a poet who seems to have all the conditions he needs. It seems a kind of freedom that other poets might envy. One might imagine, reading about Lowell's early poems, that they might be bold but serene and even playful at times. But to read the poems themselves is to feel over and over again how bitter, cranky, enraged poems can be. Lowell might have taken as his epigraph John Bunyan's lines, "God did not play in convincing of me; the Devil did not play in tempting of me; neither did I play when I sunk as into a bottomless pit, when the pangs of hell caught hold upon me: wherefore, I may not play in my relating of them."[8] Is Lowell, using prophetic poetry, trying for what was called in the forties "high seriousness"?

Possibly not. There is, in Lowell, a prosodic excess—in the alliteration, the enjambment—that does not quite correspond to the themes.

This excess, appearing in poem after poem, comes to seem a kind of se-cret, and exciting, unseriousness. There *is* play in the relating:

> The search-guns click and spit and split up timber
> And nick the slate roofs on the Holstenwall
> Where torn-up tilestones crown the victor. Fall
> And winter, spring and summer, guns unlimber
> And lumber down the narrow gabled street
>
> (*LWC*, 9)

Wallace Stevens interrupts one of his own poems to ask, "Is the func-tion of the poet here mere sound, / Subtler than the ornatest prophecy, / To stuff the ear?"[9] Lowell's early poems are about having the ability to produce the "ornatest prophecy" and, at the same time, to imagine pro-phetic poetry first of all as *sound:*

> In the great ash-pit of Jehoshaphat
> The bones cry for the blood of the white whale,
> The fat flukes arch and whack about its ears,
> The death-lance churns into the sanctuary, tears
> The gun-blue swingle, heaving like a flail,
> And hacks the coiling life out: it works and drags
> And rips the sperm-whale's midriff into rags
>
> (*LWC*, 18)

It would be hard to imagine this kind of thing done *better.* John Berry-man wrote, "The man really sounds like a prophet!" He also referred to "a talent whose ceiling is invisible."[10]

The ceiling is invisible, but the walls are in place. There are some things Lowell cannot do. The prophetic poets get their authority by convincing us that they cannot behave in any other way. "But I can't stop seeing like this," Adrienne Rich writes. "More and more I see like this everywhere."[11] But the difference between seeing and seeing *like* may trouble the prophetic poets. Poets who are highly conscious that more and more they "see like this" or "speak like this" may begin to wonder why they cannot—in some poems—see or speak differently. All speech belongs to one or another speech genre. Some poets police the boundaries of their chosen genre. Lowell has created poetic condi-tions where he cannot (as Rich can) write a poem in which he says, "I speak like this in every poem." Although he seems highly conscious of the expectations of the audience he has inherited from Eliot, his poems never address that audience directly. Intent on his own procedures, he never looks up or away. Lowell cannot talk, in the poems, about his own desire to "speak like this," his desire to take (and offer) the particular pleasure these poems afford. Whitman was always ready to dramatize his desire to give pleasure, but Lowell, probably in response to Eliot, is working at the farthest reaches of prophetic severity.

If he cannot imagine prophetic speech as just one of the ways of speaking in a poem, he cannot yet imagine what these other ways are. Wallace Stevens, in "The Comedian as the Letter C," writes, "How many poems he denied himself / In his observant progress, lesser things / Than the relentless contact he desired."[12] Readers may be able to feel, though, in the early poems the presence of the poems Lowell is denying himself. They make themselves present as a never fully felt, never fully narrated set of situations involving a family. T. S. Eliot has a provocative comment in a letter to John Hayward on his own failure to exploit the never fully felt, never fully narrated in a poem. About "Little Gidding," he says, "The defect of the whole poem, I feel, is the lack of some acute personal reminiscence (never to be explicated, of course, but to give power from well below the surface)."[13] Eliot's remark suggests the difficulty that prophetic poets have with the "acute personal reminiscence." Where should it be put? How far below the surface? What sort of power will it give the poem? And what effects will such power have on a prophetic poem? Lowell must have asked himself those kinds of questions as well. If his personal past was operating in the poems anyway, he might want to have some kind of power over that operation. Also, he may have felt that the mastery might be easy. His family may have seemed, as a topic, to *resemble* the prophetic topics; it seemed as if it would lend itself to his violent, compressed, charged style. Surely he could write about his family without having to alter the poetry?

He begins to approach the topic in a gingerly way. The first indoor setting in *Lord Weary's Castle*—although there is someone "skulking" behind "storm windows" in "New Year's Day"—is the "fifth floor attic" in "The First Sunday in Lent," the place where as a child the poet hid his possessions. Here is part 1:

> The crooked family chestnut sighs, for March,
> Time's fool, is storming up and down the town;
> The gray snow squelches and the well-born stamp
> From sermons in a scolded, sober mob
> That wears away the Sabbath with a frown,
> A world below my window. What will clamp
> The weak-kneed roots together when the damp

> Aches like a conscience, and they grope to rob
> The hero under his triumphal arch?
>
> This is the fifth floor attic where I hid
> My stolen agates and the cannister
> Preserved from Bunker Hill—feathers and guns,
> Matchlock and flintlock and percussion-cap;
> Gettysburg etched upon the cylinder
> Of Father's Colt. A Lüger of a Hun,
> Once blue as Satan, breaks Napoleon,
> My china pitcher. Cartridge boxes trap
> A chipmunk on the sabre where they slid.
>
> (*LWC*, 21)

Here the poet wants (like Elizabeth Bishop in "Under the Window: Ouro Prêto") to look at "a world below my window." But Lowell uses the more exciting as an escape from the less exciting—melodrama as an evasion of drama. The poet does not so much see an actual tree out the window as a literalized "family tree." The tree, "crooked," "tormented," is congenial. In the final stanza, the speaker prays to become an "unblemished Adam" who will be able to see "the limbs of the tormented chestnut tree / Tingle" and "hear the March-winds lift and cry: / 'The Lord of Hosts will overshadow us.'" The speaker of the poem wants, that is, to see something more exciting even than a tormented tree—he wants to see a tormented tree tremble.

"The First Sunday in Lent" opens up a kind of domestic space for the poetry, a space that will not always be "overshadowed" by the prophetic voice. Lowell's opening up of this space had consequences for other poets. Lyric poets, for centuries, avoided imagining people living ordinary lives in houses. (Epic poets, by definition, were not interested.) In "The Miller's Tale" people are in houses, but they are playing tricks on each other; in Jonson's and Marvell's country houses the people are behaving irreproachably. Nobody behaves in any *ordinary* ways. Cowper, in *The Task,* asked his readers to imagine him in and around his house puttering—but he was recommending the everyday as therapy. Wordsworth and his sister are always outside. None of Coleridge's "conversation poems" (except "Frost at Midnight") takes place in a house. Tennyson shows us himself *outside* Hallam's house—except at Christmas, but Christmas is not an everyday occasion. Dickinson writes about life inside a house, of course, but her sense of the domestic avoids two crucial elements of domesticity: boredom and desultory conversation. Whitman "installed" the muse—but no people—"amid the kitchen ware." Coventry Patmore, in order to imagine a woman in the house, had to call her an angel. George Meredith (an influence on Lowell) put a couple in a house, but they justify their presence in the poem by fighting. Yeats celebrated ancestral houses but not the ordinary life inside them. Men and women leading ordinary lives indoors was, for three hundred years, an area novelists and playwrights had almost all to themselves.

The attic in "The First Sunday in Lent" is indoors, but it is still a prophetic space. We learn more about life in the attic in another poem in *Lord Weary's Castle*, "After the Surprising Conversions":

> Once we saw him sitting late
> Behind his attic window by a light
> That guttered on his Bible; through that night
> He meditated terror, and he seemed
> Beyond advice or reason, for he dreamed
> That he was called to trumpet Judgment Day
> To Concord.
>
> (66)

There is a limit to what can be learned about such prophetic figures because nobody who knows them knows very much about them. They are safe from all inquiry, from all discourses but their own. Lowell, moving his poems indoors, often imagines his speakers in gloomy and airless spaces. (Other indoor spaces in *Lord Weary's Castle* are a "Bible House" and a prison.) Sometimes Lowell seems unable to check the inward movement, and the poem takes place in some deep interior space. The reader, and perhaps the poet, begins to miss the world, however uninhabitable, outside the rooms. Outside—outside the speaker's mind, outside the speaker's attic room—it may be Armageddon, but at least the prophet can breathe. Though he is not interested in looking and listening, he himself can feel visible and audible. It is imperative "to tell the racing world that it must die"—he is not interested in what the world itself might say (*LWC*, 22). There is a preacher in one of Lowell's early poems whose "mouthings still / Deafen my poor relations on the hill" (*LWC*, 26). There *are* some encounters between people, but when people do confront each other (one man "laughs into my face until I cry"), such confrontations are not likely to be Proustian in their nuances (*LWC*, 22).

The relationships between characters in Lowell's early poetry—even the relationship between the poet and himself—are mysterious rather than complicated. In "Colloquy in Black Rock" the only colloquy is the one that happens between the poet and his heart. Another prophetic poet might say, as Eliot does, "I said to my heart be still" or else, as Stevens does, "keep quiet in the heart." The measured, stately prophetic voice, however, is what Lowell wants to avoid. "Beat faster, faster," this poet tells *his* heart (*LWC*, 11). Lowell comes not only at the end of history but at the end of prophetic poetry: all the rules can be broken. (It is imperative that he not sound too much like Eliot or Stevens or Yeats, otherwise the *reader* might begin to think of prophetic poetry as another speech genre.) Again, the speaker's confrontation with himself is not complicated. Harold Bloom writes that Shakespeare, in his soliloquies, shows "the representation of change by showing people pondering their own speeches and being altered through that consideration."[14] The speakers in Lowell's early poetry learn nothing about themselves. There is no time to learn, there would be no time to absorb the lesson. As he tells us later in the poem, "All discussions / end in the mud-flat detritus of death." The word "discussion" would become a crucial word for Lowell, but now he is too impatient for discussion—even for a discussion with himself.

The prophetic poet can talk to himself as long as the conversation is extreme, enigmatic. He can talk about family relations as long as the same conditions pertain. Lowell's poem "Falling Asleep over the Aeneid" ends:

> Mother's great-aunt, who died when I was eight,
> Stands by our parlor sabre. "Boy, it's late.
> Vergil must keep the Sabbath." Eighty years!
> It all comes back. My Uncle Charles appears.
> Blue-capped and bird-like. Phillips Brooks and Grant
> Are frowning at his coffin, and my aunt,
> Hearing his colored volunteers parade
> Through Concord, laughs, and tells her English maid
> To clip his yellow nostril hairs, and fold
> His colors on him . . .
>
>   (*Mills*, 103)

Lowell sent Elizabeth Bishop a draft of this poem, and she wrote back, asking, "Why does the great-great aunt laugh, I wonder."[15] The question suggests that the great-great-aunt laughs only because laughter would, at that moment, be strange and arresting. Adrienne Rich, remembering her own early poetry, writes, "In those years formalism was part of the strategy—like asbestos gloves, it allowed me to handle materials I couldn't pick up barehanded."[16] A reader may feel that Lowell is, in his early poems, using a similar strategy. It is not simply the formalism of the poems—the tightly rhymed stanzas, the refrains—but also, in a sense, the *formality* of the prophetic voice that is part of the strategy. This formality is particularly noticeable when family scenes are evoked. In a poem in *Day by Day*, Lowell will write, "We are poor passing facts, / warned by that to give / each figure in the photograph / his living name" (127). The prophetic poet, though constantly calling out to people ("cousin," "my cousin," "child," "my child"), rarely uses their names. There is a formality in the address—as if the prophet were wearing not asbestos but silk gloves. A kind of fastidiousness is at work. Words denoting family relations are simply inserted into poems. In "The Death of the Sheriff," he writes, "Nothing underneath the sun / Has bettered, Uncle, since the scaffolds flamed / On butchered Troy" (*LWC*, 73). What is the word "uncle" doing in these lines?[17] The word often gives a poem a dandyish tone, as in Stevens's "Le Monocle de Mon Oncle" or Rich's "The Uncle Speaks in the Drawing Room." When Lowell uses the word "uncle" it sounds Shakespearean (in part because of all the "nuncles" in the clown speeches and in part because of the presence and force of the word "uncle" in *Hamlet*). But Lowell is after another effect that is also Shakespearean: dissociated speech is being spoken in the presence of relations. (Ophelia's last speech gets a great deal of its power from taking place in front of her family.) The word "uncle" has a destabilizing effect on the parts of "The Death of the Sheriff" that are about history and violence—but the violent, the prophetic parts of the poem equally have a limiting effect on the domestic resonance of the word.

One of Lowell's projects at this stage of his career is to keep ordinary happiness out of his poems. He is less successful, though, at keeping ordinary unhappiness out. Any emotion that might seem susceptible to solace gets assigned to personifications rather than people. In "Winter in Dunbarton," "the coke-barrel in the corner whimpers" (*LWC*, 29). In "The Quaker Graveyard in Nantucket," "the high tide / Mutters to its hurt self" (*LWC*, 17). Lowell's early poems might be compared to a poem like Coleridge's "Dejection: An Ode." In Lowell's early poems, the poet expresses the grand emotions, and the natural objects feel the lesser ones—to the extent, that is, that there are lesser emotions to be felt. No people in Lowell's early poems are given any emotions that are not extreme. If there are two brothers in a poem, they turn out to be Cain and Abel; if there is a married couple, they turn out to be Adam and Eve. If the characters in a poem are taken not from the Bible but from life, their situation will be so lurid (or so biblical) as to overshadow all other circumstances. The brother and sister in "Her Dead Brother" are engaging in incest. Relations between fathers and sons too seem melodramatic and mysterious rather than dramatic and complex. The speaker of "Christmas Eve under Hooker's Statue" says, "I am cold: / I ask for bread, my father gives me mould" (*LWC*, 23). Such moments have the crudity and emotional violence of Beckett's *Molloy* but without Beckett's humor. Sometimes the violence is not merely emotional. The "flintlock" from "The First Sunday in Lent" returns (as Chekhov demanded) in "Rebellion." The speaker addresses his father:

> You damned
> My arm that cast your house upon your head
> And broke the chimney flintlock on your skull.
> Last night the moon was full:
> I dreamed the dead
> Caught at my knees and fell:
> And it was well
> With me, my father. Then
> Behemoth and Leviathan
> Devoured our mighty merchants.
>
> (*LWC*, 35)

This is an indoor poem that wants to get outdoors as quickly as possible. The speaker of "Rebellion" may refer to a house, but he brings it, in the same line, down on his father's head. It is as if the poem cannot wait to talk about what all the other prophetic poems talk about: Leviathan devouring mighty merchants.

Lowell uses figures like Adam and Eve, in a sense, typologically. He imagines biblical families as a way to practice imagining his own. His actual family, though, being by such strategies unsatisfied, continues to press on him, and he continues to try to accommodate them. The most successful poems about his family in the first book—"The Quaker Graveyard in Nantucket" and "In Memory of Arthur Winslow"—are elegies. Elegy is a mode congenial to prophetic poets, as the examples of Milton and Whitman and Crane suggest. It can require minimal adjustment of tone. Many prophetic poets cannot write, say, about love without calling their vocation into question. (Emily Dickinson and Hart Crane are exceptions.) To write an elegy, on the other hand, a prophetic poet simply has to have heard of a death in the world. That death, then, can be an occasion for prophetic emotions—Lowell chooses disgust as his. "The Quaker Graveyard in Nantucket"—Lowell's elegy for his cousin, Warren Winslow—shows little personal grief or even family feeling. Even his disgust is upstaged by the verbal excitement. Lowell, in these elegies, turns the full force of his prophetic rhetoric on his family. ("The preacher's mouthings still / Deafen my poor relations on the hill.") Nothing his relations did in their life is as exciting as what he can do with their death. And nothing about his cousin's death hits home, nothing about it makes Lowell think of home—we learn only that his cousin's death takes place in "these home waters" (*LWC*, 15). It is as if Lowell has taken the passages in "Lycidas" that were specifically about Edward King *in the water* and perversely moved them to the emotional center of his own elegy. In "In Memory of Arthur Winslow," his elegy for his grandfather, he writes,

> the ghost
> Of risen Jesus walks the waves to run
> Arthur upon a trumpeting black swan
> Beyond Charles River to the Acheron
> Where the wide waters and their voyager are one.
> (*LWC*, 25)

The poem itself, in a sense, "runs" his grandfather to the last line, where he can become, like Lowell's cousin, one with the wide water. The wide water, in these poems, represents the power of Lowell's prophetic voice. His family is lost in it. In Lowell's elegy for his grandfather, he refers to "half forgotten Starks and Winslows." Both these elegies half-forget their subjects.

Wittgenstein, in his *Philosophical Investigations*, says that "to imagine a language means to imagine a form of life."[18] Lowell is imagining a form of life (a life lived with other people in houses), but he cannot yet imagine a language for it. These are poems about families, but they are not the family poems he has been "denying" himself. Those poems do seem to make their presence felt in these poems, though. It is in his elegies that the combination of prosodic playfulness and savagery of tone is most striking. The ferocity of the elegies—they stand out in a book of ferocious poems—suggests that the family, more than any other topic, brings forth all the expressive and repressive energies of his style. He can write about it using his prophetic voice, but it seems to require, somehow, *more* from his prophetic voice. The elegies are not only more intense but longer than most of the other poems. The first elegy is seven pages long, and the second is four. (Most of the poems in *Lord Weary's Castle* are a page long.) Lowell, writing about his family, has a kind of austere unstoppability. He is like the Puritan in Bunyan's *Life and Death of Mr. Badman* who says, over and over, "I have yet much more to say."

In Lowell's next book, *The Mills of the Kavanaughs,* the prophets, no longer in small towns but in cities, will become even more isolated. Lowell, like Allen Ginsberg, will imagine a world of "bleak rooms and coldwater flats." The two poets (remembering Crane's "subway scuttle, cell or loft") will help to urbanize the "high lonely tower" that prophetic poets from Milton to Yeats associated with prophecy. Not that Lowell's prophetic poetry is very much like Ginsberg's. Lowell would learn more from poets of the everyday (and from Ginsberg as a poet of the everyday) than he could learn from prophetic poets. Everybody in *Howl* either talks or is about to talk the way a prophet does. Lowell, unlike Ginsberg, imagines not just failed prophets but nonprophetic people. (He likes to dramatize the nonprophetic voice caught in a sort of prophetic language storm.) Ginsberg's prophets come down from their heights alone—"down shuddering mouth-wracked and battered bleak of brain all drained of brilliance in the drear light of Zoo."[19] Lowell will imagine, more and more, this "coming down" as a "coming home," and in later poems he will reimagine Ginsberg's "drear light of Zoo" as his daughter's bedroom with its stuffed animals. Ginsberg, in other words, was not helpful for Lowell in terms of showing him how to keep writing. Also, Lowell did not have access to the Beat subculture that could glamorize prophets by putting them in a specific cultural context. He was on his own.

In *The Mills of the Kavanaughs,* then, hoping to say different things than he had said before, Lowell turns to dramatic monologue. There are seven poems in that book, and the speakers of at least half of them are mad—or married to mad people. The mad speech in the poems may come in part from tensions in the poet's life but also from a desire to swerve away from prophetic speech. Mad speech offers if not an escape from elevated speech, then a different kind of elevated speech. They are, in Lowell's imagination, adjacent speech genres. The problem, as many critics noted at the time, is that the personae sound like the prophetic speakers of the earlier book, only more so. (I will have more to say in this chapter about Lowell's representations of mad speech.)

Many of the poems get close to the everyday by focusing on holidays. The ritual aspects of these holidays, the hypnotic nature of the language associated with them, tempt Lowell, but so do the ways in which holidays are intimately related to everyday life. What he knows how to do best, though, is to write about rituals. Rituals show us everyday activity, but it is extremely charged activity. When we are told that the husband in the title poem of *The Mills of the Kavanaughs* "turned the burners up / And stirred the stoup of glüg," his action seems ominous (91). Of course, Lowell is, in a sense, continually turning the burners up. The atmosphere becomes more ominous after the festivities are over. Philip Larkin, in his poem, "Talking in Bed," writes, "Talking in bed ought to be easiest, / Lying together there goes back so far." The couple in Larkin's poems struggle "to find / Words at once true and kind, / Or not untrue and not unkind."[20] In Lowell's early poetry, talking in bed goes back *quite* far: talking in bed means talking in an archaic, scary way. The wife in "The Mills of the Kavanaughs" says to her husband,

> "'You have gored me black and blue.
> I am all prickle-tickle like the stars;
> I am a sleepy-foot, a dogfish skin
> Rubbed backwards, wrongways; you have made my hide
> Split snakey, Bad one—*one!*' Then I was wide
> Awake, and turning over."
>
> (*Mills*, 92)

Talking in bed in Lowell's early poetry means finding words that are mad and cruel. "'Michael', she whispered, 'all I want to do / Is kill you'" (*Mills*, 117). The people in Lowell's prophetic poetry were living, whether they knew it or not, at the end of time; these people are living at the end of their marriages. Significantly, the atmosphere (for the reader) feels similar. In both cases there is no possibility, no question of time passing normally. In "The Mills of the Kavanaughs," the title poem of the collection, Lowell writes, "Then life went on; you lived, or lived at least / To baby-smile into the brutal gray / Daylight each morning" (*Mills*, 95). Between the phrases "Then life went on" and "each morning" there are only the brutal and grotesque.

Why was it so difficult to write a poem in the first person about ordinary life inside a house? Dramatic monologues were not, for Lowell, the answer. In a sense, all the earlier poems had been dramatic monologues. The solution might lie not in the choice of speaker but in the choice of the occasion. In some of his poems, Lowell tries to imagine not the ends of situations but their beginnings. A wedding poem, for example, might be a way to write about *incipient* domesticity, domesticity still unmarred by violence. In a wedding poem, a family would be gathered around. The prophetic poet could wish everybody well, modulating the strange harshness of his tone into, say, the strange sweetness of the Song of Solomon. The act of choosing a new family rather than being yoked to an old one might bring out something new in the poet's range of feeling. But Lowell would not modulate his tone for elegy, and he will not alter it when he writes about weddings. In "Where the Rainbow Ends," Lowell writes,

> The victim climbs the altar steps and sings:
> "Hosannah to the lion, lamb, and beast
> Who fans the furnace-face of is with wings:
> I breathe the ether of my marriage feast."
>   (*LWC*, 75)

This is a spiritual wedding and not a real one. Still, the idea of a real (and macabre) wedding is suggested in the lines. Poems about weddings are, for the early Lowell, poems about marriage—about his parents' marriage, about his own first marriage. His first wife sounds like his mother, and both of them sound like the speakers in his prophetic poems. Anne Kavanaugh, the wife in "The Mills of the Kavanaughs," says, "You must abide / The lamentations of the nuptial mass—" (*Mills*, 96). Marriage might begin in gladness, but despondency and madness come quickly. In "Between the Porch and the Altar," the speaker says to his girlfriend, "I taste my wife / And children while I hold your hands. I knife / Their names into this elm" (*LWC*, 48). (Infidelity is a constant theme in Lowell's poetry, but he does not always write about it in this macabre way.) Marriage is, like other relationships, violent, but it has, unlike other relationships, an element of the perverse about it: its victims have chosen it.

To write about childhood might be another way to write about beginnings—and to make, in the poetry, a new beginning. But Lowell's attempts to write about his own childhood, though frequently powerful, reach similar dead ends. Childhood does not, as it did for Ammons, offer Lowell a memory of preprophetic innocence. He cannot find in his childhood the kind of "lost world" that poets like Jarrell have gone there to find. The figure in the fifth floor attic in "The First Sunday in Lent," fascinated by military history, is a typical portrait of the poet as a child. Lowell remembers himself as violent, imaginative. "I played Napoleon in my attic cell" (*LWC*, 24). Lowell was—it turns out—a prophet from the start. He is like Jeremiah, who (in the King James version) tells us, "Then the word of the Lord came unto me, saying, 'Before I formed thee in the belly I knew thee; and before thou camest forth out of the womb I sanctified thee, and I ordained thee a prophet unto the nations'" (Jer. 1:4–5). In *Notebook*, Lowell writes, sardonically, "From the womb, I say, I scorned Leviathan, / found my intemperate, apocalyptic terms" (206). In "The Exile's Return," the only children in the village are "strutting children" (*LWC*, 9). Sometimes these children are figures of anarchic rage. The strutting child returns in Lowell's translation of Rimbaud's "The Poet at Seven":

> He would clap his hands on his rump,
> and strut where the gloom of the hallway rotted
> the hot curtains. He stuck out his tongue,
> clenched his eyes shut, and saw dots.
>
> (*Imitations*, 77)

To return to childhood is to return to a gloomy and airless space. Childhood, like marriage, is grotesque.

Given all this, it is somewhat startling to remember that Lowell did write fresh and wonderful domestic poems about marriage and fatherhood. He became one of the foremost American poets of domesticity— of heterosexual domesticity—as Merrill became the foremost American poet of homosexual domesticity. Lowell, like Merrill, will imagine domesticity as a shared experience. It was not inevitable, though, that he would imagine it as shared: the boy in the fifth floor attic is, in a way, domestic; he has carefully furnished the room. And there are poets (Gary Snyder, for example, in many of his poems) who imagine domesticity as cheerful solitude. It is moving that he does imagine it as shared. At the same time, Lowell will become a poet of separation and divorce. There had not been many poems about separation and divorce. Like the topic of people living ordinary lives in houses, the topics of separation and divorce were, before Lowell's generation, reserved to the novelist and playwright and the occasional poet like George Meredith. Lowell, however, makes these topics his own. There is a certain wit in his approach to the subject matter. Whereas Blake wrote a prophetic poem called "Milton," and Tennyson and Longfellow, both poets drawn to the prophetic voice, wrote sonnets called "Milton," only Robert Lowell would think to write a poem called "Milton in Separation." It is almost as if the prophetic and the domestic are joined in three words. (Robert Graves was after a similar effect in 1944 when he called a biography *Wife to Mr. Milton.*) Other postwar poets will write about separation, but Lowell is distinctive in his treatment of it. Merrill, for example, is inclined to write about the "dim wish of lives to drift apart."[21] Adrienne Rich takes a tone that is both utopian and acerbic: "the more I live the more I think / two people together is a miracle."[22] Lowell is readier to place (and accept) blame for the drifting apart; his vision of separation, perhaps because children are involved, is more interested in aftermaths and consequences. But the choice of domesticity as a central theme is fateful. It was as if many of his early poems had been devised to keep his family out. His poems will more and more be written to allow his family—especially his new family, his wives and children—in. And the idea of family will, in his later poetry, stay when all the elements of that organization—plot, narrative, syntactic connection—drop out.

There are eight years between *The Mills of the Kavanaughs* and his next book, *Life Studies*, and in that period Lowell begins to make changes in his style. I cited Wallace Stevens's lines in my introduction: "To say more than human things with human voice, / That cannot be; to say human things with more / Than human voice, that, also, cannot be." Since, if Lowell writes about domesticity in the prophetic voice it will not seem like domesticity, he tries a new voice, and since a new voice in the old prosody will seem like new wine in old bottles, he begins to write poems that don't rhyme, poems without metrical structure. He gives up the tightly organized stanzas. He gives up enjambment. He brings domesticity for the first time to the center of his poetry. The poems in *Life Studies* are still not exactly about people living ordinary lives indoors. There is still the sense of luridness, of scandal, that dominated *The Mills of the Kavanaughs*: in some poems it feels as if the book of Revelation had moved into lowercase and become a book of revelations. And he is still, in many poems, writing about his family with the abrupt devotional ardor ("Grandpa! Have me, hold me, cherish me!") that he had used in *Lord Weary's Castle*.[23] But now he allows the members of his family more personality, that is, a wider ranger of tonalities: they aren't always being sent off to become one with the wide water. With the introduction of his family comes the introduction of new speech genres.

In the early poetry, aspects of the ordinary world were yoked by violence to the hurtling forward motion of the poem. The poetics of yoking was reflected, for example, in the practice of excessive hyphenation. There were eight hyphenated words in "The Exile's Return," the first poem in *Lord Weary's Castle*. It is as if words had to be yoked to other words, or they would fly off and make a poem of their own. Images from the ordinary world were also chastened, sometimes by being neglected. The "watermelons gutted to the crust" in "Colloquy in Black Rock" brought nothing from the world of watermelons: they were there because Lowell needed victims of violence. In the elegy "In Memory of Arthur Winslow," there was a reference to "longshoreman Charon." Watermelons and longshoremen: these elements from pastoral and georgic were yoked to the prophetic mode, and any other resonance in them was curtailed.

With *Life Studies,* Lowell begins to explore new speech genres. Another poet might simply have tried to yoke speech genres together or juxtaposed thematic material, writing poems full of references to Jeremiah and kitchen sinks. Such a poetics—though he does experiment with it in some poems—is too literal minded for Lowell. What he wants to juxtapose within speech genres is tone. The language experiment is, above all, a tonal experiment. In the introduction to *Imitations,* apologizing for the extreme freedom of his translations, he writes, "I have been reckless with literal meaning, and labored hard to get the tone." He adds, "In poetry tone is of course everything." Ideology (even Catholicism, as he himself admitted later) must have seemed to Lowell too full of literal meaning. Although he calls one of his later books *History,* he does not have a theory of history and is not really a poet of ideas. Merrill calls Yeats's *A Vision* "that maze of inner logic, dogma, dates."[24] Lowell's later poems are the maze without the dogma. Although his commitment to the dogma was always, as I said, somewhat theatrical, he is, nevertheless, surrendering access to a tremendous and reliable source of authority when he gives up access to dogma. Dogma is not interesting to him anymore, I think, because he has something more absorbing to work with.

When James Longenbach writes that *Life Studies* "has lost some of its power because the battles in which it engages no longer seem quite so meaningful," I think he misunderstands the battles in which Lowell is engaging in that book, and that misunderstanding allows him to underestimate Lowell's value as an example to other poets.[25] Lowell is struggling to construct a postreligious voice that will not be like Eliot's or Stevens's, that will not have to have, as its groundnote, majestic sonority. How can he get access to as wide a variety of tonalities as possible, and how can he achieve mastery over them while writing poems that have some sense of freedom and play? This emphasis on tone is a gamble. It could have made Lowell seem trivial: writers who emphasize tone tend to move toward ever more defiant instances of it. In fiction such an emphasis may produce Ronald Firbank and in poetry the Sitwells. But by tone Lowell means (to use Merrill's phrase) "contrasts and disruptions of tone."[26] Lowell's experiments seem neither trivial nor limiting because he shows how an interest in speech genres may be linked (in complicated but not mysterious ways) to the experience of being in the world and to the survival of his poetry.

In "Waking Early Sunday Morning" (from his next book, *Near the Ocean,*) Lowell interrupts a prophetic stanza, but not to write, "That was a way of putting it—not very satisfactory." Instead he writes, "Sing softer!" Then he wonders, "But what if a new / diminuendo brings no true / tenderness, only restlessness, / excess" (*NTO*, 20). Lowell's struggle for "a new diminuendo" presents him with difficulties. Although he knows that domesticity is a language, he also knows, as Eliot did, that he cannot have it without problematizing it. Eliot is not a guide: his juxtapositions in *Four Quartets* were too stately, too ceremonial. Lowell wants to be quick, unceremonial. "Man and Wife," one of his first attempts to juxtapose speech genres, is also one of his first successful poems about domesticity.

To say that something has been "domesticated" is usually a way of saying that it has been made simple, safe. In Lowell's work, it often means that something has been made complicated:

> Tamed by *Miltown,* we lie on Mother's bed;
> The rising sun in war paint dyes us red;
> in broad daylight her gilded bed-posts shine,
> abandoned, almost Dionysian.
> At last the trees are green on Marlborough Street,
> blossoms on our magnolia ignite
> the morning with their murderous five days' white.
> All night I've held your hand,
> as if you had
> a fourth time faced the kingdom of the mad—
> its hackneyed speech, its homicidal eye—
> and dragged me home alive. . . . Oh my *Petite,*
> clearest of all God's creatures, still all air and nerve:
> you were in your twenties, and I,
> once hand on glass
> and heart in mouth,
> outdrank the Rahvs in the heat
> of Greenwich Village, fainting at your feet—
> too boiled and shy
> and poker-faced to make a pass,
> while the shrill verve
> of your invective scorched the traditional South.
>
> Now twelve years later, you turn your back.
> Sleepless, you hold
> your pillow to your hollows like a child;
> your old fashioned tirade—
> loving, rapid, merciless—
> breaks like the Atlantic Ocean on my head.
>
> (*LS,* 87)

This is a powerful poem about a marriage. It is, at the same time, a poem about various speech genres—some, in the context of the poem, real and others unreal.

Mad speech is back. Lowell had explored the resources of this language in *The Mills of the Kavanaughs* and in some of the other poems in *Life Studies*. Now he sees it as "hackneyed." (In one of the poems in *History*, a painter friend says, "I had to say what every madman says" [181].) There is a suggestion in the poem that, for the husband, any elevated speech (prophetic speech, for example) would be too hard to tell from mad speech; there is the suggestion that any elevated speech, in other words, would be hackneyed. In an early essay, Lowell uses the word "hackneyed" where we might expect the word "prophetic": "I rolled out Spenserian stanzas on Job and Jonah surrounded by recently seen Nantucket scenery. Everything I did was grand, ungrammatical, and had a timeless, hackneyed quality."[27] Mad speech is a speech genre Lowell will continue to struggle with. Now the poet places the husband's voice against the wife's voice—what Larkin would call the "talking in bed" voice. The wife's "talking in bed" voice is, in this poem, sane, tough, pragmatic. But it is more than that. The husband addresses his wife, "Oh my *Petite*, / clearest of all God's creatures, still all air and nerve." The husband wants, himself, to be small rather than grandiose, clear rather than incoherent, all air and nerve rather than chemically victimized and frightened. What the speaker wants is what John Ashbery (in a poem quoted in the introduction) wants, "to be small and clear and free."[28] But he cannot be—no speaker in *Life Studies* can. The husband in "Home After Three Months Away" may call himself "frizzled, stale and small," but it is not the same thing (*LS*, 84).

The speaker's tone is ardent and at the same time scared. The domestic space is as small as the space of the bed, and the boundaries of that small space are being threatened. Already the bedposts are Dionysian. The husband, feeling that there is no *place* to escape, escapes back in time. He remembers himself twelve years earlier as happily inarticulate—"too boiled and shy / and poker-faced to make a pass." It is a relief to remember being, like Our Lady of Walsingham, "expressionless," even if his inexpressivity expresses nothing more mysterious than shyness. His wife, he remembers, had a "shrill verve" that was not Dionysian, a fury that had as its focus a real region, not "the kingdom of the mad" but the "South." The wife is not simply a pragmatic figure, a helpmate, not simply "small and clear and free," not simply someone whose "household motions" are "light and free." Twelve years earlier she scorched one region; last night she dragged him back from another, more formidable one. The wife in this poem is helpful because she has access to powerful speech, a speech that is the enemy of, the treatment for, hackneyed speech. In one scene she speaks the language of feeling, in the other she speaks the language of ideas. (The husband seems not to be interested in ideas except insofar as they scorch him or break on his head.) These languages correspond to the everyday and the prophetic speech genres. The woman's version of everyday speech is not "frizzled" but full of "verve." Her version of exalted speech is not mad speech but political speech. (I will return to the significance of political speech later.)

Lowell refuses to oversimplify or give the poem a sentimental ending. His wife, having faced the kingdom of the mad and the traditional South, now turns on the husband. "Your old fashioned tirade— / loving, rapid, merciless— / breaks like the Atlantic Ocean on my head." The ending of the poem is ambiguous. In early Lowell, if the Atlantic Ocean was breaking on your head, you were one of the sailors in "The Quaker Graveyard in Nantucket," and you were drowning. The wife's voice here, though merciless, is also loving. The word "loving" in the description of the tirade recalls the terms used by R. P. Blackmur, reviewing Lowell's first book in 1945, "Dante loved his living Florence and the Florence to come and loved much that he was compelled to envisage in hell, and he wrote throughout in loving metres. In Lowell's *Land of Unlikeness* there is nothing loved unless it be its repellence; and there is not a loving metre in the book."[29] Lowell's tirades in his early poems were rapid and merciless but never loving— they were harangues. His wife's voice seems to offer what the figures in Lowell's earlier poetry longed for. In "In Memory of Arthur Winslow," the speaker implored the Virgin Mary for "buckets of blessings on my burning head" (*LWC*, 28). In a later poem he will say to his wife, "Your rapier voice—I have had so much— / hundred words a minute, piercing and thrilling . . ." (*Dolphin*, 70). Her voice offers excitement but not consolation. It is interesting to compare Adrienne Rich's version of this "invective":

> You want to say
> to everything:
> Keep off! Give him room!
> But you only watch,
> terrified
> the old consolations
> will get him at last[30]

In many of Lowell's poems, someone (either a speaker within the poem or the speaker's companion or child) is keeping some version of these speech genres—the prophetic and the everyday—safe. The poetry is at its most pessimistic on those occasions (frequent in *For the Union Dead*) when nobody is keeping them alive. If there is anything consoling in this poem, it is only that someone is keeping two crucial speech genres safe.

It might seem odd to say that a version of the prophetic voice is valued in Lowell's later poetry. Many critics argue that, though the prophetic voice makes appearances in, say, "Beyond the Alps" or "Waking Early Sunday Morning," it becomes less and less important as Lowell's career progresses. Lowell says in the poem "Reading Myself" that he never wrote anything in this period to go back to. It is true that these are the poems he does not try to rewrite, but this does not mean that he rejected the voice. The prophetic language might have become for Lowell what "the oppressor's language" was for Rich, but it does not, and, in fact, he remains preoccupied by the registers and tonalities of the prophetic voice. James Longenbach writes that "the 'breakthrough' narrative offers a narrow and inadequate reading even of Lowell's career."[31] My own position is that there are many breakthroughs in Lowell's career and that Lowell wanted, each time, to bring as much with him from before the break as he could. And he is not at all inclined to revel in the rhetoric of endless reinvention of self. At one point, he even doubts how much he, as a poet, has changed. Writers from Ovid to Rilke have imagined change that is turbulent and complete. Lowell wonders whether "things that change us only change a fraction" (*Dolphin*, 72). This intuition, though it keeps him from moralizing, makes him, in a way, more helpful to some readers than he might otherwise have been.

His insight that prophetic poetry is a speech genre—is a kind of *sound*—does not mean that he rejects it but that he begins to hear versions of that sound in other prophetic poets. The prophetic remains fresh and alive for Lowell because it seems interesting, as a poet, to try to do the prophet in different voices. He begins to experiment this way early on. In an early poem, "The Fens," Lowell plays with the type of rural political prophecy associated with William Cobbett's *Rural Rides* as well as with Joanna Southcott and Richard Brothers—the uneducated equivalents of prophetic poets like Blake and Shelley. In "The Slough of Despond" from *Lord Weary's Castle*, he returns to the equally unlettered prophetic world of John Bunyan. (This is Lowell's attempt, not very successful, to investigate the line of prophetic poetry that starts with

Langland.) In "At the Indian Killer's Grave," Lowell appropriates the voice of King Philip, the Indian prophet who says, "The judgment is at hand." In another poem he notices "the Bible-twisting Israelite" who "fasts for his Harlem." Lowell has a poem for Che Guevara, "the last armed prophet," as he calls him. In an interview he calls Freud a prophet. Marx, too, is one of the "prophets." In one poem he refers to "bygone Reichian prophets." Lowell sees prophetic speech as not, in fact, a rarefied, cast-off kind of speech but a speech fragments of which are everywhere.

As he pays attention to varieties of prophetic experience, he becomes more and more fascinated by prophetic language gone wrong. How does it go wrong? What happens when it does? One way (which we have noticed before) is mad speech, usually manic speech. This is prophetic speech as nothing but fast talking—rapid, merciless, not loving. Lowell writes of one prophetic figure who

> talked for thirty-two hours
> on everything, everybody,
> read Cervantes and the Bible aloud
> simultaneously with shattering rapidity . . .
> 　　　　　　　(*DBD,* 134–35)

Lowell may have been inspired in these poems by Ginsberg, who writes of prophets whose "whole intellects disgorged in total recall for seven days and nights," prophets "who talked continuously seventy hours from park to pad to bar to Bellevue to museum to the Brooklyn Bridge . . . yacketayakking screaming vomiting whispering facts and memories and anecdotes."[32] In some poems Lowell mixes irony and admiration for the prophetic voice gone wrong. Listening to a student leader of the sixties, he says, "His voice, electric, was a low current whir; / by now he'd bypassed sense and even eloquence" (*Notebook,* 185). One misses the poems he might have written about Jim Jones and David Koresh. As his career continues, though, Lowell develops more and more of an appetite for the sound of other prophetic voices working well. (Where will he find what Stevens found in George Santayana or in the woman singing in "Ideas of Order at Key West"?) He is listening for a voice that keeps going, with no "diminuendo." In a poem in *The Dolphin* he writes about hearing the sound he seeks. It is a

> persistent cry without diminishment
> or crescendo through the sleepless hours.
> I hear its bland monotony, the voice

that holds, and never shortcircuits the transcendence
I fiddled for imperiously and too long.

(76)

Lowell knows too much now about what was restrictive and limiting
about his early voice. The voice he hears, the "cry without diminishment," is, in fact, a police siren.

The fact that Lowell never gives up his interest in the prophetic voice
complicates his search for a plausible everyday voice. It is a search that
is, at the same time, complicated by a lack of role models. As he tells his
readers in his version of Rimbaud's "The Drunken Boat," "I felt my
guides no longer carried me" (*Imitations*, 81). He cannot be a purely
prophetic poet like Eliot or Allen Tate, nor can he be a poet like William
Carlos Williams, committed to celebrating the everyday. Lowell is not,
instinctively, a celebrator of the everyday; he is not, like Stevens, interested in "the rhapsody of things as they are."[33] Lowell may bring to the
everyday what he brought to Catholicism, the zealotry of the convert,
but his zealotry is more in evoking than celebrating. Nor does he naturally celebrate his own heroism. Although he writes in *Imitations* about
"ris[ing] to the heroism of the quotidian," he is not generally interested
in that kind of heroism (110). Lowell maintains a nineteenth-century
idea of greatness; his idea of greatness is like Emerson's or Carlyle's: it
involves Alexander the Great and Margaret Fuller. (*History* was originally going to be called *Heroes*.)[34] Lowell generalizes and moralizes
about such figures—what else are they for?—but rarely about everyday
people.

This refusal to moralize about the ordinary is not a refusal of knowledge. What Lowell celebrates is another kind of knowledge, one that
comes (or is supposed to come) as a sort of reward for living every day.
It is the knowledge people living together have of each other. If the people in his prophetic poems know nothing about each other, the people
in his everyday poems know too much: they have a kind of stamina in
the face of endless accumulation of domestic knowledge about one another. The knowledge accumulates, yet it never becomes ponderous.
Awareness of the knowledge—knowing that they know—is as close as
the people in his poems come to happiness. In a postdivorce poem to
his second wife, Elizabeth Hardwick, Lowell writes, "Our light intimacy of reference is unbroken" (*DBD*, 44). Where prophetic poetry offers a ponderous and estranging litany of references (often, as in Eliot's
poetry, broken), everyday poetry offers a light intimacy of reference.

Like Merrill and Ammons and Rich, Lowell is fascinated by the healing
properties of an intimate circle involving the poet, the loved ones, and
all readers. This light intimacy of reference (alienating to those who
want to get all the references) is, in fact, what Lowell, in the late poems,
has to offer his readers.

Sometimes domestic knowledge can seem not ponderous but still
burdensome. In *The Dolphin*, Lowell appropriates (once again) the voice
of Elizabeth Hardwick. Near the end of a sonnet, addressing him, she
says, "You [are] doomed to know what I have known with you" (31).
Sentences that enact the entanglement they evoke seem always about to
turn into the never-ending sentence that begins *I know that you know that
I know.*[35] Adrienne Rich, in a poem about her father, shows the dangerous side of such sentences.

> That terrible record! how it played
>
> down years, wherever I was
> in foreign languages even
> over and over *I know you better*
> *than you know yourself   I know*
>
> *you better than you know*
> *yourself   I know*
> *you*   until, self-maimed,
> I limped off, torn at the roots
>
> stopped singing a whole year[36]

(In a later poem she says, addressing a lover: "I can't know what you
know / unless you tell me.")[37] Lowell is aware of the dangers made explicit by Rich's version of the sentence, yet he brings to his own versions of the sentence tenderness and, most of all, patience. The knowledge he is doomed to know is easier to bear than the knowledge the
prophetic poet was doomed to know. It is shared knowledge. The first
poem in *Lord Weary's Castle* ends with the phrase, "your life is in your
hands." After "Man and Wife" Lowell writes more and more about the
experience of knowing his life (by which he means also his creative life)
is, in part, in the hands of others.

If Lowell never seemed completely comfortable as a purely prophetic
poet, neither is he very comfortable in the everyday. "Household motions" are, in his poetry, rarely "light and free." Because he has come late
to the everyday, he is always conscious of the domestic as a provisional

arrangement. It could be altered (just as poems evoking it can be altered) at any moment for better or worse. In his early poetry he "memorized the tricks to set the river on fire," and now he is learning tricks to let the river seem just to flow by (*History*, 194). (Certainly, it never occurs to him that the everyday might be another speech genre in which a poet might show off.) As a purely prophetic poet he wanted to be seen, to be heard, but now, because he wants to see and hear the world, he worries about his nearsightedness, about becoming hard of hearing. His infidelities fill him with remorse, his manic depression fills him with bewilderment; he rarely feels himself, as Williams does, to be "the happy genius of [his] household." Lowell understands, though, that readers might value him precisely because everyday life does not come easily to him. He wrote to Stanley Kunitz, "It may be some people have turned to my poems because of the very things that are wrong with me, I mean the difficulty I have with ordinary living, the impracticability, the myopia."[38]

If there is unhappiness in his version of the day to day, there is also a kind of happiness in it. I suggested earlier that happiness arises in Lowell's poetry from representations of people having known each other a long time. The idea of mutual knowledge is central to Lowell's experiments in juxtaposition. Tonal juxtapositions are important to Lowell because he wants the prophetic and the everyday to have what Merrill, in *The Changing Light at Sandover*, calls "a workable relation"—Lowell wants them to have a kind of relational knowledge of each other. He has a number of strategies for achieving this. For example, he often revises by moving lines from one poem to another. (Vereen Bell writes about the "portability of fragments" in Lowell.)[39] It is as if, having seen the effect of some lines in one poem, Lowell wants to see what work the lines will do in another poem. He likes to insert a word from one register into a line written in another register just to see what will happen— this is not so different from the "bad boy" image of himself he evokes in some of his poems and in his translations of Rimbaud. Words come in that don't belong, crashing the party of his poems. Mikhail Bakhtin writes, "The transfer of style from one [speech] genre to another not only alters the way a style sounds, under conditions of a genre unnatural to it but also violates or renews the given genre."[40] Lowell wants to see if one speech genre will violate or renew another. Lowell is interested, for example, in what the word "human" will do to this opening line of one of his sonnets. "The night blowing through the world's hospital is human" (*History*, 58). The archangel Michael tells JM and DJ in *Scripts for the Pageant:* "ALL GOOD DISCOURSE MUST, LIKE FORWARD MOTION, / KNOW RESISTANCE."[41] Resistance is what Lowell wants; he wants "contrasts and disruptions of tone." Like Merrill, again, he distrusts "unrelenting fluency"—something both poets mastered at the beginning of their careers.[42] Lowell revises not to avoid contrasts and disruptions of tone but to achieve them. They are what he revises *for*. (It is the same impulse that led A. R. Ammons to begin a poem with the line, "So I said I am Ezra," and Jorie Graham to begin a poem with the line, "So Look I said this is the burning bush we're in it it has three faces.")[43] In *Four Quartets,* Eliot writes that he believes in poetry

> where every word is at home,
> Taking its place to support the others,
> The word neither diffident nor ostentatious,
> An easy commerce of the old and the new,
> The common word exact without vulgarity,
> The formal word precise but not pedantic,
> The complete consort dancing together[44]

This is exactly the effect Lowell does not want. He does not want every word to be at home, he wants words that are diffident, ostentatious. An *uneasy* commerce of the old and new is what he looks for. In everyday life people use common words that are vague, vulgar, pedantic, imprecise. Why not in poetry? Above all, he doesn't want anything as ceremonial as a complete consort dancing together—that sounds too sacramental. (Eliot can turn any of his readers into Williams. One imagines the later Lowell reading *Four Quartets* and saying "Phew!") Like Rich and Ammons, Lowell does not know how far he will go or where his experiments will lead him. Fidelity to experience is paramount; he is enormously patient with the unpoetic and increasingly impatient with "poetry." "This year," he writes, ". . . must be written / in bad, straightforward, unscanning sentences—" (*Notebook,* 172). He wants to write a "random, haggard sentence" (129). Why? Because events seem random, and because he feels haggard.

Such gestures are more serious than they might seem. Some of Lowell's poems are experimental in ways that can make other experimental poetry seem complacent about its procedures. Juxtaposition is, in part, a way for Lowell to avoid a poetics of vacillation, of endless back and forth. The back-and-forth rhythm (so much a part of the poems in *For the Union Dead*) has been ruined, in a way, by his experience with manic depression. As I suggested earlier, both everyday and prophetic speech are implicated in and have to be won from the silence of depression and the mad speech of mania. It presents a difficulty for Lowell that the language of mania is already a "poetic" language. Lowell knows that prophetic speech is like mad speech. (In "Man and Wife" he calls it "hackneyed" as a way of exercising a kind of preemptive literary criticism.) The prophetic voice might sound mad, but it was not the *same* as mad speech. Mad speech cannot make the sense Lowell wants to make. He refuses to see madness as, in Theodore Roethke's phrase from "In a Dark Time," "nobility of soul / at odds with circumstance."[45] Manic depression was, for Lowell, also a literary problem, a technical problem. Lowell writes, "Sometimes, my mind is a rocked and dangerous bell, / I climb the spiral steps to my own music" (*Notebook*, 57). Everyday poetry, too, must not simply be a surrender to glumness, dumbness. Lowell cannot always simply attend happily to "the music of what happens," because that music may be weirdly competitive with the music of his poetry.

His consciousness of that competition is, in part, what keeps the later poems from being merely playful experiments. The title of his last book, *Day by Day*, has two meanings. "Day *by* day" suggests a poetics of juxtaposition. There is also its colloquial meaning: "Take it day by day." Take nothing for granted. Never take home for granted. Frost imagined home as a place where, when you have to go there, they have to take you in. Lowell, in poems like "Man and Wife," sees home as a place to which someone "drags" you back alive. The domestic in Lowell is not a safe haven, but neither is it a place with an ideology that must be unmasked. Domesticity is too necessary to Lowell for him to want to satirize its vocabularies. It is something to be achieved—in life and in art.

Lowell's evocations of the domestic (like those of Cowper and the early Wordsworth) are colored by the fact that the ordinary is periodically defamiliarized. For Cowper (who, like Lowell, had to battle mental illness), the domestic meant a safe place in which to attempt ordinary life. Wordsworth had forcibly to remind himself of everyday life. He wrote to Isabel Fenwick that he was "often unable to think of external things as having external existence, and I communed with all that I saw as something not apart from, but inherent in, my own immaterial nature. Many times while going to school have I grasped at a wall or tree to recall myself from this abyss of idealism to the reality."[46] Lowell, bracing his hand against a wall, is not reassured.

> Earth's solid and the sky is light,
> yet even on the steadiest day, dead noon,
> the sun stockstill like Joshua's in midfield,
> I have to brace my hand against a wall

to keep myself from swaying—swaying wall,
straitjacket, hypodermic, helmeted
doctors, one crowd, white-smocked, in panic, hit
stop, bury the runner on the cleated field.
                                        (*Notebook,* 25)

How can he be reassured when the wall is swaying too? His attempts to
achieve the ordinary life often fail. Cowper called his long poem "The
Task," and there is an implication that achieving a kind of everyday life
may be a "task" for some poets, and it is a task to which they will not always be equal. Whitman too must reassure himself about the reality of
the world. "The domestic joys, the daily housework or business, the
building of houses—they are not phantasms . . . they have weight and
form and location."[47] It is because he wants to remind himself that "domestic joys" are real that Lowell is so intent on giving them "weight
and form and location" in his poetry. The attempt to be sure tends to involve grasping, reaching out, putting them in relation to his own body.
It is as if the ultimate arbiter of "weight and form and location" is the
body. Lowell puts this insight to work immediately: it is as if, rereading
his poetry and discovering how bodiless his prophets were, Lowell
grants them bodies in retrospect. One of his key words in this regard is
"swelled." (Ben Jonson's work seems his particular inspiration here.)
"Do you still / swell your stomach with oracle?" he is asked by an un-
named interlocutor in one of the poems in *History* (183). And his sonnet
on Pound ends with the words, "To begin with a swelled head and end
with swelled feet" (*Notebook,* 120). The prophet might wish he had no
body, but to be bodiless is worse. Nevertheless, Lowell will not make
too much of it. Although he is grateful for moments when he can believe in the reality of the body, he refuses a poetics of constant gratitude,
a refusal for which some readers will be thankful. Instead he brings,
from *Life Studies* on, a mordant wit to his sense that ordinariness is
going to be, for him, only intermittent, that he is not always going to
feel "human." Pozzo, in *Waiting for Godot,* says, "I am probably not particularly human, but who cares?"[48] And Lowell, in a poem for his
mother in *Day by Day,* says to her, "It has taken me the time since you
died / to discover you are as human as I am . . . / if I am" (79). He takes
nothing for granted, neither the world nor the body nor domesticity
nor the everyday nor ordinary life.
    Lowell is, for example, aware of what can surround domestic
space—in his case, there are the spaces of prophecy, of madness on one

side and the spaces of depression and exhaustion on another. It would be the death of his poetry to police the boundaries too much. Many of his poems are about, in part, his awareness of these spaces, about the way he seems to make them aware of each other by placing their characteristic tonal registers in relation to each other, generally within a domestic space. Speech genres too in Lowell's imagination can have a kind of relational knowledge of each other. This relation may be felt merely as "contrasts and disruptions," but that is better than nothing. Considerably better: a poetry of no contrasts, no disruptions (Lowell wrote many such poems in his first three books) would be a poetry that denied itself the version of happiness that *this* kind of relational knowledge also provides. It is not happiness for the people in the poems but happiness for the poet.

Lowell cannot have access to this happiness unless the crucial speech genres, prophetic speech and everyday speech, are working well for him. After *Life Studies*, Lowell came out with *For the Union Dead* (1964) and *Near the Ocean* (1967). If, as Helen Vendler has said, they are his "two weaker volumes," it may be because his juxtapositions are insufficiently confident.[49] Many of the poems in *For the Union Dead* look back at the speech genres explored in the earlier poems, but they do not have the same energy. The prophetic poetry sounds merely manic. (The poem "For the Union Dead" is an exception because it is a political poem. I will have more to say about the political in Lowell's poetry later in this chapter.) One reader felt that Lowell, writing the prophetic poems, was simply putting "a series of violent words . . . next to each other," and there are poems where this seems to be true.[50] It is as if he is producing a parody of juxtaposition. Lowell, in these books, feels dissatisfied with himself both as a person in the world and as a prophetic poet. In "Eye and Tooth" he writes, "I saw things darkly / as through an unwashed goldfish globe" (*FTUD*, 18). What kind of prophetic poet is he? In "Hawthorne" he writes an enervated version of Bishop's "The Sandpiper." The poem ends:

> Leave him alone for a moment or two,
> and you'll see him with his head
> bent down, brooding, brooding,
> eyes fixed on some chip,
> some stone, some common plant,
> the commonest thing,
> as if it were the clue.
> The disturbed eyes rise,

> furtive, foiled, dissatisfied
> from meditation on the true
> and insignificant.
>
> (*FTUD*, 39)

Many of the poems in *For the Union Dead* and *Near the Ocean* lack confidence about both the prophetic and the everyday. Only in poems like "For the Union Dead" and "Waking Early Sunday Morning" can Lowell imagine plausible speakers for these speech genres.

In *For Lizzie and Harriet*, Lowell includes a poem called "Harriet" that is about keeping prophetic language safe by trusting it this time not to the verve of his wife's invective but, in part, to the verve of his ten-year-old daughter's vocabulary.

> A repeating fly, blueblack, thumbthick—so gross,
> it seems apocalyptic in our house—
> whams back and forth across the nursery bed
> manned by a madhouse of stuffed animals,
> not one a fighter. It is like a plane
> gunning potato bugs or Arabs on the screen—
> one of the mighty . . . one of the helpless. It
> bumbles and bumps its brow on this and that,
> making a short, unhealthy life the shorter.
> I kill it, and another instant's added
> to the horrifying mortmain of
> ephemera: keys, drift, sea-urchin shells,
> you packrat off with joy . . . a dead fly swept
> under the carpet, wrinkling to fulfillment.
>
> (*FLH*, 13)

The poem is, first of all, about resisting the temptation represented by the fly. An early poem, "As a Plane Tree by the Water," included the refrain, "Flies, flies are on the plane tree, on the streets" (*LWC*, 47). Here the fly is in the house—it "seems apocalyptic in our house." (YET U HOUSE ME, Merrill would have had the fly reply.) For a prophetic poet things are or are not apocalyptic—usually they are. To say that something "seems" apocalyptic is (hardly noticeable though it might be) to mix diction. In one of the sonnets in *History*, Lowell writes about his "apocalyptic disappointments." The word "apocalyptic" is hyperbolic, but hyperbole has, in ordinary language, its own precision and accuracy. In *Day by Day*, Lowell writes, "only by exaggeration / could I tell the truth" (18). In another poem in *For Lizzie and Harriet*, he writes, "For / the hundredth time, we slice the fog, and round / the village with our headlights on the ground" (13). The phrase "the hundredth time" is hyperbolic, but it is different from the hyperbole in the early poems: it is colloquial hyperbole. It is the difference between the phrases "the mudflat detritus of death" and "the horrifying mortmain of ephemera." To exaggerate at all must feel charged to a poet like Lowell. He exaggerates in these poems for the same reason he brings the fly into the poem: as a way of staging his resistance to temptation. As a younger poet, he would, like Roethke, have written, "My soul, like some heat-maddened summer fly, / Keeps buzzing at the sill."[51] The fly does not get compared to the soul in Lowell's poem. He calls the fly's presence apocalyptic, and that keeps him from being reminded of anything less (and therefore more) serious. (Merrill's late poem, "The House Fly," is a similarly deft treatment of the subject.) Lowell's poem is not about the coming end of time but something more challenging to the imagination—time uneventfully passing, events occurring and recurring. Nothing, as I said in the introduction, is as threatening to the prophetic poet as everyday time.[52]

It is safe to exaggerate, safe to talk about the fly because his daughter is the presiding genius of the poem. "Whamming" is a violent word that, like the word "gross," is tamed by its place in a child's vocabulary. The fly "bumbles and bumps its brow on this and that." The language parodies the violence of Anglo-Saxon poetry as well as the hectic alliteration of Lowell's early poems. In the early poetry, "blue-lung'd combers lumbered to the kill"; now a fly "bumbles and bumps its brow on this and that." Those words hint at a world that is "all mind and violence and nothing felt." (And, in fact, Lowell kills the fly.) The line "one of the mighty . . . one of the helpless. It" is a return to one of Lowell's early prosodic devices—putting a caesura just before the last foot of the line. The mannerism is back, but here it emphasizes the mild, unimpressive word "It." Many of the devices return in the sonnets, but—as with the many ellipses in the sonnets—they are no longer being used for melodramatic purposes. Melodrama does not have to be replayed as farce, though. It can return as a kind of play. Many of Lowell's poems about his daughter are a kind of meditation on his daughter's infancy and childhood—an improvement over his own. In another poem for his daughter, he writes, "Downstairs, you correct notes at the upright piano" (*FLH*, 14). Again, many of the later poems are about a father, influenced by his daughter, correcting his own notes. In one of his sonnets in *Notebook*, he writes, "Heidegger said that time is ecstasy" (180). The prophetic writer quoted here may be Heidegger, but the one quoting is, in this poem, a ten-year-old girl's pet guinea pig. The poem is called "Words for a Guinea-Pig."

The prophetic voice and the everyday voice are important to Lowell, but he is, like Ammons, easily bored. Seamus Heaney, one of Lowell's shrewdest readers, writes that Lowell's early poems had "an unremitting verbal determination to secure our dazed attention." His early style created a "*monotone* of majesty which was bound to drown out the human note of the poet who had aspired to majesty in the first place."[53] Lowell does not want a "monotonous sublime" (as he calls it in a later poem), but neither does he want a monotone of "humanness." Mixed diction would become monotonous if it were always the same "Lowellian" prophetic voice mixed with a "Lowellian" everyday voice. When he quotes Elizabeth Hardwick in one poem the lines seem to reflect his suspicions about his own work. "I guess we'll make Washington this weekend; / it's a demonstration, like all demonstrations, / repetitious, gratuitous, unfresh . . . just needed" (*Dolphin*, 58). Lowell's *poems* can seem like demonstrations of a voice obsessively repeating itself. In his afterword to *Notebook*, he says that he is "famished for human chances"; this seems, in part, to mean that he is famished for other voices. The poems in his later books—*Notebook, History, The Dolphin, For Lizzie and Harriet*—open themselves up, over and over, to other voices. Seamus Heaney, at the end of *Station Island*, imagines being told by a voice, "You've listened long enough. Now strike your note."[54] Lowell, feeling that he has struck his note often enough, now wants to listen. The early poems took as their organizing unit the unstoppable line; the poems beginning with *Life Studies* are notable for their "extraordinarily phrasal construction."[55] Seamus Heaney writes, "Lowell always had an inclination to launch such single lines and phrases across the sky of the poem and indeed, in the blank verse sonnets had so tried to make poems blaze line by line that the reader could feel at times he was out bareheaded in a meteor shower."[56] This way of writing is peculiarly vulnerable to criticism. Robert von Hallberg, commenting on Lowell's focus on lines and phrases, writes that "he was always trying for the memorable line within his reach" and argues that "this is just the problem of *History*: too often lines or quatrains, rather than poems, stand out in memory."[57] Poets themselves may be suspicious of this way of constructing a poem. Stevens interrupts one of his own poems to say, self-mockingly, "Phrases!"[58] If Lowell is interested in achieving the effects of a meteor shower, he also wants, I think, to create the impression that he is standing *with* his readers bareheaded in it. What does this mean? Phrases are interesting to Lowell, I think, in part because they will make it easier for him to accommodate fragments of other people's speech.

Other people's speech is starting more and more to preoccupy him. Lowell's poetry, more even than the poetry of William Carlos Williams, more even than the poetry of Allen Ginsberg, gives the sense of having been spoken language first. The words Lowell chooses are often words he heard. (They come less often from books.) Spoken language, whether his own or others', whether overheard or heard, is a way of happening that seems congenial to the ways he now wants his poetry to happen. Sometimes it is voices of the dead to which he wants to listen. In a group elegy for the dead poets of his generation, he writes, "Sometimes for days I only hear your voices" (*History*, 157). Sometimes he writes poems about the desire to hear the voices of the dead. In a poem written for his mother after her death, he writes, "I almost lifted the telephone to dial you, / forgetting you have no dial" (*DBD*, 78). What he hears sometimes is just his own voice. In *Notebook* he has a poem, dedicated to his daughter, that consists of a sort of greatest hits collection of his own lines. (The poem is called "Familiar Quotations.") Not every poet introduces a sequence of thoughts (as Lowell does in "Epilogue") by saying, "I hear the sound of my own voice" (*DBD*, 127). He is, though, in the later poems, mostly listening to other people—living people. It is as if, having written the most monologic poems of his generation, he will now write the most heteroglossic. Lowell ends his book *The Dolphin* with the words: "My eyes have seen what my hand did," but he could have written: My ears have heard what my voice said, or, rather, My ears have heard what our voices said.

Lowell is fascinated by the way people talk, particularly people who didn't fall from prophetic speech but have spoken everyday speech "from the womb." Sometimes these speakers are well-meaning, hapless. In "Publication Day," Lowell makes a poem out of a letter from a woman whose book was rejected for publication and who wants help from him. In "Under the Dentist," Lowell gives what sounds like a verbatim account of a visit to the dentist, offering the reader not his own but his dentist's undramatic monologue. Examples could be multiplied— in fact, one of the projects of the sonnet books seems precisely to multiply them. The poems offer a sort of benign version of the auditory hallucinations in John Bunyan's *Grace Abounding to the Chief of Sinners*. Bunyan writes, "I felt as if there were nothing else but these voices from morning to night within me, as though indeed there could be room for nothing else."[59] Readers instinctively want to be generous to poems that are themselves so hospitable. Grossman writes about "the paralyzing specificity with which [Lowell] views the world," but of course what is paralyzing for Grossman keeps Lowell feeling alive, moving.[60] Some of his readers, in fact, noticing Lowell's generosity, want to be the object of it. He is ready to oblige them. Why not? When someone tells him, "what I say should go into your *Notebook*," he puts the comment in a sonnet in *The Dolphin* (52).

People who collect examples of speech in America work, whether poets or not, in the tradition of Whitman or Mencken. They either celebrate the speech (like Studs Terkel) or correct it (like William Safire). Lowell doesn't want to satirize American speech, nor does he want simply to hear America singing. His ambition is more modest. He just wants to hear the people around him talking. Like Adrienne Rich, what he wants to hear is "a conversation of sounds melting constantly into rhythms."[61] The "surprise and sparkle" of slang, for example, even slang nobody ever spoke, pleases him (*DBD*, 89). He can (now) take as much pleasure in clichés—words yoked together—as any contemporary poet, but he also likes the opposite of clichés—words that were never before juxtaposed. When he picks his daughter up from summer camp, he takes pleasure in hearing language spoken in unison. "The campers . . . harden in their shyness, / their gruff, faint voices hardly say hello, / singing 'Do we love it? *We love it*'" (*FLH*, 40). ("Gruff" is a word that keeps appearing in the sonnets. The word looks backward to the stern, uncompromising prophetic figures in the early poems, but it also carries with it a sense of the social: the man in the fifth floor attic might, if he talked to someone from the world below his window, seem gruff. People are gruff in *conversation*.) Lowell likes to write sentences that begin with "We talk like . . . " In one poem he writes, "We talk / like room-mates bleeding out the night to dawn" (*FLH*, 45). In *Day by Day*, he writes of a couple: "They talk like two guests / waiting for the other / to leave the house" (4). How people say things is often more compelling than what they say. In *Day by Day*, Lowell begins a poem for his first wife, Jean Stafford: "*Towmahss Mahnn:* that's how you said it . . . / 'That's how Mann must say it,' I thought" (29). Not everything he overhears is so conveniently "phrasal." The voices can sometimes seem merely chaotic. One poem, the aptly titled "Open House," consists entirely of voices overheard in a mental hospital. The inclusion of the voices (no matter how chaotic) seems, though, to satisfy an appetite in the poet. There is a kind of happiness in these poems: they are each an "open house"; indoors and outdoors are finally one. Seamus Heaney says in a poem that he thinks of his own voice as consisting of "echo soundings, searches, probes, allurements."[62] Lowell, too, wants an aesthetic of openness, hospitality, readiness.

Lowell's poems are, of course, not completely open. There are certain allurements he is not drawn to. He is not intent, as Merrill is, on showing people being "ravishingly polite" to each other.[63] Nor is he interested, as Williams is, in small talk. Nor is he very interested in representing flirtation. The most famous moment of flirtation in his poetry is about a failure to flirt: "Too boiled and shy / and poker-faced to make a pass." He is impatient with preliminaries, with incipience—he seems happiest imagining long-married couples. Voices are rarely seductive in Lowell, and when they are, they are made deliberately grotesque. The sexual is, like the prophetic, chastened by being brought back to a body that is not itself very grand or very alluring. He writes about "flirting seniles, their conversation three noises" (*Dolphin*, 64). He drifts off, "Adrift in my sweet sleep . . . I hear a voice / singing to me in French, *O mon avril* / Those nasals . . . they woo us" (*History*, 25). Berryman writes frequently about sex. Lowell rarely does. The sexual is a territory that is neither prophetic nor everyday. This fact might make it useful to Lowell if it were not for the fact that, unlike the political, the sexual is not obviously helpful in bringing the two speech genres together.

What Lowell wants, first and foremost, from the voices he incorporates is relief from his own voice, which tends to be immensely authoritative in whatever it does. Lowell, writing lines like "Cured, I am frizzled, stale and small" sounds, somehow, unfrizzled, fresh, large. (Just as Merrill, writing "Already I take up / Less emotional space than a snowdrop," makes the reader instantly feel that space to be charged and desirable.) The other voices are a way for Lowell to escape from his own voice, his own characteristic ways of speaking. They are Lowell's way of recognizing that there are many ways of sounding prophetic, everyday, manic, depressive. Not all of them belong to him, but all of them can go in his poems. The other voices are also Lowell's way of bringing voices that are none of the above into his poems. Grossman writes, "The poem wholly in quotation marks seems his characteristic invention," and one senses that Lowell feels excited by and grateful for the possibilities of quoted speech.[64] Critics who use Bakhtin's terms sometimes forget what complicated motives are involved and what passionate intention is required to maintain a heteroglossic space.

Lowell is not interested only in the heteroglossic but in the dialogic: his appetite is not just for random speech but also for conversation. For Lowell—as for Ammons, Rich, and Merrill—the representation of conversation is crucial. Lowell, in an interview, remembered Delmore Schwartz telling him that "if you got two people talking in a poem you could do anything."[65] Conversation takes place in the later poetry, as it can in life, in the middle of, in the context of random things people say: it can feel like a sudden focusing, a turning of the phrases *to each other.* If psychoanalysis was once a secular version of confession, conversation is, in later Lowell, a secular version of psychoanalysis. Conversation begins to equal survival—and particularly the survival of his poetry. It is a version of happiness and freedom that he can trust. In a poem called "New York Again" in *The Dolphin,* he writes, "survival is talking on the phone" (74). Rapport offers safety and excitement—in *History,* he talks about "the velocity of conversation" (169) and in *Day by Day* "a whiplash of voices" (108). In a sonnet in *Notebook,* he talks about being "lost in the dark night of the brilliant talkers" (119). This "dark night" rather than the "dark night" of "Skunk Hour" is where he now wants to be lost.

Wallace Stevens writes, "Two things of opposite natures seem to depend / On one another." He continues,

> Morning and afternoon are clasped together
>
> And North and South are an intrinsic couple
> And sun and rain a plural, like two lovers
> That walk away as one in the greenest body.[66]

Lowell is becoming more and more interested in how opposites come not only to depend on but to resemble each other. Lowell writes, "Our *New York Times Cookbook* looks like *Leaves of Grass*—/ gold title on green" (*Notebook,* 219). (Both are big books of instructions on the good life, one domestic, one prophetic.) Lowell is not interested in the "correspondences" that interested Baudelaire and Roethke but, instead, in the idea of rough resemblance, of family resemblance. Lowell's poems suggest, though, that the daydream behind juxtaposition, the dream behind the emphasis on relational knowledge, is the possibility that opposing words, opposing tones, opposing speech genres might move toward each other—that there might be a reconciliation at the heart of language.

There is more to the daydream. Conversation is, for Lowell, juxtaposition not just of speech but of speakers. Many of Lowell's poems, beginning with "Man and Wife," have been, as I said, about people keeping kinds of speech safe for each other. His poems get their life from the lesser speech genres that flourish in domestic situations. His poems are full of bantering, bickering, interrupted stichomythia, shared reminiscence, speech after short silence, brilliance at breakfast, boredom at breakfast, talking in bed, talking in the car: the domestic version of Heaney's "echo soundings, searches, probes, allurements." The intimacy, built up out of decades of such moments, is very great. People who live together in such prolonged intimacy come to resemble each other. Lowell is fascinated by that resemblance and particularly by the idea of interchangeability of speakers. His poems are full of the kind of speech that could be assigned to either husband or wife. The poems dramatize the idea of interchangeability, and the speakers in the poems dramatize it as well. Elizabeth Hardwick's voice recurs in Lowell's poetry: his description and evocation of the voices of his wives and children are part of what readers think of as the sound of a Lowell poem. In a letter to Stanley Kunitz about his incorporation of Elizabeth Hardwick's voice, he calls it "a mixture of my voice and another voice in my head, part me, part Lizzie, italicized, paraphrased, imperfectly, obsessively heard."[67] Hardwick, too, is very conscious of the ways Lowell has sounded over the years. He can do her voice, and she can do his. He quotes, in a poem in *The Dolphin*, lines from a letter she wrote him:

> I'm watching a scruffy, seal-colored woodchuck graze
> on weeds, then lift his greedy snout and listen;
> then back to speedy feeding. He weighs a ton,
> and has your familiar human aspect munching.
>
> (41)

The possibility of speakers becoming interchangeable is central to "Dear Sorrow I" in *For Lizzie and Harriet.*

> If I can't whistle in the dark, why whistle?
> One doubts the wisdom of almighty God
> casting weak husbands adrift in the hands of a wife.
> We need the mighty diaphragm of Job
> to jangle grandly. Pain lives in our free discussion,
> like the Carlyles fighting meat from the mouth of their dog.
> Luckily the Carlyles couldn't bear children—
> ours sees me, "Genius, unwise, unbrilliant, weird,"
> sees you, "Brilliant, unwise, unweird, nerves."
> Barbaric cheek is needed to stay married. . . .
> Lizzie, I wake to the hollow of loneliness,

I would cry out *Love Love*, if I had words:
we are all here for such a short time,
we might as well be good to one another.

(25)

Many of the words in the second sentence of this poem—"doubts,"
"wisdom," "almighty God," "casting," "weak," "adrift," "in the hands
of"—belong to an anguish we associate with Job or the Psalms. But
Lowell does not give the sentence the "I" it needs and instead supplies it with the urbane "One," once again, undercutting the effect of
the prophetic language. He has accumulated all these words simply to
make a joke about uxoriousness. Indeed, the fact that this poem is
about a couple subverts our expectations. Lowell doesn't say, "I need
the mighty diaphragm of Job." (He already had it; his purely prophetic poems were a tour de force of stamina.) Instead, like Merrill, he
imagines *two* people occupying the prophet's role: "We need the
mighty diaphragm of Job." And, like Merrill, he plays this for comedy.
There is something comic, he knows, about two people being Job with
each other. Lowell, always eager to discriminate between kinds of
prophets, here discriminates between kinds of prophetic couples. Elizabeth Hardwick and Robert Lowell are like Jane Welsh and Thomas
Carlyle but also unlike them: Lowell and Hardwick have a child.[68] This
makes a difference in the writing only because Lowell continually
pays attention to the difference it makes. Lowell wants, in his poems,
to pay attention to his daughter in ways for which there are few precedents in father-daughter poems. Male poets have not usually written
about their daughters, unless, like Yeats, their daughters have just
been born or, like the Pearl Poet or Ben Jonson, their daughters have
died. Children in Lowell's poetry—even other people's children—are
very much alive. In a poem in *For Lizzie and Harriet*, the poet is at another woman's house, and he says to her, "Your child, she's nine,
keeps shrewdly, inopportunely / reappearing" (23). Children repeatedly appear in Lowell's poetry—shrewdly, inopportunely, keeping the
poetry's perspectives surprising. Ammons tries to escape the solip-
sism of the prophet by saying (in "Gravelly Run"), "It is not so much
to know the self / as to know it as it is known / by galaxy and cedar
cone."[69] Lowell wants to know himself as he is known by his wife and
daughter. Both poets should perhaps be compared to Bunyan, who
once again strikes the characteristic Protestant prophetic note: "So I
saw in my Dream, that the Man began to run; Now he had not run far
from his own door, but his Wife and Children perceiving it, began to

cry after him to return: but the man put his fingers in his Ears, and ran on crying, Life, Life, Eternal Life: so he looked not behind him, but fled towards the middle of the Plain."[70] The middle of the plain is a prophetic space: it is where Ammons, in his early poetry, continually found himself. Lowell never, in the late poetry, runs far from his own door.

The early poems, though so many of them took place outdoors, could make the reader feel claustrophobic. The later poems, though so many take place indoors, can, because of their openness, make the reader feel agoraphobic. There are two forces outside the poetry that rescue it from too great an openness to random or familiar voices. The first one is the poet's interest in politics.

It is unclear, though, how deeply Lowell, as a *poet*, cares about the political. While Adrienne Rich instinctively makes the personal political, Lowell instinctively makes the political personal. This can make for some surprises. His political poems are often original in their points of departure. Who else would begin a poem for Eugene McCarthy with the words, "I love you so" (*History*, 175). That line—Lowell's version of Merrill's line, "However seldom in my line to feel, / I most love those for whom the world is real"—brings the weight of everything he knows about himself to his consideration of politics.[71] Everything is personal for Lowell now. Although the political world often enters the domestic world from the television screen, Lowell does not think of the political as a collection of impersonal forces. In the work of a poet like Lowell, a television set is likely to be a humanizing rather than dehumanizing force. Merrill mentions in *The Book of Ephraim* that he does not own a television set and adds that he barely reads the newspaper. Both, again, should be judged against not Bunyan but Emily Dickinson, who tells us, "The Only News I know / Is Bulletins all Day / From Immortality."[72] Lowell gets his bulletins from the television news and then talks to people about them. Politics, for Lowell, is something that happens between people. Knowledge of politics is a relational knowledge: political discussions take place between wives and husbands, between fathers and daughters. The father in one of Lowell's poems talks politics with his daughter and says afterward, "It's funny-awkward; I don't come off too well" (*Notebook*, 231). This line, itself "bad, straightforward, unscanning," is Lowell's version of "that was a way of putting it—not very satisfactory." (His way of putting it, though, is, unlike Eliot's, a way of putting it to another person.) It is as if Lowell wants to be clumsy, as if he wants to not "come off too well"—and political discussion offers him an opportunity. He is always patient with political beliefs—his own and others'. He is interested, as a poet, not so much in his own political beliefs but in what it feels like to have such beliefs. To have political beliefs offers the pleasure, now and then, of discovering that you, like other people, have presupposed a stable reality. Because he understands what beliefs can do for the people who have them, he is more forgiving than others might be. He observes, for example, in an interview, "Pound's social credit, his fascism, all these various things, were a tremendous gain to him; he'd be a very Parnassian poet without them. Even if they're bad beliefs—and some were bad, some weren't, and some were just terrible, of course—they made him more human and more to do with life, more to do with the times."[73] There is an implication that the more awkward the beliefs, the more human the believer.

Clumsiness—both verbal and physical—is important to Lowell's sense of the political. Politics are human, clumsy.[74] When Jean-François Lyotard asks, "What else remains as 'politics' except resistance to the inhuman?" the question has a Lowellian ring.[75] The human, in order to resist the inhuman, must sometimes consent to become part of a crowd and to march. The crowd will be clumsy because it will consist entirely of people trying to put off individuality. In one poem he asks, "What is history? What you cannot touch" (*Notebook*, 103). History is inhuman. The political, the attempt to change the course of history, is human—it is what you *can* touch. Here is "The March I."

> Under the too white marmoreal Lincoln Memorial,
> The too tall marmoreal Washington Obelisk,
> gazing into the too long reflecting pool,
> the reddish trees, the withering autumn sky,
> the remorseless, amplified harangues for peace—
> lovely to lock arms, to march absurdly locked
> (unlocking to keep my wet glasses from slipping)
> to see the cigarette match quaking in my fingers,
> then to step off like green Union Army recruits
> for the first Bull Run, sped by photographers,
> the notables, the girls . . . fear, glory, chaos, rout . . .
> our green army staggered out on the miles-long green fields,
> met by the other army, the Martian, the ape, the hero,
> his new-fangled rifle, his green new steel helmet.
>
> (*History*, 148)

Lowell calls the harangue "remorseless" rather than "relentless," the word a reader might expect. The word "remorseless" belongs to a vocabulary of private scruple: it is as if a harangue is something one might feel remorse about afterward. He sees the political as clumsy, human, and also as something one can easily participate in, as not discontinuous with life. Lowell focuses here on the awkwardness of trying to walk—to march—with arms locked. The marchers stagger out "on the miles-long green fields": they do not "walk away as one in the greenest body." Another poet might have satirized the act of linking arms. For Lowell, it is "lovely to lock arms, to march absurdly locked / (unlocking to keep my wet glasses from slipping)." Although he makes the political personal, his political poems are not personal in the same way as his domestic poems. In a poem called "The Couple," he writes, "The sidewalk was two feet wide. We, arm in arm, / walked . . . / Our manner had some intimacy in my dream" (*Dolphin*, 50), and Lowell suggests in "The March 1" that there is a dreamlike intimacy about the marchers as well.[76] But the poems are different: it is the difference between a "miles-long green field" and a sidewalk that is "two feet wide." In the early poems, the prophetic chastens the domestic; in some of the later poems, the domestic chastens the domestic.

Lowell is, though, constantly searching for ways to avoid poems of chastening. The political offers him the chance to link the two speech genres. To speak politically is to speak a kind of prophetic speech in order to intervene in the everyday. On other occasions speaking politically may involve a recontextualizing of everyday speech. The space of domestic speech is, as I said earlier, surrounded by other spaces. But these spaces, too, are surrounded. Political speech works in Lowell's poetry to fill a surrounding space that, in other poets (Merrill, for example), is empty. In the passage from Bunyan there is only the house and the middle of the plain. Lowell's political poems introduce the idea of countless houses on countless plains.

The other force outside the poetry that keeps it from a kind of chaotic openness is death. In his early poems, Lowell is preoccupied by violent death; in his later poems, he is more likely to think about "mortality." Death, as he might have said, is the one change that changes more than a fraction. Lowell wants his poems to be open, to be free, to be experimental, but he never forgets that "all discussions // End in the mudflat detritus of death" (*LWC*, 11). Helen Vendler writes that "Lowell has made a certain trajectory his own: the curve which begins in possibility and ends grimly in necessity."[77] He is, though, often comic in his evocation of "the one life offered from the many chosen" (*Dolphin*, 20). Here is a sonnet, quoted earlier, from *For Lizzie and Harriet*:

Two buildings, scaffolds, go up across my street;
one owned by Harvard, the other owned by Harvard;
they keep on hammering from five till five.
Man shouting resounds on the steel ribs—
thus from a rib of the Ark and in his cups,
Noah harangued a world he said would drown . . .
How could the reckless, authoritative young
bear me, if I had their life expectancy?
Their long hair, beads, jeans, are early uniforms—
like the generation of leaves, the race of man.
A girl straddles a car hood, and snuffs the dust of the headlights:
"I want to live," she screams, "where I can see."
The pale green leaf clings white to the lit night
and shakes a little on its stiff, tense twig.

(16)

Some of his readers might be trying to escape from a binary view of the world—Lowell implies, in this poem, that we're lucky if we have *two* choices. His sentences enact that intuition. He tells us about two buildings, "one owned by Harvard, the other owned by Harvard." This line (and there is a hint of it in "from five till five") is a kind of parody of the claustrophobic self-reflexivity of his early poems, themselves inspired by the stern (what he might now call "gruff") tautologies of the Hebrew Bible. There is something wonderfully straight-faced about such lines. He begins another poem in *For Lizzie and Harriet* with the line, "Four windows, five feet tall, soar up like windows" (22). Simile usually offers a hope of escape: similes like these awaken that hope to thwart it. Other poets make use of similes like these so that they have the force of epiphany. For Lowell the epiphany that x is like x may be a source of comedy but not of happiness. Some of his later poems are able to reverse the trajectory to some extent; in some of these poems he imagines a movement from necessity to possibility. The presence of other voices in the poem can make that possible. And in many of the later poems there is no trajectory at all. In some poems he juxtaposes narratives of necessity and narratives of possibility just to see what will happen.

In his last book, *Day by Day,* he writes a poem called "Marriage." It is about his third wife (who already had three daughters) and the son he had with her.

I

We were middle-class and verismo
enough to suit Van Eyck,

when we crowded together in Maidstone,
patriarch and young wife
with our three small girls
to pose in Sunday-best.
The shapeless comfort of your flowered frock
was transparent against the light,
but the formal family photograph in color
shows only a rousing brawn of shoulder
to tell us you were pregnant.

Even there, Sheridan, though unborn,
was a center of symmetry;
even then he was growing in hiding
toward gaucheness and muscle—
to be a war-
chronicler of vast inaccurate memory.
Later his weird humor
made him elf and dustman,
like him, early risers.
This summer, he is a soldier—
unlike father or mother,
or anyone he knows,
he can choose both sides:
Redcoat, Minuteman, or George the Third . . .
the ambivalence of the Revolution that made him
half-British, half-American.

II

I turn to the *Arnolfini Marriage,*
and see
Van Eyck's young Italian merchant
was neither soldier nor priest.
In an age of Faith,
he is not abashed to stand weaponless,
long-faced and dwindling
in his bridal bedroom.
Half-Jewish, perhaps,
he is freshly married,
and exiled for his profit to Bruges.
His wife's with child;
he lifts a hand,
thin and white as his face
held up like a candle to bless her . . .
smiling, swelling, blossoming . . .

Giovanni and Giovanna—
even in an age of costumes,

they seem to flash their fineness . . .
better dressed than kings.

The picture is too much like their life—
a crisscross, too many petty facts,
this bedroom
with one candle still burning in the candelabrum,
and peaches blushing on the windowsill,
Giovanni's high-heeled raw wooden slippers
thrown on the floor by her smaller ones . . .
dyed *sang de boeuf*
to match the restless marital canopy.

They are rivals in homeliness and love;
her hand lies like china in his,
her other hand
is in touch with the head of her unborn child.
They wait and pray,
as if the airs of heaven
that blew on them when they married
were now a common visitation,
not a miracle of lighting
for the photographer's sacramental instant.

Giovanni and Giovanna,
who will outlive him by 20 years . . .

(69–71)

The poem is memorable not least because Lowell, without seeming
to be making any effort, manages to bring—as if for the last time—so
many of his themes together. I said earlier that he began, with *Life Studies*, to write poems that could allow him to write about his successive
families. And the topic of family has, in fact, stayed in his poetry when
plot and narrative and structure have dropped out. He refers in the
poem to "the shapeless comfort" of a "flowered frock," and the poem itself seems to offer a kind of shapeless comfort. The *comfort* comes, for
Lowell and for his readers, from the presence in the poem not only of
his themes but also of so many of his sounds, his rhythms. "Marriage"
begins with an echo from the period of *Life Studies* and *For the Union
Dead*. It was in those books that he first began using the past tense and
first person plural to signal friendship and intimacy. Sometimes the intimacy was with another writer. "We couldn't even keep the furnace
lit!" he wrote to Delmore Schwartz (*LS*, 53). But more often the intimacy
was with one of his wives or with his mother. "How quivering and
fierce we were," he wrote to his first wife, Jean Stafford (*FTUD*, 6). In

another poem, he wrote, "Often with unadulterated joy, / Mother, we bent by the fire / rehashing Father's character—" (*LS*, 79). When he begins "Marriage" with the line, "We were middle-class and verismo," it is as if he is using one of his "Familiar Quotations."

Lowell is offering a kind of coda to the poetry he has been writing since *Life Studies*, but he is also thinking about the poems he wrote in *Lord Weary's Castle*. Words that might have appeared in (or been used to describe) his early prophetic poems are used here to describe his family. Lowell describes his son, Sheridan:

> This summer, he is a soldier—
> unlike father or mother,
> or anyone he knows,
> he can choose both sides

The father would like to choose both sides; he would like to be both prophetic and domestic. The "ambivalence" the son feels is felt by the father as he remembers the prophetic poems. Lowell calls himself a patriarch. Although in a poem by another poet the word "patriarch" would seem simply arch, in a poem by Lowell the word has other resonances. It is a biblical word that is being domesticated. The word no longer suggests a towering figure spouting prophetic speech but instead a corny, hyperbolic word for a father. In *Lord Weary's Castle* references and allusions were crowded together in the poem; here it is the poet and his family who are crowded together in a house. His early poems were praised for their formality; here it is only the "family photograph" that is "formal." "Rousing" and "brawn," words that might be used for the combination of manic energy and power in the early poems, are, in this poem, used to describe his pregnant wife's shoulder. Principles of composition Lowell learned from the New Critics have already been mastered by his son in the womb. His son *is* a principle of composition: he is a "center of symmetry." In his poem "Harriet," Lowell kept his prophetic language safe by trusting it in part to the vocabulary of his ten-year-old daughter. Here he does something similar with Sheridan. Sheridan is described as having "muscle." He is (like the young Lowell in the attic in "The First Sunday in Lent") a "war- / chronicler." He is drawn to George the Third. In "Sheridan," Lowell describes his son playing with his "whole plastic armory, claymore, / Nazi helmet, batwings" (*DBD*, 68). In that poem the son seems to have a kind of demonic force. In another poem, "For Sheridan," he describes his son as having "brute cherubic force" (*DBD*, 82). In "Marriage," he does two things at once with his own prophetic energy: he domesticates it by using its vocabulary to describe domestic matters, but he also (as his description of his son suggests) *hides* that energy in the domestic, as if it, like his son, might grow in hiding.

In the second half of the poem, Lowell turns to Jan van Eyck's painting of a married couple, *Giovanni Arnolfini and His Wife* (1434). He identifies the couple in the painting, Giovanni and Giovanna, with himself and his wife. The husband "is not abashed to stand weaponless." This poem, like the poem "Sheridan," has been preoccupied by weapons. To stand weaponless is, in these poems, to be a purely domestic figure. The poet, in the third of the poem's long narrow stanzas, expresses more of his ambivalence about domesticity. The stanzas will get shorter, and the poem will end with a stanza of only two lines. When Lowell describes the husband as "long-faced and dwindling," he is also describing the shape of his poem. It is as if poems of pure domesticity will inevitably take their own shape, unaffected by the words that are used in them: "formal," "rousing," "brawn," "vast."

Another poet might have let the poem allegorize the dissatisfactions of marriage. Lowell chooses to complicate this reading by shifting his own interpretation of the shape of his stanzas. The stanzas are not merely pictures of life offering less and less and then running out. The stanzas are also pictures of a lifted hand and a candle: "He lifts a hand, / thin and white as his face / held up like a candle to bless her." This is not going to be a poem only about the "woe that is in marriage." Lowell chooses from the painting now not an image of Calvinist austerity but of Flemish opulence:

> Giovanni and Giovanna—
> even in an age of costumes,
> they seem to flash their fineness . . .
> better dressed than kings.

He calls the painting a "crisscross," and the poem is itself a crisscross of opposing images from the prophetic and the domestic worlds. Images of a solitary prophetic life—the "one candle still burning," suggesting the figures in "Penseroso" and "Auroras of Autumn"—are crisscrossed with images of the shared life of domesticity: "Giovanni's high-heeled raw wooden slippers / thrown on the floor by her smaller ones." At the same time, hopeful images of the prophetic (a single candle) are crisscrossed with pessimistic images (the "restless marital canopy"). And optimistic images of the domestic ("homeliness and love") are crisscrossed with unhappy images ("too many petty facts"). It is an extraordinarily open, exploratory poem. At the end of the poem, all the crisscrossing images come together with the use of the phrase "as if":

> They wait and pray,
> as if the airs of heaven
> that blew on them when they married
> were now a common visitation

There is a kind of hidden *ars poetica* in these lines. It is as if Lowell is saying, in part, that the extraordinary complexity he worked so hard for at the beginning of his career can be achieved now with so much less appearance of effort. He cannot, like his son, "choose both sides," but he can make the force of both sides felt in the poem.

I said that Lowell's poems are kept from a kind of chaotic openness by the presence in many of them of politics and death. "Marriage" is not political, but it is historical. Lowell is, in this poem, highly conscious not only of the controlling force of his own personal history but of the controlling force of larger historical movements. Words that the earlier couple believed in must now be used ironically: Lowell uses the word "sacramental" ironically, and he uses the word "miracle" to mean "trick." The couple in the painting "flash their fineness." The couple in the photograph "pose in Sunday-best." The couple in the painting can seem to bring the prophetic and the domestic together in part because they lived in a different time, in an "age of Faith."

Death is also a controlling figure. Even Sheridan is a memento mori: death, too, is a "dustman" who can "choose both sides"—the couple in the painting and the couple in the photograph. The poem ends with the simple lines, "Giovanni and Giovanna, / who will outlive him by 20 years." Although the poem ends with a reference to death, it is not a dark ending, in part because the last line refers not to death exactly but to an act of "outliving." The poem itself does not seem dark, and the poet does not seem overly melancholy.

"Outliving" is a powerful word for Lowell, who had outlived so many of his own poetic strategies. Some poets, Stevens and Merrill, for example, present themselves at the end of their careers as possessing a kind of graceful mastery. In the poems of *Day by Day,* Lowell brings back many of the ways he has sounded in the past—and adds a new note. In "Marriage," he writes, in admiring terms, of "gaucheness" and "homeliness." In many of the other poems as well, he characterizes himself as hapless, clumsy. Lowell may present himself this way because of

his awareness of the difficulty and complexity of his project. He wants
to make poetry out of the crisscross of voices "imperfectly, obsessively
heard" and bring those voices into relation with each other, and it is crucial that he never oversimplify or sentimentalize. A purely prophetic
poet might imagine that Lowell, at the end, saw himself as a failure.
Grossman writes, "In *Day by Day* Lowell gives an account of his latest
style as if it were felt by him to be an instrument no longer responsive to
his purpose and not yet replaced by a more powerful means."[78] What
Grossman does not and perhaps cannot acknowledge is that Lowell has,
in fact, found an instrument that is extraordinarily responsive to his
purposes and desires. Lowell's project is what Adrienne Rich, in a poem
called "Transcendental Etude," describes as her project: "a half-blind,
stubborn / cleaving to the timbre, the tones of what we are / —even
when all the texts describe it differently."[79]

2

"Both ways is the only way I want it"

A. R. Ammons

In his first long poem, *Tape for the Turn of the Year* (1965), Ammons tells a story about a friend of his, a self-made man, now very wealthy: "thirty yrs ago he didn't / have nothing: / now there's nothing he / can't have."[1] I want to describe, in this chapter, the stages by which Ammons himself came to a sense that there was nothing he couldn't have.

"Thirty years ago he didn't / have nothing." What Ammons did have (in his first book, *Ommateum*) was a way of writing that seemed impossible for him to escape from. How can poets free themselves from what Wallace Stevens, in "The Comedian as the Letter C," calls "the strict austerity / Of one vast, subjugating, final tone"?[2] The problem is especially difficult if one stumbles on this tone at the start. The voice sounds final in the sense that it is a voice suited to talking about last things, and it sounds final as well in that it leads nowhere. Strictness and austerity are difficult to resist when one finds them in one's own voice, especially early on when one is looking for signs of election. What saves Ammons from its subjugation is what saved Lowell: a consciousness of all ways of speaking as speech genres. Ammons calls them "countermotions," and his openness to them is what makes his poetry continually fresh (*TT*, 9). Ammons is patient with these countermotions: he refuses to understand by them what other poets or critics have understood. The relationship between the prophetic and the everyday rarely appears in Ammons's work merely as "a contest of dictions."[3] He is after something more interesting. What fascinates him almost from the start are the relationships between them—the ways they move toward and away from each other, the ways they resist and accommodate each other.

Other poets who share these preoccupations are more fastidious than Ammons. Ammons is willing to let the prophetic and everyday voices play themselves out in his poems. In the introduction I quoted Marianne Moore's *Paris Review* interview: "The accuracy of the vernacular! That's the kind of thing I'm interested in, am always taking down little local expressions and accents. I think I should be in some philological operation or enterprise, am really much interested in dialect and intonations. I scarcely think any of that comes into my so-called poems at all."[4] Ammons begins, after *Ommateum*, to let as much of "that" into his poetry as he can, but he does not want his poetry to consist only of everyday language. Again, he is like Lowell in this regard. Retaining the prophetic voice of the early poetry, he modifies it by letting it come into contact with, compete with, collaborate with everyday language. He is also like Lowell in that he does not want simply to be a poet who can do either voice. What if he could find a speech genre that would allow him to do both at the same time?

Ammons is interested not only in "the accuracy of the *vernacular*" but also, from the start, in the accuracy of scientific language. His interest in scientific language complicates, as I will show, the relationship between the everyday and the prophetic. The scientific voice can sometimes resemble the everyday voice (in its interest in particulars, in its openendedness), but it is not the same as the everyday voice. The scientific voice can also (in its authoritative tone, its strangeness) sometimes resemble the prophetic voice, though, again, it is not the same as that voice. In the nineteenth century, as poets like Tennyson demonstrate, the scientific voice could be a rival to the religious prophetic voice. But if the scientific voice is one of the countermotions in Ammons's poetry, it can also act as a motion that absorbs countermotions. The scientific voice is important for Ammons because it can be a way of being prophetic and everyday at the same time.

Of course, the scientific voice is in the poetry from the start, but Ammons is, at the beginning, more preoccupied by the creation of a purely prophetic voice. Roland Barthes, in his essay "The Grain of the Voice," writes about "the encounter between a language and a voice."[5] Much of the interest—the suspense—of Ammons's earliest poems comes from listening to this encounter. The very early poems are, in a sense, *about* a poetic voice taking its chances with a language, trying to stay alive *in spite of* that language—a language in which it is, in poem after poem, not—to use Stevens's phrase—finding a satisfaction.

In an important early poem, "Rack," Ammons writes,

> The pieces of my voice have been thrown
> away I said turning to the hedgerows
> and hidden ditches
> Where do the pieces of
> my voice lie scattered
>
> (*CP,* 5)

He thinks the pieces of his voice are scattered in the hedgerows and hidden ditches of a prophetic space—and his early poems are about looking for them there. A prophetic space is a space put in the place of the world: poets create a prophetic space by imagining that the every-day world can be made to mean what they want it to mean. (Prophetic space is not the same as utopian space, a space explored in the poetry of Adrienne Rich, among others.) The objects in the landscape, whether an arrangement of three or four images (a mountain, a desert, hedge-rows, hidden ditches) or a heap of broken images, are not complicated. Objects are emblematic rather than mimetic: no object is more many-sided or textured than it needs to be. Each element of this space (which may be rural or urban) is charged with significance. Events, too, are charged. No event can occur unless it either is itself momentous or por-tends momentous events. The trivial is permitted, is interesting, only as evidence of *triviality*. Blake in *The Four Zoas* and Rilke in the *Duino Ele-gies* create such spaces with utter conviction, and their spaces are, at every moment, convincing. Ammons cannot rival their conviction.

It began to seem that every prophetic poet could create this space with more conviction than Ammons could. For many prophetic poets the landscape is not a prophetic space until it is occupied. The poet im-agines a body—a prophetic figure—entering (once and for all) an in-hospitable landscape in order to perform some consequential act, usu-ally a speech act of some kind. The speech act may be a threat or a vow (Allen Grossman writes, "I stood in the Avenue, and vowed"), but it turns the landscape into a prophetic space.[6] The landscape may resist the prophet, present impediments. An early poem by the twentieth-century Welsh poet R. S. Thomas begins,

> One night of tempest I arose and went
> Along the Menai shore on dreaming bent;
> The wind was strong, and savage swung the tide,
> And the waves blustered on Caernarfon side.[7]

But the poet triumphs. Similarly, Geoffrey Hill begins an early poem, "Genesis," with the words, "Against the burly air I strode / Crying the miracles of God."[8] The air is burly, the wind strong, and the tide savage, but the prophetic figure arises and strides and establishes the inhospitable landscape as a prophetic space. If prophetic poets abandon this landscape, they do so decisively. Blake writes in his preludium to *America a Prophecy:*

> *The stern Bard ceas'd, asham'd of his own song; enrag'd he swung*
> *His harp aloft sounding, then dash'd its shining frame against*
> *A ruin'd pillar in glittring fragments; silent he turned away,*
> *And wander'd down the vales of Kent in sick & drear lamentings.*[9]

The figure in Ammons's early prophetic poems can scarcely enter and can barely occupy this landscape, can hardly make it a prophetic space, and when he can, can occupy it only with the greatest difficulty.

Once the prophetic poets dominate the prophetic space, once they put themselves at the center of it, they can look about and begin to name landmarks. Some of the place-names will be those of the world outside the poem: Blake, in "London," wanders near "the charter'd Thames." T. S. Eliot's "Unreal City" features London Bridge and King William Street. R. S. Thomas evokes Caernarfon, Lowell sees the "sky descending . . . / . . . on Boston." The prophetic poets want their readers to understand that they have been living their small lives not in the day-to-day world but inside this prophetic space. Ammons's prophetic space is, by contrast, largely unmarked. Helen Vendler writes, "The poetry [Ammons] is best able to write is deprived of almost everything other poets have used, notably people and adjectives."[10] A prophetic poet might get along without people and adjectives, but few interesting poets tried to get along as long as Ammons did without referring to a shared world. When Ammons does mention place-names they are places like Sumer, places distant from him (and us) in time as well as space.

Having occupied the prophetic space, the prophetic poets may allude not only to the geography of a shared world but also to other prophetic spaces. (The prophetic poets whose sense of vocation comes from the Bible imagine landscapes that are similar to each other.) These spaces may border each other, may be laid over each other, may be a resketching of the same space in later time. References to other spaces can be a way of acknowledging these relations. Ammons knows this. In *Tape for the Turn of the Year,* he sees "peaks relate across / thin / & / icy air" (130). Nevertheless, he resists this knowledge. Only a confident prophetic poet is willing to imagine a prophetic space as (also) a literary space. If Ammons offers few place-names from a world his readers know well, there are also few references to other poems. Allen Gross-man often uses epigraphs in his poetry. Ammons never does. Nor does Ammons dedicate poems to other poets. It is as if, for Ammons, literary echoes belong to the world of the finely crafted lyric, poems with punc-tuation, what Ammons calls the "self-conscious POEM" (*TT*, 144). When he does mention another poet, he does so in a way that is almost parod-ically self-conscious and, as a consequence, highly *un*charged. In the body of his poems, as well, references to poems by other poets are scarce. Ammons's line, "Blind in the wide land I" from "The Wide Land" may echo Milton's phrase from *Samson Agonistes*. Ammons's speaker, though, is not "eyeless" but "blind," and he is not in "Gaza" but in "the wide land." Is this a literary echo? If so, Milton's phrase has been—to use a word Ammons uses often in *Ommateum*—"bleached." One very early poem mentions "wattles" and "lapis lazuli," and an-other mentions "gyres," but in neither poem does Ammons invoke Yeats with much energy or seem to want to borrow Yeats's own prophetic en-ergy. It is as if Ammons hopes, by making his prophetic space inhospit-able to other spaces, to retain the inhospitality of the landscape he is trying to convert.

Still, in poem after poem Ammons does send his prophetic figure into this inhospitable landscape, hoping for the best. Not only can the prophetic figure not dominate the space, he can hardly stay upright in it. "The Sap Is Gone Out of the Trees" concludes with the lines, "and I said Oh / and fell down in the dust" (*CP*, 1–2). Poem after poem ends in this way. Although there is something comic, even absurd, about the repetition in the very early poems, the poems are rarely coherent enough to accommodate absurdist humor. Another poem (forty-seven pages later in the *Collected Poems*) begins, "I picked myself up from the dust again" (49). In another poem he writes, "With ropes of hemp / I lashed my body to the great oak" (*CP*, 14). It is all the prophet can do to remain inside the landscape. John Hollander, in his prose poem "On the Calendar," offers his readers a more human version of this predica-ment: "I will start a second time, awake again to an old alarm, move in-evitably among the echoes of the previous day . . . and so I shall die once again of aggravated commencement."[11] Ammons is writing poems of aggravated commencement.

He does, nevertheless, maintain a sense that something momentous is going to happen. The reader is not sure what it will be but can guess what it won't be. It will not, for example, involve masses of people. Whitman saw "hooded hordes swarming over endless plains," and later poets like Eliot, Auden, and Fenton have sent crowds swarming through their prophetic spaces. Ammons's poems will become crowded, but not with people. His early poems are full of a sense of imminent endings, but these endings seem disconnected from historical or political outcomes. The suspense in his early poems centers only on the fate of one solitary figure. Something will happen to *him.*

This suspense is so pervasive that it gets into the titles of the poems. One early poem is called "The Wind Coming Down From," and another is called "I Came in a Dark Woods Upon." In "The Wide Land" Ammons offers us the (previously quoted) line, "Blind in the wide land I" (*CP*, 48–49). Ammons suspends this "I" frequently in the early poems: it is one of his first mannerisms, although not one he retains. This "I" has come to the end of the line and might do anything. Another early poem, "Driving Through," begins, "In the desert midnight I said / taking out my notebook I" (*CP*, 33). Something will happen to this prophetic figure, but first there will be postponements, setbacks. In the next line of "Driving Through," for example, he tells us that he is "astonished." Does he mean "surprised and happy"? The word here seems more likely to have its Miltonic sense of "turned to stone." Turning to stone is one way the poet can stay (or stay upright) in the prophetic space—although the poem's title, "Driving Through," suggests that this will not be a poem about staying in the space. If Ammons had written Geoffrey Hill's poem "Genesis," it would begin, "Against the burly air I / Said Oh, and fell down." This suspense, this aggravated commencement, can be maddening: in one poem Ammons alludes darkly to "possibly incipient sorrow" (*CP*, 6). The prophetic figure, that is, may or may not come to grief. What sort of sorrow would he feel? Will it be the fate he waits for, a prophetic sorrow that he can make poetry of, or will it be another setback? The sorrow (which was only *possibly* incipient, in any event) does not come. Nothing does. The poet begins to suspect that something may be wrong with his settings. The space in Ammons's early poetry is often stark but rarely vividly so; it is almost always a little hard to see. It doesn't seem to justify the work— largely, one feels, of exclusion—necessary to establish it. Corrective measures begin to be taken. In poems like "I Came Upon a Plateau," Ammons tries to give his space more density, more particularity; in poems like "Having Been Interstellar," he tries to expand it. None of these measures seems to make much difference. The prophetic figure never does quite learn to arise and stride through the landscape; he never comes much closer to a speech act than the word "Oh." Allen Grossman writes, "Place a man in the center, and he becomes / The man who has prepared for a lifetime / To answer, and now is ready."[12] Ammons has tried to move that man to the center of the space but without success, and the prophetic figure never does have the adventures poet and reader may have wished for him.[13] But Ammons does figure out, at least, how to keep the prophetic figure in the space. He sets him moving. Not that he can move the way he wanted to at the start. Ammons can keep his prophetic figure in the prophetic space, it turns out, only by moving him, perpetually, up and down.

The narrator of *Paradise Lost* narrates his own motions up and down, but each of these countermotions is momentous, belongs to one narrative; each is, as he puts it in the proem to book 3, "hard and rare." Wordsworth advances, horizontally, from one scene of instruction to another. In the generation after Wordsworth, the prophetic figure, no longer sure what it means to be a prophetic figure, begins to move, frenetically, up and down. There can be no scenes of instruction when there are hardly *scenes* at all. Keats, for example, writes that Endymion is

> as one
> Who *dives* three fathoms where the waters run
> Gurgling in beds of coral: for anon,
> I felt *up*-mounted in that region
> Where *falling* stars dart their artillery forth[14]

Directional chaos is often found where there is anxiety about prophetic speech. Elizabeth Bishop, for example, writes in "At the Fishhouses":

> *Down* at the water's edge, at the place
> where they haul *up* the boats, *up* the long ramp
> *descending* into the water, thin silver
> tree trunks are laid horizontally
> *across* the gray stones, *down* and *down*
> at intervals of four or five feet.[15]

Because motion is better than paralysis, Ammons's prophetic figure begins, early on, to move in this way as well. In "The Wide Land," Ammons refers to "sudden // alterations of height." In the poem "Still," he writes, "I whirled through transfigurations up and down" (*CP*, 140–42). He calls one early poem "Sitting Down, Looking Up." In one of his long poems, he writes, "Call me down from the high places."[16] Coming down, he is—instantly—called up again. John Ashbery is right to say that Ammons "is always on the brink of being 'whirled / beyond the circuit of the shuddering Bear' from the safe confines of backyard or living room."[17] Ammons's preoccupation with the fact of motion begins to show up in the titles of the poems. "Motion," "Two Motions," "Motion for Motion," "What This Mode of Motion Said" (*CP*, 146, 143, 127, 116). Not surprisingly, signs of motion sickness appear. In his poem "The Upshot," Ammons writes, "It's hard / to live / living it / up down."

What this mode of motion says is that if the prophetic figure stopped moving, the poet would have to recognize, finally, the limitations of the space he has been trying, in poem after poem, to make plausible, to make inhabitable. In a poem called "Choice," Ammons tells us that he is "idling through the mean space dozing / blurred by indirection" (*CP*, 35). The space of his early poems *is* a "mean space . . . blurred by indirection." The reader begins to suspect that Ammons's prophetic space is simply the day-to-day world inadequately imagined. The poet too seems to guess at this but does not know what to do about it. Maurice Blanchot writes that the artist "now finds himself as if at the beginning of his task again and discovers the proximity, the errant intimacy of the outside from which he could not make an abode."[18] This sense of having to start over again and again, each time failing to "make an abode," is at the center of Ammons's early poetry.

Something begins, though, in certain poems to happen. Moving up and down in this space, Ammons starts to notice aspects of it. The poet begins registering his sense that this space—whatever kind of space it will prove to be—is more crowded than empty. In one early poem, "Bees Stopped," he writes of many "populations":

> Bees stopped on the rock
> and rubbed their headparts and wings
> rested then flew on:
> ants ran over the whitish greenish reddish
> plants that grow flat on rocks
> and people never see
> because nothing should grow on rocks:
> I looked out over the lake
> and beyond to the hills and trees
> and nothing was moving
> so I looked closely
> along the lakeside
> under the old leaves of rushes
> and around clumps of drygrass
> and life was everywhere
> so I went on sometimes whistling

> (*CP*, 5)

In Frost's poem "The Most of It," a "great buck" appears from a "tree-hidden cliff." In Ammons's poem nothing moves—but the speaker is nevertheless not, as Frost's speaker is, "keeping the universe alone."[19] The prophetic figure is noticing small things like bees and things smaller than bees like their "headparts and wings" and also ants running over the "whitish greenish reddish / plants that grow flat on rocks." In other Ammons poems the rock would be bare, but in this poem the rocks are covered by flat plants. Ammons is distracted by the leaves as leaves: they are no longer simply emblematic. Rewriting this poem (again and again in the books to come), Ammons will have learned the name of the "plants that grow flat on rocks." Here he notices simply that the leaves are "whitish greenish reddish." This willingness to be ineloquent for the sake of exactness is something readers do not associate with prophetic poets.[20] When Rilke writes about "the more and more crowded gaze," he seems to be talking about a gaze crowded by symbols.[21] Ammons's gaze is simply becoming more crowded. More important, this kind of seeing is not something prophetic poets associate with themselves, yet no cognitive dissonance is registered in the poem. Instead, he is only (a little) surprised at his fate: "So I went on sometimes whistling."

Nothing should grow on rocks, and yet something is growing, and he notices it. This knowledge is hard to know what to do with. In his poem "The Woodspurge," Dante Gabriel Rossetti tells of a figure who, throwing himself in the grass in despair, notices, after a moment, a woodspurge. Here are the last two stanzas:

> My eyes, wide open, had the run
> Of some ten weeds to fix upon;
> Among those few, out of the sun,
> The woodspurge flowered, three cups in one.

> From perfect grief there need not be
> Wisdom or even memory:
> One thing then learned remains to me—
> The woodspurge has a cup of three.[22]

If we imagine Ammons as only a prophetic poet, then the fact that the leaves are "whitish greenish reddish" seems a not very important message. The fact that the leaves are "whitish greenish reddish" is not something that, as he will put it cheerfully in Garbage, "someone somewhere may be at this very moment / dying for the lack of" (13). But if we imagine him as a failed prophet casting about in his perfect or imperfect grief for help, then the plants don't seem to answer any of his needs. A fundamental shift occurs when prophetic poets can find something "interesting"—it means they have been distracted from their task. Something more profound, perhaps, shifts when they allow the word "interesting" itself into their poetry. In the poem "Identity," for example, the prophetic figure notices a spider web and writes,

> It is
> wonderful
>   how things work: I will tell you
>   about it
>   because
>
> it is interesting
>   (*CP,* 114–15)

In another early poem, he interrupts an exalted, forlorn passage to tell the reader, "So I touched the rocks, their interesting crusts: / I flaked the bark of stunt-fir." He seems, after this interruption, somewhat less exalted but also less forlorn.

Elizabeth Bishop, in a letter I quoted in the introduction, writes, "What one seems to want in art, in experiencing it, is the same thing that is necessary for its creation, a self-forgetful, perfectly useless concentration."[23] Ammons's poems start organizing themselves around such moments of "self-forgetful, perfectly useless concentration." I mentioned the poem called "I Came in a Dark Woods Upon" (*CP,* 27). The next time the poet nears that part of his imagined space he is "coming to a pinywoods" (*CP,* 36). It is as if the dark woods had been a piney woods all along, but Ammons hadn't noticed. In "Interval," he tells us that he

> picked up some dry pineneedle bundles from the ground
> and tore each bundle apart a needle at a time
>   It was not Coulter's pine
>   for *coulteri* is funnier looking
>   and not Monterey either
>
>   (*CP,* 36)

The prophetic figure is engaged in self-forgetful, perfectly useless concentration and cannot remain unchanged by it.

Ammons begins explicitly criticizing his earlier voice, hoping to get some distance from it. He sees himself as

> one over by a rock
> making up songs

as if there were no
world at all.
(*TT,* 186)

The prophetic figure did not notice that the rock had leaves. In another self-critical poem, Ammons refers to "confusing hills, disconcerting names / and routes" (*CP,* 38). We've seen these hills (dimly) and heard some of these disconcerting names and routes. Real place-names, as I said, rarely got into the early poems. It was as if the prophetic space, presented with real place-names, might fade into the light of common day. In the early "Dying in a Mirthful Place," Ammons says he "hurried away to a hill in Arizona," but Arizona, in that poem, was like Tennessee in Stevens's "Anecdote of a Jar." When Ammons writes "Arizona," he is establishing that his soon-to-be-abandoned desert landscape is in America (in a sense, he is saying farewell to it by naming it), but he does not (yet) intend "Arizona" to bring with it any excess reality.

Something is happening in Ammons's poetry, and it is apparent again in an early poem called "Batsto." Batsto seems at first like one of the "disconcerting" names; in fact, it is the name of a town in New Jersey. The poem begins like his other poems, but in the fifth line, Ammons tells us, "We took Route 9 north through / Pleasantville" (*CP,* 50–52). Another poet might have mentioned Paterson. Ammons wants to move from prophetic to everyday space without occupying a literary space. Instead of Paterson, he mentions Pleasantville, a town with a wonderfully bland and undisconcerting name, and a few lines later we hear about housing developments and golf links. He is not moving up and down, he is not "driving through" in the sense of driving into and out of the landscape. He is *touring* it.

In a later poem, "One: Many," Ammons writes, "I think of California's towns and ranges, / deserts and oil fields, / highways" (*CP,* 138–40). What do California's towns and ranges have to do with Ammons's prophetic space? Or with the places we associate with his day-to-day life: North Carolina, New Jersey, upstate New York? Not much. The poet is relaxed and expansive, a little giddy. He seems to be reading Whitman, who writes lines like, "I see the cities of the earth and make myself at random a part of them!"[24] He is, in a sense, on vacation, finding California's towns and ranges "interesting." Ammons never does manage a formidable prophetic place-naming manner, never has anything to rival Eliot's line from *The Waste Land,* "Jerusalem Athens Alexandria / Vienna London / Unreal." Making the real

unreal is something he never learns how to do. Just as the purely prophetic figure never does have his adventures, so Ammons never does
get to pretend that his prophetic space can have the same place-names
as the world, can be the world transfigured. While he does transfigure
the world, he doesn't make it a prophetic space. Instead, he makes it a
(huge and various) space where the prophetic figure from the early
poems can thrive along with everybody else. It is a space where anything can happen.

  Neither Ammons nor Lowell ever experiences a moment of conver-
sion. The transition from a poetry where nothing can happen to a
poetry where anything can happen is gradual in Ammons—there are
turning points, but there are points where he turns back. Ammons
writes,

> my story is how
> a man comes home
> from haunted
> lands and transformations
>   it is
>   in a way
>   a great story:
> but it doesn't unwind
> into sequence
>   (*TT*, 9)

The reason why the story doesn't unwind into sequence is because it is
not, I think, exactly Ammons's story. Once he finds the scattered pieces
of his voice, he doesn't throw any of them away. The haunted, prophetic voice, a version of it, will be retained. The introduction of a "perfectly useless concentration," for example, does not necessarily mean a
relief from the prophetic voice—it can also mean a complication of it. A
change of subject is not always a change of style. Inarticulate prophetic
poets are perfectly capable—driven by their desire to keep writing—of
making a raid on the articulate. John Ruskin wrote, "The greatest thing
a human soul ever does in this world is to see something and tell what
it saw in a plain way."[25] Ammons, like Ruskin, wants to see clearly and
speak plainly, but the "plain way" is as problematic for Ammons as it
was for Ruskin. Ruskin, in such declarations, represents the high voice
wanting access to the tonalities—what Ammons calls the "suasions"—
of the middle range. Ammons is still in love with the prophetic voice.
The desire to be accurate about the natural world puts pressure on the
language the prophet speaks, but another desire survives that puts

pressure on the desire to be accurate. Ammons *remains* "counter, original, spare, strange"—to use Hopkins's phrase from "Pied Beauty." In the poem "Bees Stopped," Ammons writes of the "plants that grow flat on rocks and people never see" (*CP,* 5). Like Ruskin's, Ammons's seeing takes place in a context of other people not seeing. At the same time, Ammons's seeing is, itself, an odd thing. ("Bees Stopped" begins with the strange, arresting line, "Bees stopped on the rock.") It matters also that he is looking, as he says in "Bees Stopped," "closely." Elizabeth Bishop, in the letter quoted above, writes about Darwin: "One *feels* the strangeness of his undertaking, sees the lonely young man, his eyes fixed on facts and minute details, sinking or sliding giddily off into the unknown."[26] With Ammons too the *strangeness* of the undertaking is what we feel; with Ammons too we have to think of what giddiness might be as a mode of seriousness. The natural world enters the poems in odd ways: in the extreme foreground, on the periphery. Just as the prophetic figure could never establish himself in the center of the prophetic space, so the day-to-day world can never occupy the center of the new space Ammons makes. That space will, in fact, have no center. As Ammons writes, "Reality is abob with centers."[27]

It is as if Ammons has been learning to see and needs, at the same time, to learn to speak. In "The Sap Is Gone Out of the Trees," Ammons didn't see anything that he couldn't talk about in his prophetic voice. Now the space of his poems is changing, and he wants to be able to describe these changing spaces. What is the point of seeing clearly if he can never speak plainly? Everyday language enters his poems the way the day-to-day world does—little by little, peripherally. The world is restored to him in pieces, and his voice too is delivered to him piece by piece. Ammons learned in writing his first long poem, *Tape for the Turn of the Year,* that one way to escape from "aggravated commencement" is to use the journal form. Blanchot writes, "The journal roots the movement of writing in time, in the humble succession of days whose dates preserve this routine."[28] Eliot had written, "The only wisdom we can hope to acquire / Is the wisdom of humility: humility is endless."[29] Humility can seem ubiquitous as well, ubiquitous because contagious, as if even the days had caught it. The "humble succession of days" is, as we have seen, the circumstance most to be feared by the prophetic poet. Still, a journal poem might be a way of submitting to while at the same mastering the everyday, a way of being "strange" about it and "strange" in it.

The humility that Ammons is interested in is closer to Moore's than Eliot's. In 1949 Moore wrote an essay called "Humility, Concentration and Gusto" in which she says, "With what shall the artist arm himself save with his humility?"[30] The notion that humility might serve as a kind of defense—even as a kind of defense against other aspects of one's own creativity—was useful to Ammons. Jeredith Merrin called his study of Moore's and Bishop's poetry *An Enabling Humility*. Humility can have an immediate enabling effect on poetry, and Ammons's poems do start to become less spare, less strange.

In a passage from a 1987 poem, Ammons tells the reader that a poet-friend has handed him a poem to read. The poet-friend is worried about whether the poem represents his true voice. Ammons tells the poet:

> the way
> is to say what you have to say
> and let the voice find itself
> assimilated from the many tones and sources, its
> predominant and subsidiary motions
> not cut away from the gatherings:
> but that is passive, he says:
> no, I retort (for effect), it is passive
> to do the bidding of the voice you
> have imagined formed: freedom engages,
> or chooses not to, what in the world is
> to be engaged[31]

Ammons could be addressing his younger self. Earlier he said he wanted to find the pieces of his voice. Now he has the sense of a voice looking for *itself* and finding itself in "many tones and sources." He remembers his own struggle not "to do the bidding of the voice you / have imagined formed." He remembers his search for freedom, which, for him, means freedom to be interested (or not) in what the world shows him, freedom to be prophetic or not, to feel humility or not, to be everyday or not.

He also remembers his own fear, the fear of how day-to-day language would sound when it entered his poems. What kind of shifts would be necessary to accommodate it? What sorts of sacrifices? He has already noticed that his everyday voice is (sometimes) expansive and confident, while his prophetic voice is (often) diffident, frightened. Some prophetic poets might hesitate, delaying the entry of everyday language into their poems because they do not know how to contain it. Ammons refers, in an early poem, to the "massive, drab constant of experience."[32] What poetry could survive the introduction of something massive, drab, and constant? At the same time, what poetry could seem important to its readers (and to the poets themselves) without talking about or incorporating in some way those aspects of experience? The everyday world for some poets may enter the poems only little by little, as a series of *assignments*. Rilke, for example, writes that "this Here and Now, so fleeting, seems to require us and strangely / concern us."[33] Ammons, though he does let the everyday world into his poetry little by little, never sees it as an assignment. All his gestures will happen now in an atmosphere of freedom.

Those poets for whom the language of assignment seems self-important or histrionic might be drawn to the idea of correspondences. The idea of correspondences between the everyday space and prophetic space suggests another way the everyday world might get into poems. Theodore Roethke, in his poem "In a Dark Time," exults in "a steady storm of correspondences!"[34] Ammons, though fascinated by the possibility of having things both ways at once, doesn't feel that these ways need to correspond to each other. Never much drawn to metaphor and simile, he writes,

> this is that & that is this
> & on and on: why can't
> every thing be just itself?
> what's the use of the
> vast mental burden
> of correspondence?
>   (*TT*, 14)

This question is turned to again in his poem "Gravelly Run." In that poem, nothing he sees corresponds in *any* way to his inner state—nothing corresponds to *anybody's* inner state. The poem ends:

> no use to make any philosophies here:
>   I see no
> god in the holly, hear no song from
> the snowbroken weeds: Hegel is not the winter
> yellow in the pines: the sunlight has never
> heard of trees: surrendered self among
>   unwelcoming forms: stranger,
> hoist your burdens, get on down the road.
>   (*CP*, 55–56)

If the sunlight has never heard of trees, it has certainly never heard of Ammons. He had written earlier, "Turning to the sea I said / I am Ezra /

but there were no echoes from the waves." In that early poem the absence of echoes was bewildering. Now, getting no echoes, he decides not to flee over the bleached and broken fields but just to "get on down the road." He is calm now because he has something better than a Romantic faith in—or doubt in—correspondences. The idea of correspondences turns out to be just another assignment. He never had an assignment as a purely prophetic poet except to try to occupy a space and speak from it. There were no "ideas" then: his motto in *Ommateum* could almost have been "no ideas and no things." Ammons has imagined himself from the start as a figure looking at a landscape and trying to speak about where he is. He still sees himself that way—it is that figure, that imagination he wants to redeem. Correspondences won't save him. Ordinary weeds would no longer be ordinary weeds if they could produce a song. Correspondence will not bring day-to-day life into his poems. Ammons will get access to the everyday world—will rescue his prophetic figure—through acts of seeing and speaking.

Ammons had already learned by looking that the visual world was more various than he thought. Now he is learning by speaking that words may be more helpful, because more *versatile*, than he thought. He can't save himself by thinking ("no use to make any philosophies"), and he can't save himself simply by becoming a different poet. Nor can he, like some poets, reinvent himself with each book. But he does want, as he says in his poem "Mechanism," to "Honor a going thing" (*CP*, 77). Ammons progresses by putting pressure on words and phrases, seeing whether these words are going things. This will be Ammons's version of the puns to which Merrill is addicted, but in Ammons it takes place over the course of many books of poems—its effects are deferred.

One of the words he puts pressure on is "say." In the early poems, he was never able to say *I say* but only *I said*. And he said it frequently: there was hardly a poem in *Ommateum* that doesn't include that phrase. But never *I say*. His utterances were never able to take place in present time; the poem was never the cry of its occasion. The present time, the present place were never right, were never safely to be spoken about. A reader, coming to the later poems ("First Carolina Said-Song" and "Second Carolina Said-Song"), might think that all the poems in *Ommateum* had been trying to be "said songs." Ammons, remembering his earliest poems, writes,

> who was that I was?
> who's that from
> rumblings, dark baffles,
> trying to
> break, overriding,
>   into song?
>   (*TT*, 170–71)

This purely prophetic figure doesn't know how to break into song but does his best with "rumblings, dark baffles." "Rumblings" and "dark baffles" are resorted to not only because he doesn't know how to sing but because he doesn't even know what to say. In a very early poem, "Doxology," Ammons tried to say something plausibly prophetic:

> You have heard it said of old time
> the streets shall flow blood, but the streets
> swept out with the flood
> shall be deposited upon sand.
>   (*CP*, 15)

It's not clear what this means: it's apocalyptic but hard to visualize. And he couldn't even say "I said" but, instead, settled for "You have heard it said of old time." Milton and Blake are aware of an audience, however small. Their poems are about hearing and saying. The early Ammons offers, in such lines, only hearsay. He adds, "You have this word for a fulfillment" (*CP*, 15). But the word "say" begins to change. The word starts to modify itself, starts to discover all the ways it can be used. In "Corsons Inlet" Ammons will refer to his own poetry as constituting "sayings." Somehow, without having ever said "I say," he has accumulated *sayings.*

It is the unremarkable words, the monosyllables, that are most vulnerable. The word "so," for example, in the early poem "So I Said I Am Ezra," is crucial.

> So I said I am Ezra
> and the wind whipped my throat
> gaming for the sounds of my voice
>   I listened to the wind
> go over my head and up into the night
> Turning to the sea I said
>   I am Ezra
> but there were no echoes from the waves
> The words were swallowed up
>   in the voice of the surf

or leaping over the swells
lost themselves oceanward
   Over the bleached and broken fields
I moved my feet and turning from the wind
   that ripped sheets of sand
   from the beach and threw them
   like seamists across the dunes
swayed as if the wind were taking me away
and said
      I am Ezra
As a word too much repeated
falls out of being
so I Ezra went out into the night
like a drift of sand
and splashed among the windy oats
that clutch the dunes
of unremembered seas

                    (*CP,* 1)

The word "so" has a variety of registers here. It is spoken by a voice confident of the "suasions" of the *high* voice. "So," the speaker begins. "So I said I am Ezra." The speaker hopes that, in saying this, he will be performing some kind of speech act. But nothing happens. The wind whips his throat. What he has said is irrelevant; the wind, it turns out, is interested only in the *sound* of his voice. Allen Grossman has a poem called "The Sound of a Voice Is the Story of Itself."[35] Grossman means the story of *itself* and not the story of the person using that voice or the fate of the message that the voice brings. But the wind is right to notice only the sound of the voice—it seems to be all that the prophetic figure himself is interested in here. The sound of the voice is, in fact, unstable. "So" is a word that looks in one direction toward portentous words like "therefore" or "thus" and, in another direction, toward the casual, the conversational, to the "so" in "so what." Reading the first line again after reading the entire poem, it seems to say, *So I said I am Ezra, so what.* (There may be more sadness in *this* "so," but there is also less strain.) Ammons foregrounds the word again in *Tape for the Turn of the Year.* Stevens writes of the moment when the voice is able to "suddenly, with ease, / [say] things it had laboriously spoken."[36] Ammons creates such a moment by simply (momentarily) giving his poem over to the word:

      & so & so & so &
      so & so
      &
      so & so & so & so so.
          (*TT,* 39)

In "So I Said I Am Ezra," he writes that "a word too much repeated / falls out of being." It is as if he hopes that this word, too often repeated, will fall out of one kind of being and into another.

Ammons is looking forward: he sees that his language is no longer purely prophetic, and he is trying to imagine what it will become. At the same time, there is a looking back. There was a vocabulary that preceded his first poetic vocabulary, and he is interested in getting access to it. Both projects are urgent. The prophetic figure, whom he is trying to rescue, is in danger of vanishing. In poem after poem, the prophetic figure has been surrendering himself. In "Mansion," he writes,

> So it came time
> for me to cede myself
> and I chose
> the wind
> to be delivered to
> (*CP*, 75)

By now the prophetic figure is, as Ammons writes in "Gravelly Run," a "surrendered self among / unwelcoming forms." Eliot, in his essay "Tradition and the Individual Talent," writes about the "continual surrender of [the artist] . . . The progress of an artist is a continual self-sacrifice, a continual extinction of personality."[37] Ammons has begun his career with self-sacrifice, has been continually extinguishing his personality: his self is already surrendered. Where can he go from there? He wants, as he says at the end of "Gravelly Run," to "get on down the road." The line recalls the end of "Lycidas": "At last he rose, and twitched his mantle blue: /To-morrow to fresh woods, and pastures new."[38] By "pastures new" Milton means prophetic (and epic) poetry: he is going to surrender his human self and take on a larger self. Ammons is simply heading for pastures new, new because he had never looked at them closely before.

Ammons makes progress, moves down the road, precisely by writing lines like "stranger, / hoist your burdens, get on down the road." Prophetic poets who want (however ambivalently) the power of the colloquial, who want what Marianne Moore called the "little local expressions," have usually opted for *reported* speech. Not trusting the speech they grew up with, they record only random overheard phrases. Taking what is unfamiliar to them, they further defamiliarize it in their poems. In some poems the phrases will be chastised for their triviality. The prophetic space, which is an auditory space as well, makes itself an echo chamber, and the emptiness of the space in which the phrases echo indicates the inanity of the phrases themselves. (Frank O'Hara, as usual, offers the comic view of this project. "To be idiomatic in a vacuum," he writes, "it is a shining thing!")[39] The quoted phrases are removed from the complexity and richness that might have been theirs in their original context outside prophetic poetry—outside poetry itself.[40] Eliot, for example, in *The Waste Land* writes, "He'll want to know what you done with that money he gave you / To get yourself some teeth."[41] The word "teeth" and the phrase "what you done" sound grotesque and scary, and "what you done" sounds doom-laden. Hart Crane, in *The Bridge*, seeks a similar effect:

> if
> you don't like my gate why did you
> swing on it, why *didja*
> swing on it
> anyhow—[42]

Lowell too used overheard speech, though his relation to the fragments was more benign. Ammons is not interested in unfamiliar speech. When he uses "little local expressions," the expressions are local to him. "Stranger, / hoist your burdens, get on down the road." This sounds, at least in retrospect, like a piece of Ammons's own voice.

He takes possession of that part of his voice little by little. In the second stanza of the early poem "Rack," telling us about his search for the pieces of his voice, he writes,

> Tomorrow I must go look under the clumps of
> marshgrass in wet deserts
> and in dry deserts
> when the wind falls from the mountain
>
> (*CP,* 5–6)

Wind, mountains, desert: these make up a landscape in early Ammons. (A covert and a sky make up a landscape for early Keats; all Bishop, in *North & South*, needs is an apartment window and a sky.) Ammons's lines in "Rack" include what so many of his lines have (the tone of urgent inquiry, of hectic quest), but now there is something new: he says he must "inquire of the chuckwalla what he saw go by." He could have said "lizard," but instead he surprises the reader (who is not used to being surprised by Ammons) with a tone of mock-dignified whimsy. Again, in the early poem "Coming to Sumer," the speaker, after eight lines, tells us, "I said." We already know he is Ezra—he said so in the second line. Instead, he says, "It has rained some here in this place" (*CP,* 22). He could have written, "It has rained here in this place," and he would have sounded solemn, truth telling, terse. But it has not rained forty days and nights, there is no blood in the streets, it has only rained "some." This is a poet who is "coming to Sumer" from Whiteville, North Carolina, and is remembering, for the length of a line, the way they talked there. (We are also getting one of the first and shortest of the "weather reports" Ammons will become famous for. Weather reports— because they demand some degree of natural description and informal speech—are of interest to Ammons.) Always learning from his effects (there is no effect that shows up in one poem alone), Ammons goes further in *Tape for the Turn of the Year:* "thank it's agonna snow / some: / don't keer if it do" (146).

Phrases from his childhood appear in more and more poems, and soon he begins to write childhood poems. He begins to give himself what no prophetic poet *has* to have: a vividly remembered childhood. The prophetic poets' memory of their childhood is usually not much more revealing than, say, Job's childhood anecdote: "My root was spread out by the waters, and the dew lay all night upon my branch" (Job, 29:19). (Allen Grossman took "The Dew Lay All Night upon My Branch" as the title of one of his early books of poetry.) Ammons, similarly, began by writing like this: "The sap is gone out of the trees / in the land of my birth / and the branches droop" (*CP*, 1). Now he begins to remember more. One of his most powerful poems about childhood is called "Hardweed Path Going." He remembers being a boy on a farm in North Carolina:

> Every evening, down into the hardweed
> going,
> the slop bucket heavy, held-out, wire handle
> freezing in the hand, put it down a minute, the jerky
> smooth unspilling levelness of the knees,
>   meditation of a bucket rim,
> lest the wheat meal,
> floating on clear greasewater, spill,
> down the grown-up path:
>
>   don't forget to slop the hogs,
>   feed the chickens,
>   water the mule
>   cut the kindling,
>   build the fire,
>   call up the cow:
>
>   supper is over, it's starting to get
> dark early,

better get the scraps together, mix a little meal in,
nothing but swill.

"To think clearly," says Charles Simic, "what I need is a pig and an
angel." Toward the end of "Hardweed Path Going," Ammons introduces Sparkle, his "favorite hog."

> Down the hardweed path going,
> leaning, balancing, away from the bucket, to
> Sparkle, my favorite hog, sparse, fine black hair,
> grunted while feeding if rubbed,
> scratched against the hair, or if talked to gently:
> got the bottom of the slop bucket:
>   "Sparkle . . .
>   You hungry?
>   Hungry, girly?"
> blowing, bubbling in the trough
>
>   Waiting for the first freeze:
> "Think it's going to freeze tonight?" say the neighbors,
> the neighbors, going by.
>
>   Hog killing.
>
> Oh, Sparkle, when the axe tomorrow morning falls
> and the rush is made to open your throat,
> I will sing, watching dry-eyed as a man, sing my
>   love for you in the tender feedings.
>
>   She's nothing but a hog, boy.
>
> Bleed out, Sparkle, the moon-chilled bleaches
>   of your body hanging upside-down
> hardening through the mind and night of the first freeze.
>   (*CP*, 66–68)

Ammons was specific about time and place in the early poems only
when the place was distant and the time was far away: one of the
poems in *Ommateum* is called "In Strasbourg in 1349," and another is
called "At Dawn in 1098." It is as if he were afraid of evoking a closer
time and place, as if he wanted what he called "the . . . safety / of multiple origins" (*CP*, 23). The language of "Hardweed Path Going" is prior
to prophetic language, but it anticipates that language: it too is cold, uncompromising, austere, primitive. The child is father to the prophet.
Nevertheless, it is a language on which everyday life exerts pressure,
and that makes the difference to the poet.

In poems such as "Hardweed Path Going" and "Easter Morning,"

Ammons returns not to "multiple origins" but to his one origin. It is not a safe place (he loses, for example, two beloved pets in the former poem), but it is, in some ways, a safer place than his adulthood. There is, for one thing, no sense of impending doom. The child in this poem is not only safe but *busy*. He is not idling through a mean space dozing, nor is he moving pointlessly up and down. Later he will be a prophetic poet trying to get a prophetic narrative under way, but now he is still living in a world of the georgic, a world in which things are always already under way. In fact, the child gets things going: he slops the hogs, feeds the chickens, waters the mule. The prophetic poet is likely to talk about a long dark night of the soul or a night coming when no man can work. The child's time is a time of "every evening," of many evenings. He tells us, "It's starting to get / dark early." (In *Tape for the Turn of the Year*, Ammons quietly evokes not tumultuous biblical darkness but "country darkness" [149].) In the prophetic poems, the adult will be worried about the scattering of his voice, will try to "run down all the pieces" and mix them together. The child says to himself, "Better get the scraps together, mix a little meal in." He is thinking about small tasks, easy to accomplish, crucial, but not extremely urgent. In "So I Said I Am Ezra," the wind will whip his throat, and in "The Sap Is Gone Out of the Trees," the wind will whip his carcass. Here it is the pig's carcass that is at the center of the poem. He writes, "Bleed out, Sparkle, the moon-chilled bleaches / of your body hanging upside-down / hardening through the mind and night of the first freeze." In "So I Said I Am Ezra," the fields he flees over are "bleached." In this poem the pig's body is bleached: the hyperbolic adjective from the prophetic poems has been sent back in time to find the noun it was meant to modify. Ammons may have begun to feel, after writing such poems, that his experiments with the everyday were more than some hit-or-miss emergency measure, but they had, because of their connection with—in a sense because of their endorsement by—this child, a kind of trustworthiness.

The poems that want to be purely prophetic are full of compulsions: *Tomorrow I must go look . . . I must go out beyond the hills . . . I set it my task to gather . . . I will have to leave the earth . . . So it came time / for me to cede myself.* But a reader notices, more and more, other compulsions in the poems: the desire to talk about chuckwallas, the desire to say it has rained some here in this place. T. S. Eliot wrote, in "Ash-Wednesday," "Teach us to care and not to care."[43] Ammons wants to teach himself to write "keer." One of Ammons's very early poems is called "In the Wind My Rescue Is." He must have sensed that his rescue would be achieved by letting his poems put pressure on words like "so" and "say" and "some" and "chuckwalla." Allowing his poems to register the pressure of phrases like "get on down the road" and "don't keer if it do" is a momentous act of permission. Those are the words, the phrases, that enabled him to keep writing, that kept him from having to send a prophetic figure hurtling up and down forever in an underarticulated space.

How could other kinds of poems besides memory poems be opened up to everyday language? Again, little by little. Colloquial moments, getting their effects by their proximity to prophetic speech, have often only the limited force of surprise. Roethke worried that such juxtapositions would be jarring. Ammons, by contrast, wants to be jarring, he wants to jar *himself*. Donne yoked together (violently or gently) whatever opposites occurred to him. Eliot assembled fragments of contrasting weight and tonality. Donne could not comment on his juxtapositions, and Eliot could comment—but only in his footnotes and in certain places in his poems. Ammons wants to comment *whenever he wants*. Just after the beginning of *Tape for the Turn of the Year,* he writes, "today / I feel a bit different: / my prolog sounds phony & / posed." And in "Essay on Poetics," he writes, "I / have the shaky feeling I've just said something I don't trust."[44] The voice is often folksy. Folksiness is, for Ammons, what it was for Frost: an intermediate speech between prophetic speech and everyday speech, a speech that hopes to participate in the force of both, that hopes to be both authoritative and open-ended. It can seem, unfortunately, often to contain what is least trustworthy about each. But if folksiness does not work as a hybrid speech genre, it is still useful as a tone in which to comment. And to be able to comment on his writing is crucial to Ammons. Why? Partly because he is allowing his own poetry more and more freedom, and he needs to keep some sort of control over that freedom. It is also partly because a certain distance from himself has been crucial to his progress as a poet. John Ashbery may seem, in some ways, a freer poet than Ammons, but Ashbery doesn't tell us very much in his poetry about achieving this freedom. Ammons writes poems that are about their own freedom, and it is a sign of that liberation that he be able to talk about the freedom. But he likes to comment also because the commentary will annoy so many readers. Ammons, more and more fascinated by effects, will sometimes do things for effect. His poetic motto, at such moments, might be: "I do it just because you think I can't." Ammons, remembering all the constraints under which he once operated, seems to give himself a greater variety of permissions than other poets writing at his level. A sense of freedom and permission is crucial to him if he is going to find all the pieces of his voice. What is notable in Ammons is that he wants only his own permission and that he takes a certain mischievous pleasure in proceeding without ours.

Meanwhile, he continues to try out effects. Some effect are jarring when juxtaposed with his own prophetic voice but even more jarring when juxtaposed with earlier prophetic voices. A poet like Eliot would write, in "Ash-Wednesday," "I rejoice that things are as they are."[45] Ammons wants to say, "reality, I've got a feeling / you can be awful nice!" (*TT*, 47). Ammons, bored by trying to match the solemnity, the scrupulousness of Eliot's lines from "Ash-Wednesday," "At the first turning of the second stair . . . At the second turning of the second stair,"[46] wants to say,

> Up the stairs you go
> up the stairs you go
> beddybye &
> snooze snooze
> up the stairs you go.
>   (*CP*, 251)

Ammons wants (tired of the drama of almost human phrases like "It has rained some here in this place") to say, "today ben / der clouds / downwashen" (*TT*, 189). His readers may wince, but he doesn't care. In "Coon Song," after telling a story about a raccoon trapped by dogs, Ammons, addressing the reader, moves the poem out of its grim dark rural Robert Penn Warren territory into a different territory:

> I do not care what
> you think: I do not care what you think:
> I do not care what you
>   think: one two three four five
> six seven eight nine ten: here we go
>   round the here-we-go-round, the
>   here-we-go-round, the here-we-
> go-round
>   (*CP*, 89)

Rarely able to come up with, rarely able to sustain the defiance, the scorn, the derision appropriate to a prophetic voice, he does manage a version of it here. It is cranky, curmudgeonly—folksy. David Bromwich refers to Bishop's "good natured defiance of the readers she does not want."[47] This describes Ammons at such moments.

He is not always commenting, of course—and not always commenting in a folksy way. If he were, his poems might be intolerable, but he is always experimenting with countermotions—with "predominant and subsidiary motions." If he can get all the pieces of his voice to work together, he might achieve what must be the dream of even the stingiest, most unprolific poets: to be able to go on forever.

Fewer and fewer obstacles stand in his way. One obstacle, of course, is boredom—his own. Boring the reader might be acceptable, even enjoyable, but he doesn't want to bore himself. (One definition of a minor poet might be a poet who never bores himself. Conrad Aiken never bored himself.) Robert Lowell was sometimes boring to himself: "I was tired / of pencilling the darker passages," he writes, "and let my ponderous Bible strike the floor."[48] Ammons, like Lowell, wants to remain interesting to himself because he wants his writing life to be coterminous with his actual life. If there's a way to keep writing, poets like Lowell and Merrill and Rich and Ammons will find it.

Ammons is always looking for ways to keep going without going stale. Conversation poems are a strategy he discovers early. Engaged in conversation, voices may be lured into new tonalities. The prophetic voice will surprise itself, but so will other voices. The everyday voice, happy to be in its element, will become expansive, experimental. The folksy voice, unable to talk to the reader, may be able to talk to another folksy voice. Voices in conversation may alienate some readers, but they are, in Ammons's poems, manifestly not alienating each other. The charmed circle is unbroken, and conversations are always productive of new effects. Michel de Certeau writes, "The rhetoric of ordinary conversation consists of practices which transform 'speech situations,' verbal productions in which the interlacing of speaking positions weaves an oral fabric without individual owners, creations of a communication that belongs to no one." He adds, "Conversation is a provisional and collective effect of competence in the art of manipulating 'commonplaces' and the inevitability of events in such a way as to make them 'habitable.'"[49] Ammons, whose early spaces were uninhabitable, is fascinated by the act of making space habitable. "The Wide Land" is one of his conversation poems.

> Having split up the chaparral
> blasting my sight
> the wind said
>   You know I'm
>   the result of

forces beyond my control
I don't hold it against you
I said
It's all right I understand

Those pressure bowls and cones
the wind said
are giants in their continental gaits
I know I said I know
they're blind giants
Actually the wind said I'm
   if anything beneficial
      resolving extremes
filling up lows with highs
No I said you don't have
to explain
It's just the way things are

Blind in the wide land I
turned and risked my feet
to loose stones and sudden

alterations of height
                                    (*CP*, 48–49)

The tenderness of the dialogue—reminiscent of Hardy's "The Subalterns"—is more striking when we recall that the speaker has been blinded by the wind: "Having split up the chaparral / blasting my sight." This is, once again, a prophetic space of a kind, but now the prophetic figure is engaged in conversation; he is learning the benefits of "resolving extremes."

More and more voices enter Ammons's poetry, sometimes to instruct him, sometimes to delight him. In "Corsons Inlet" the swallows enter the space of the poem for a moment to say "cheet, cheet, cheet, cheet." And the poet has more and more conversations, though they are generally not with people. Almost always, he is talking to the wind or a mountain. There is no intimacy in these conversations; he does not, for example, have a conversation with any part of nature he can call "mother" (as Robinson Jeffers calls the ocean "mother" in his address to it), but at least the wind and the mountain answer Ammons. The ocean does not answer Robinson Jeffers.[50] These conversations in Ammons's poems, of course, are missing something. One can speak of the everyday in Ammons and (sometimes) of the domestic but not very often of the human. He knows this and comments on it, but he doesn't mind.

The space of his poems is crowded enough. And he is writing more and more happy poems, poems about finding the pieces of his voice, poems in which he shows the pieces working together.

They don't always work together very well. In "Corsons Inlet," for example, the mixture is unstable. The poem is, explicitly, a celebration of the everyday, the provisional. The left margin keeps moving: this is one of the first of Ammons's shape-shifting poems. Playfulness (rather than, say, humility) is ubiquitous here, and not the heavy-handed or hostile playfulness of some of his other poems. We get, for example, a weather report: "It was muggy sunny." The two adjectives, with their *y* endings, have a childlike feeling about them.[51] The poem is hortatory in some parts, though, and readers will have different appetites for the hortatory tone when the topic is provisionality. The poem begins, "I went for a walk over the dunes again this morning / to the sea" (*CP*, 147–51). The speaker rounds a naked headland and returns. Robinson Jeffers, finding himself on a naked headland, would declaim against humanity; Ammons muses about shapes and forms. But he doesn't just muse—he *looks*. Although much of the poem is given over to what he sees, he doesn't want merely to be Dorothy Wordsworth, taking notes, noticing, but to be William as well, generalizing, holding forth. This does not always work. Wanting to celebrate openness he sounds instead—in lines like "I have reached no conclusions, have erected no boundaries"—somewhat ceremonial. The tone seems to come, most immediately, from *Four Quartets*. Eliot writes,

> There is, it seems to us
> At best, only a limited value
> In the knowledge derived from experience.
> The knowledge imposes a pattern, and falsifies,
> For the pattern is new in every moment
> And every moment is a new and shocking
> Valuation of all we have been.

And, again, later in the poem,

> every attempt
> Is a wholly new start, and a different kind of failure
> Because one has only learnt to get the better of words
> For the thing one no longer has to say, or the way in which
> One is no longer disposed to say it. And so each venture
> Is a new beginning[52]

Ammons ends "Corsons Inlet" with the lines,

> I will try
>   to fasten into order enlarging grasps of disorder, widening
> scope, but enjoying the freedom that
> Scope eludes my grasp, that there is no finality of vision,
> that I have perceived nothing completely,
>   that tomorrow a new walk is a new walk.
>
> (*CP,* 151)

Ammons's diction works against the flexible, nimble sensibility he wants to celebrate. "There is no finality of vision." "I have perceived nothing completely." These assertions sound final, sound complete. The (halting, anguished) speech about commencement in the early poems has here become a commencement speech.

John Ashbery is so appealing because he can never pontificate about provisionality without understanding that there is something comic about it. In "Soonest Mended," he writes,

>   Better, you said, to stay cowering
> Like this in the early lessons, since the promise of learning
> Is a delusion, and I agreed, adding that
> Tomorrow would alter the sense of what had already been learned,
> That the learning process is extended in this way, so that from this standpoint
> None of us ever graduates from college[53]

It's hard to talk about new beginnings so much without sounding complacent; Ashbery's humor helps. Ammons—like Eliot—pontificates. In an early poem, he called himself a "spent / seer," but the prophetic voice is not spent, it is only modified. Folksiness has got into it, the colloquial has got into it, it has learned to talk about itself but it is still there, and Ammons is not sure what to do with it.

It might be that "Corsons Inlet" isn't strange enough. Ammons seems strongest when he isn't trying so hard to be "less strange." Willard Spiegelman writes, "For all his fascination with the details of the natural world, and despite his precise attempts to capture its dappled, Hopkinsesque grandeur, Ammons often seems alone and uncomfortable out of doors."[54] Readers may prefer the poems in which he doesn't pretend to be comfortable, when, for example, in poems like "Cascadilla Falls" or "Clarity," he gives his solitude and discomfort more room, when he allows himself to be strange, by which I mean eccentric but not charming. In a poem called "Prospecting," he writes,

> and my loneliness
> like an inner image went

> out and shook
> hands with the willows
> (*CP*, 56–57)

The image of loneliness shaking hands with the willows is weird. "Corsons Inlet" seems insufficiently aware of the oddity of its project.

The poem "Saliences"—often discussed together with "Corsons Inlet"—may be more successful. The long lines of "Corsons Inlet" suggest, in spite of themselves, prophecy, the King James Bible, Whitman, Robinson Jeffers. The short lines of "Saliences" recall the experiments of William Carlos Williams and Robert Creeley, different as Ammons is from those poets. The poem begins:

> Consistencies rise
> and ride
> the mind down
> hard routes
>   walled
> with no outlet and so
> to open a variable geography,
>   proliferate
> possibility, here
> is this dune fest
>   releasing
> mind feeding out,
> gathering clusters,
> fields of order in disorder,
> where choice
> can make beginnings,
>   turns,
>   reversals
> (*CP*, 151–55)

T. S. Eliot can claim that "every moment is a new and shocking / Valuation of all we have been," but the contemporary reader doesn't quite feel the newness, the shock in the lines. The very short lines of "Saliences" convincingly enact the "turns" and "reversals" the poem wants to celebrate.

A poem like "Saliences"—what Ammons calls a "skinny" poem—can enact turns and reversals, but there are other poems in which the skinniness feels like a kind of warding off. It is as if Ammons is worried that these "skinny poems" may be "mean spaces," and he wants to give room to a countermotion. (As he writes, "Maybe you're sick of / domestic details & long / for some swept / transfigurations.") "He Held Radical Light" is a poem about the poet's continuing desire to return to the space of his early poems and speak as he was never quite able to speak in those early poems.

> He held radical light
> as music in his skull: music
> turned, as
> over ridges immanences of evening light
> rise, turned
> back over the furrows of his brain
> into the dark, shuddered,
> shot out again
> in long swaying swirls of sound:
>
> reality had little weight in his transcendence
> so he
> had trouble keeping
> his feet on the ground, was
> terrified by that
> and liked himself, and others, mostly
> under roofs:
> nevertheless, when the
> light churned and changed
>
> his head to music, nothing could keep him
> off the mountains, his
> head back, mouth working,
> wrestling to say, to cut loose
> from the high, unimaginable hook:
> released, hidden from stars, he ate,
> burped, said he was like any one
> of us: demanded he
> was like any one of us.
>
> (CP, 192–93)

This is not quite an *ars poetica* but a subcategory of that genre: a poem about the kind of music the poet occasionally needs to make. (The poem stands out from Ammons's poetry in the way "Anglais Mort à Florence," with its explicit connection between music and emotional crisis, stands somewhat apart in the poetry of Stevens.) Ammons's poem begins: "He held radical light / as music in his skull: music." This is not at all what we've come to expect from Ammons: this prophetic space is unlike the prophetic space of the earlier poems. For one thing, it feels *literary*. Not mind or memory, Ammons says, but skull. The word "skull" recalls the menacing Jacobean atmosphere of Eliot's "Whispers of Immortality," another poem about seeing the skull beneath the skin. Who is this new prophetic figure? He isn't "Ezra." Ammons is using words that are not part of his vocabulary (music, skulls, the word "rad-ical"), and he is telling us about someone for whom they are crucial. The tone is, like Eliot's, at once clinical and breathless—breathless be-cause the "he" in the first line is an "I," though not quite the "I" of "I Ezra." Clinical because the phrase "he held radical light . . . in his skull," put in the past tense, sounds like a phrase from an autopsy. But the speaker's tone is intimate, he knows about the furrows of "his" brain, he seems to identify with, to be, the prophetic figure. The coroner *is* the prophetic figure or, rather, is that figure from time to time.

The second stanza begins with the wonderfully straight-faced line "reality had little weight in his transcendence." The speaker continues, "so he / had trouble keeping / his feet on the ground." The contest between the short lines and the long lines is crucial to the poem. It is as if the poet is anxious about shooting out again in "long swaying swirls of sound." He tries to make the poem behave with lines like the spon-daic "so he"—short lines suggesting, again, the decorums of Williams and Creeley, an aesthetic prizing modesty, hesitation, if not quite hu-mility. Nothing very bad can happen in lines so short. The two lines "turned, as" and "rise, turned" offer a symmetry that the poem doesn't really believe in. The word "radical" in the opening diagnosis—"he held radical light"—seems to suggest that there is a *root* problem, a problem that will be evident even in lines of two beats. "So he / had trouble keeping / his feet on the ground." The "so" here is mumbled: the speaker doesn't know what kind of "so" it is. Now we get the line "his feet on the ground, was." The word "was" is tacked on. In a poem as tense as this poem, anything extra hints at extravagance. Something is going to start up again.

The next stanza tells us that nothing can keep him off the moun-tains. The poem is not about nostalgia so much as continued appetite. The speaker's voice is somehow sympathetic here, almost tender. The tenderness is unexpected: it is as if Ammons has come to terms with the prophetic figure of the early poems. He doesn't have to be a figure representing failed speech, he can become a figure representing pure desire—and the desire can be, to some degree, satisfied. The prophetic figure now knows about roofs, now hopes to be "like any one of us." But he also has, now, an adequate prophetic space, and nothing can keep him from it. At the same time, nothing can keep him, now, from everyday space.

Ammons knows what many other prophetic poets have seemed not to know because he was, in a sense, present at every stage of the creation of his voice. He knows the history of all the desires that operate as countermotions in his poems. And he knows that all these desires had to be given a language and a voice in which to make themselves real. Ammons understands, also, that every motion awakens in us an appetite for its countermotion. He writes "He Held Radical Light," for example, and then he produces comic versions of it. A later poem begins with the lines, "The wind is still my subject," and another begins with the lines, "I'm stuck with the infinity thing / again this morning." Another is called "A Tendency to Ascendancy." A poem expressing the opposite impulse is called "Weight":

> He loved cloud covers
> went into woods
> to hide from stars: he
> wept under bridges,
> noticed weeds, counted
> frog calls
> till a stone in
> his belly hardened
> against infinity, the
> grievances of levitation.[55]

Ammons is equally happy to undermine his tendency to keep his feet on the ground. In an early poem, "Guide," Ammons tries to think about what could be wrong with his trips to the mountains in search of "unity." The wind tells him that "a peachblossom blooms on a particular / tree on a particular day: / unity cannot do anything in particular." The poet, finding the wind persuasive, tries to think good thoughts about particularity, but then he asks, "Are these the thoughts you want me to think" (*CP,* 79–80). Ammons is a powerful poet because he knows that the desire to speak prophetic speech can also be called "a tendency to ascendancy" and because he knows that nobody can know what the everyday feels like if he is simply trapped in its rhetoric. In one long poem he writes,

> It's impossible anyone should know anything about the concrete
> who's never risen above it, above the myth of concretion
>
> in the first place.[56]

Many contemporary poets are caught in "the myth of concretion"— they hope that a continual hortatory evocation of concreteness will "suffice." But the concrete is, for Ammons, just one more exciting way to sound.

Ammons seems, of all contemporary poets, least trapped, least impeded. His poems occupy a space that is difficult to characterize.
They are full of turns and reversals. In *Tape for the Turn of the Year*, he
writes,

> we praise Your light:
> give us light to do what
> we can with darkness:
>
>> courage
>> to celebrate Your
>> light
>> even while the
>> bitterdrink
>> is being drunk:
>>
>> give us the will
>> to love
>> those
>> who cannot love:
>>
>> a touch of the dark
>> so we can know how one
>> hungry for the light,
>> can
>> turn away:

Then, farther down the page, he tells us:

>   I had
> lunch after
> "who cannot love" —
> soup, sandwich, milk,
> chocolate fudge cookie, &
> coffee
>   (*TT*, 60–62)

Ammons's inventiveness is most apparent when read against the high
modernists. It's hard to imagine Eliot writing "I had lunch after 'What
are the roots that clutch,'" nor is it easy to imagine a collection called *The
Really Short Poems of H.D.* Blanchot would see such inventiveness as an
example of a kind of mastery: "The writer's mastery is not in the hand
that writes . . . Mastery always characterizes the other hand, the one that
doesn't write and is capable of intervening at the right moment to seize
the pencil and put it aside. Thus mastery consists in the power to stop
writing, to interrupt what is being written, thereby restoring to the
present instant its rights, its decisive trenchancy."[57] Ammons likes to

play with this kind of interruption, but he is also interested in another kind of mastery, the mastery of what Blanchot called "the incessant." He is drawn to long poems because, as he writes,

> I've been
> looking for a level
> of language
> that could take in all
> kind of matter
> & move easily with
> light or heavy burden:
> a level
> that could
> without fracturing, rise
> & fall
> with conception &
> intensity:
> not be completely
> outfaced
> by the prosaic
> & not be inadequate
> to the surges.
>   (*TT*, 143–44)

He wants to

> make a
> dense, tangled trellis so
> lovely & complicated that
> every kind of variety will
> find a place in it
>   (*TT*, 44)

The long poem may be the place where the prophetic and the everyday find their real home. They are both voices that need time and space; they can't be placated with a few lines. ("I can't be human," Roethke wrote in his journal. "I haven't the time.")[58] Ammons wants to write enough poems—and enough long poems—so that all the pieces of his voice can be accommodated.

So many of his short poems have one or another trajectory. He is always having it one way, then another:

> One can't
> have it
>
> both ways
> and both

> ways is
> the only
>
> way I
> want it.

In an early poem he writes,

> So when the year had come full round
> I rose
> and went out to the naked mountain
> to see
> the single peachflower on the sprout
> (*CP*, 39–40)

That is one trajectory—the prophetic to the everyday. It's an odd trajectory; it's a little as if Yeats went out to the hazel wood to see the hazel trees. Sometimes the move from prophetic to everyday space can be clever in the way it subverts our expectations. An early Ammons poem called "The Watch" begins, "When the sun went down and the night came on / coming over the fields and up the driveway / to the rose arbor and the backporch posts" (*CP*, 43). It's not clear which way this poem is going to go. This time, it stays in the prophetic space. We are used to poems (Coleridge's "Dejection: An Ode" or Tennyson's *In Memoriam*) in which a poet, quickly or gradually, cheers himself up. A long poem in which the poet has many moods but in which these moods do not, to adapt Emerson, have to believe in each other can seem appealing. It can seem appealing, as well, to avoid an *intellectual* trajectory, to write notes but not notes toward.

Stevens said of the everyday that "it is the one / Discovery still possible to make."[59] The spirit of discovery has led Ammons outside (what even he may consider) poetry. It is as if he wants to see how deep he can go into ordinariness and still find poetry. Poetry may be, though, for someone like Ammons, hard to leave behind. He uses the quaintly colloquial word "bumfuzzlement," but that's still poetry: Cummings would have sent it sprawling down the page. Ammons looks into the meanest, most banal spaces imaginable, but unpromising spaces have always brought out the best in him: his hard-won, highly resourceful sense of language goes to work on them.

Ammons sometimes writes as if he thinks that a poetic gift is the last obstacle. What if he were to surrender it? What if he tried to replace it with nonpoetic language? Nonpoetic language is, though, at the end of the twentieth century, in short supply. In his long poem "Pray without Ceasing," he writes, "I send / empty statements, slip-shoddiness, / incredible breeziness and such." Incredible breeziness is everywhere in Ammons, but it feels too intimately related to the big wind of the early poems to be really nonpoetic. Incredible breeziness is not, in Ammons, uninteresting. What about its opposite? What about language which is *not* empty, *not* slipshod?

Scientific speech is a speech genre to which Ammons was drawn from the start. I cited earlier Barthes's discussion of "the encounter between a language and a voice." Scientific language may have been appealing to Ammons at first because of the possibility that he could surrender his inadequate prophetic voice to it, that that voice would be lost in the encounter. He does try to surrender his voice. Toward the end of one long poem, for example, Ammons incorporates a prose paragraph from a book about the sea, then follows it with a prose paragraph from a textbook called *The Science of Botany*. James Merrill incorporates prose paragraphs in his long poem "The Thousand and Second Night," but the paragraphs come from invented books. Ammons is not drawn to that kind of game. On the last page of that long poem, saying, "Here is something I have always wanted to quote," he quotes a long paragraph from an article about estuaries in *Scientific American*. Then he writes, "Isn't that beautiful?"

The long poem is called *Essay on Poetics:* it is clear that the language of science will be a crucial part of Ammons's poetics. But it is not a relief from his struggles with voice—it is, itself, simply another piece of his voice. Every speech genre is another countermotion, complicating (as each of them does) the trajectory of his poems. It is an impediment but a productive one. Here, for example, "the happy genius of his household," Ammons imagines the scientific impulse as part of a rhythm of hurry and delay—in this case, as a postponement of prophetic speech.

> I should go out and measure the diameters of
> the branch, secondary branches, small limbs, and twigs
> and their extensions from base
> and devise a mathematics
> to predict the changes of located average birds: it
> would give me plenty to do for weeks
> and save me from the rigors of many heights:
> or scoot me to them: conceiving a fact stalls the
> imagination to its most threatening dimension:[60]

Mathematical calculations, he writes, "would give me plenty to do for weeks / and save me from the rigors of many heights." This line glances at the restorative power of everyday facts, but Ammons rejects that restorative power as too familiar from other poems, too much like a book by John McPhee or Tracy Kidder. Ammons is not sure, in fact, whether this immersion in diameters and extensions *will* save him from "many heights"—it may reawaken in him an appetite for them.

What is compelling is the absence of urgency. The speaker doesn't say, "I *must* go out and measure the diameters." Instead he says, "I *should* go out." Wordsworth, in his "Ode to Duty," wrote, "My hopes no more must change their name, / I long for a repose that ever is the same."[61] Ammons knows that any motion is simply a postponement of another. His hopes change their names frequently. Conceiving a fact only stalls the imagination: he will be back on the mountains, "wrestling to say." It is very difficult for an Ammons poem to go wrong, and if it does it will soon go right. In any event, it will not be impeded.

Ammons is not, like Cowper in *The Task,* going on and on because he fears the interruption of other kinds of speech—he is not going on and on in order to calm himself. Nor is he, like Tennyson in *In Memoriam,* going on and on in order to console himself. He can calm himself when he wants—or console himself or shore fragments against his ruin or include history. He just wants to be allowed—to allow himself—to go on and on. Ammons seems at first to illustrate Wayne Koestenbaum's ideas about logorrhea: "Logorrhea—addiction to talk—is inevitably a matter of solitary binge, of isolation. The malaise is never interpersonal, never dialogic." Koestenbaum adds, "Logorrhea is writing against the aphorism. Writers who mince words, writers of few words, are not troubled by logorrhea." Ammons, of course, who subverts any descriptions but those formulated specifically to describe him, writes poems of few words and many words. Koestenbaum's discussion is, however, intriguing in this context and suggests ways in which Ammons, like Ashbery, resists close reading. "Logorrhea—the term—denies the ubiquity of subtext, secrets: denies that everywhere, in every sentence, however loose, a message lies hiding, waiting to be interpreted. Saying logorrhea, we momentarily refuse language's invitation; we stop listening."[62] Ammons will still be talking when we start listening again. "Writing," according to Blanchot, "is the interminable, the incessant. . . . To write is to surrender to the interminable."[63] This is the only surrender Ammons wants to make and the only surrender he has made. In a 1983 interview Ammons recommended that poets not "concentrate on

voice and tone in a narrow sense: what happens is that the poet begins
to identify in himself something he calls voice but which is really becoming only a mannerism. But voice . . . is a resolved action of many
voices."[64] Ammons has the exuberance of a poet who has had to give
nothing up. His poetry is prophetic, folksy, scientific, playful, everyday.
He has made his poetry out of a resolved—or, in a sense, an *unresolved*
action of many voices, many countermotions.

> I wouldn't give up a hair of
> the beautiful
> high suasions of language,
> celestial swales, hungering the
> earth up into heaven, no,
> I would just implicate
> the language with barklike beeps,
> floppy turf
> of songsound, I would lift up so much
> of the whatnot
> it would pull the heavens down
> commingling with things and us
>
> I would give up nothing
> if I had my way[65]

3

"Some kind of workable relation"

James Merrill

In James Merrill's trilogy, *The Changing Light at Sandover*, one of the two heroes, JM, says that he is trying to find "some kind of workable relation // Between the two worlds."[1] The worlds to which he refers, of course, are the everyday and the supernatural. The statement is extremely odd in many respects, not the least being the immediate narrative context, which is the effort to find potential mothers for reincarnated souls. Negotiation even between people who share a world can be arduous. To negotiate with spirit voices would appear to redouble the difficulty while at the same time adding pointlessness. There is no spirit world—and if one were to invent such a world, wouldn't it make more sense to have it answer in every particular to one's deepest wishes? Why the rhetoric of effort when life itself is hard enough? Why not three volumes—if the poem had to be so long—of people talking to *each other*? In this chapter, I want to trace the development of the relationship between the everyday and the supernatural in Merrill's work.

Merrill had been including highly concentrated interplays of voices in earlier poems, though the people in the poems are not always talking *to* each other. In "Matinées," there is a quatrain in which the poet captures what he calls "one's household opera":

> The pipe's aubade. Recitatives.—Come back!
> —I'm out of pills!—We'd love to!—What?—*Nothing,*

Let me be!—No, no, I'll drink it black . . .
The neighbors' chorus.

(*CP*, 269)

The speakers here are histrionic, polite, irritated. What people in houses can want from each other is not the intimate, exactly, but the social. The demand can seem intense (recall the first couple in *The Waste Land*) but, at the same, a little ridiculous. The occasions are trivial, and yet one has to rise or descend to them. Any response, whether willingness or reluctance, can make one feel one is performing in a "household opera." In "Days of 1935," a poem about his childhood fantasy of being kidnapped by gangsters like Bonnie and Clyde and held for ransom, Merrill writes,

> Their names were Floyd and Jean. I guess
> They lived in what my parents meant
> By sin: unceremoniousness
> Or common discontent.
>
> "Gimme—Wait—Hey, watch that gun—
> Why don't these dumb matches work—
> See you later—Yeah, have fun—
> Wise guy—Floozie—Jerk—"
>
> (*CP*, 303–4)

Merrill enjoys their language for its own sake. With their machine gun delivery, screwball comedy timing, gangster lingo, slangy throwaway insults, each trying to make the other think for as long as possible that they mean the insults, Floyd and Jean already believe they're in the movies. What could be better than the way they talk? Merrill is interested in seeing what he could do with already stylized language, and he transforms their language while remaining faithful to it. He offers the couple what they would not have thought to ask for—a version of their story in which their phrases rhyme. They may be themselves "a dumb match," but in this poem the match works. It works aesthetically, which is not unlike the way they themselves had hoped to work. Nothing could be better than such rapport, and Merrill, wondering what it could do in his poetry, what it would do for his poetry, goes to work on it.

But Floyd and Jean use the same lingo, have the same speech rhythms. What if the voices had different word banks, different rhythms, different tonalities? Merrill is fascinated, thrilled, by otherness—not simply in the pious sense of "acknowledging" it but by the endless twists and turns of interacting with it. In his memoir, *A Different Person*, he writes, "Among friends we are no doubt free to be 'ourselves'—giddy, vague, sullen, unforthcoming. We can say what we don't mean, and still be understood. Or we can say nothing, like couples long married who speak hardly at all. A stranger's ear and a stranger's grammar, by contrast, keep us at concert pitch."[2] What if the characters in these stanzas were "human and otherwise"? Human grammar and "a stranger's grammar," human voices and spirit voices talking endlessly, completing each other's thoughts, their phrases crashing into each other, narrowly avoiding each other, racing side by side? What if one voice were to speak with "rushing eruptive intensity," while another "booms and raves," and yet another says, "Come back" and "We'd love to" and "Let me be"?[3]

The three books that make up *The Changing Light at Sandover* were published separately: *The Book of Ephraim* in 1976 as part of *Divine Comedies; Mirabell* in 1978; and *Scripts for the Pageant* in 1980. All three were collected in 1982 as *The Changing Light at Sandover*. The poem, which runs to 560 pages, consists largely of transcripts (with commentary) of the more than twenty years James Merrill (JM) and his partner, David Jackson (DJ), spent talking with spirit voices at the Ouija board. JM and DJ have conversations with, among others, Ephraim (a first-century Greek Jew), then with Mirabell (a bat who turns into a peacock), and finally with the archangels Michael, Emmanuel, Raphael, and Gabriel. The speech of the supernatural is indicated by capital letters in the text. Over the course of the three volumes, an immensely complicated cosmology is revealed.[4] As Judith Moffett explains, "After an unspecified number of incarnations and degrees of development, each human soul is promoted to the first of nine States, thenceforth no longer to be reborn. At this point he becomes a 'patron' with an earthly soul (called a 'representative') to oversee, and the patron who had been overseeing *him* moves to a higher Stage."[5] The cast includes Pythagoras, Gertrude Stein, Montezuma, Akhnaton, T. S. Eliot, Maria Callas, Wallace Stevens, God Biology, and Mother Nature. God Biology speaks. JM and DJ also have conversations with friends who have died. The two most important of these friends are W. H. Auden and Maria Mitsotáki, a friend from Athens. At the end of the poem, "august presences from the other world convene to hear JM read the beginning of the trilogy."[6] Among them are Dante, Eliot, Rilke, and Yeats.

Merrill wrote *Sandover* because nobody else could have done it and because he had been, from the first book, teaching himself how to write it. Although he began the trilogy with the words "Admittedly I err," a reader can imagine Merrill asking himself how he can take the most possible pleasure from what he has taught himself to do in poems. Many critics felt that he *had* erred. Stanley Poss saw the first volume as all style and no substance. The second volume of the trilogy was, according to Peter Stitt, "an intellectual sham." Denis Donoghue wrote that parts of the second volume were "heartbreaking" but that it felt "wretched to have to cross such a dismal terrain to reach them." The trilogy spent much of its time, according to William Harmon, "floundering in chit-chat and mumbo-jumbo." Calvin Bedient, reviewing the first book of the trilogy, argued that Merrill had misunderstood his gifts.[7] I will argue that Merrill had a profound understanding of his gifts. Over the course of his career he had gained an intimate working knowledge of what everydayness meant to his poetry, and it is this knowledge that is celebrated in *Sandover.* Poets who can write memorable poems about everyday life may feel, at a certain point, as if there is nowhere to go. Merrill's life was not interrupted by madness or physical illness or haunted by suicide, and though he is probably the most resourceful poet of his generation in writing about what was an uneventful life, he would not have wanted to feel condemned to a life of finding and celebrating ever-new aspects of the everyday. He may also have had a sense that the everyday was unusually strong in him and wanted to test it.

James Merrill's sense of the everyday would be formidable because it would be supported by the domestic and the human. It is important, though, to remember that his ability to write poetry of the everyday, the domestic, and the human did not come to him (as everything else seemed to come) immediately. He had to gain access to these voices, poem by poem. Lowell and Ammons developed the prophetic voice first and then the everyday voice; their everyday voices, because they had been buried alive under the earlier prophetic voices, carried with them a sense of that fate. Merrill had to extricate the everyday and domestic and human voice not from the prophetic voice but from what one might call his poetic voice.

One can trace the progress of this extrication over the course of his career. His first book, *First Poems,* was published in 1951. The next books were *The Country of a Thousand Years of Peace* (1959), *Water Street* (1962), *Nights and Days* (1966), *The Fire Screen* (1969), *Braving the Elements* (1972), and *Divine Comedies,* in which *The Book of Ephraim* appeared. After the trilogy he published three books, *Late Settings* (1985), *The Inner*

Room (1988), and his final book, *A Scattering of Salts* (1995), which came out after his death. In his memoir, Merrill said his early poems "remained verbal artifacts, metered and rhymed to be sure, shaped and polished and begemmed, but set on the page with never a thought of their being uttered by a living voice" (*DP*, 6). The poems are conscious of themselves as verbal artifacts—they may even be organized around epiphanies about their own precariousness, but these epiphanies do not offer any relief or interruption. The early poems seem uninterruptible, while *Sandover* will seem almost to revel in interruption.[8] Whatever enters the rarefied world of the early poems takes on the manner of the poem—that is one of the conditions of its entry. It is as if one needed a password and then discovered that, once inside, all one could speak were passwords. It is not easy to know in some poems what, if anything, is being said. Merrill, in a late poem, "The Parnassians," writes of poems in which "the mere exchanged glance between word and word / Took easily the place, the privilege / Of utterance" (*CP*, 529). The poems are often about their own inadequacy, but this inadequacy seems to be an unspoken understanding between the poet and his readers. The poems do not seem to require emergency stylistic relief, as Ammons's early poems did. The mood of the poems is melancholy. About one such poem Merrill wrote in his memoir, "It had the obligatory note of sadness struck without exception by my early poems, regardless of my state of mind during their composition" (*DP*, 70). In a section of his memoir called "My Favorite Words," Merrill wonderfully captures the atmosphere of these early poems.

> What were my recurrent words? No longer, as at sixteen, "pale" or "dim," or even the irresistible names of colors—"violet" or "rose," scented respectively by turbulence and upward movement. The words I never wearied of were rather those adverbs like "still" or "even," or adverbial phrases like "by then" or "as yet" or "no longer," which, sharpening a reader's sense of time, suggested a reality forever in the process of change, that had "only now" come into being or was "already" on the point of vanishing. "Still" with its triadic resonance of immobility, endurance and intensification ("Eleanor grew still more animated") was perhaps the hardest to resist. Deep in the pinewoods of my vocabulary, it yielded an intoxicating moonshine I would keep resorting to in small, furtive sips. (*DP*, 260–61)

Immobility, endurance, and intensification. To one critic, though, it seemed that the early poems "didn't dare move."[9] It is as if any motion might attract countermotion, motion of a kind that Merrill was not yet ready or able to control with his "poetic" voice. Ammons, in his early poems, seemed over and over to imagine spaces that the human figure finds impossible to occupy. Merrill's figures—whether human or not—sit perfectly still in the space of his. There is no hurry. Merrill was, as he said, in love with the language of "by then," "as yet," and "no longer" and is happy to watch and see what changes and what remains in the poems as he writes them. Ammons uses the word "idling": "Idling in a mean space dozing," he writes early in his career. Merrill's is not a mean but an elegant space, but he too, as he says, is idling.

Merrill has his own way of idling, though: he uses the word "idlesse." Merrill's diction, especially in his early poems when there was little to distract from it, has received much attention. Richard Howard, for example, calls attention to Merrill's use of words such as "gracile," "idlesse," and "chryselephantine" and phrases such as "roulades of relinquishment" and ("better and worse still," writes Howard) "the night was a warm nubility."[10] But it might be worthwhile to look more closely at what kind of "affected" language Merrill uses. Helen Vendler, writing about the later Merrill, observes that his "diction, though it can be fully literary, is also colloquial and topical, and in that way, though he generally writes in meter, he writes in the current language of America."[11] He was not "colloquial and topical" in the early poems, the poems before *Water Street*, but it is valuable to look at what else he was not. He does not, like Robert Duncan, another poet who was under a spell in the forties and fifties, use words like "'twas" and "ere" and "wrake." "Among my friends," Duncan writes, "love is an answer to a question / That has not been askt."[12] Some readers who enjoy the early Merrill will feel obscurely disappointed by Duncan's decision to use the word "askt"—it is as if the answer would have to adapt itself to the question, as if everyday life will only be able to happen in a language that has been prepared to decorate and muffle it. In fact, there is not going to be an everyday in Duncan's poetry: he is not heading there; he has seen it and detoured.[13]

In "The Black Swan," Merrill refers to "a private chaos warbling in [the swan's] wake." What is surprising here is not that the chaos is called (and remains) private but that Merrill characterizes it as "warbling." There is a difference between words like "wrake" and "warbling." In an interview, Merrill says of Stevens, "I think he continues to persuade us of having had a private life, despite—or thanks to—all the bizarreness of his vocabulary and idiom."[14] We can sense a private, an everyday life behind Merrill's early vocabulary and idiom as well: it is there as a pressure. The poems seem to be taking place in this world and this time. Gertrude Stein felt that Joyce had made a terrible mistake in making up words, as if his relationship to language had been corrupted. One feels, moving from Merrill's poems to Duncan's, that Duncan, by his archaisms, has cut off possibilities for himself. Robert von Hallberg writes, "Merrill's poems proudly occupy a special corner of the language where the possibilities of play are unlimited by mundane considerations of democratic usage."[15] I would argue that there are many special corners of the language, and each is different: The "mundane" and "democratic" are, in the world of poetry, just one more corner.

Merrill does get a little restless. In "The Country of a Thousand Years of Peace," he writes of

> the toy city where
>
> The glittering neutrality
> Of clock and chocolate and lake and cloud
> Made every morning somewhat
> Less than you could bear
>
> (*CP*, 57)

His poems of this period can seem like that toy city. Merrill knows he won't always write this way and wonders idly what his future poems will sound like. He imagines some violent end to the voice, some "turbulence and upward movement." In "Medusa," he writes, "Tonight may one of us" (it doesn't matter who, though there is the suggestion that he means some inner figure of capable imagination) "[r]aise his quivering sword, and think to kill." He tries parody. In his poem "In the Hall of Mirrors," a guard, speaking to the mirrors, says, "'Your seeresses of sheer Space / In argent colloquy despise / Anything personal or commonplace'" (*CP*, 121). Weary of sheer space, he wants detailed (domesticated?) space, not argent colloquy but simple conversation, conversation about the personal and commonplace, among other things. In the same poem, he says, with wonderful understatement, "You feel that something must begin."

Merrill stands out among contemporary poets for the way in which he writes about creative development, traditionally a subject for anguish and self-doubt. In the opening paragraph of his memoir, *A Different Person*, he remembers the spring of 1950, a time when he could see no way into the next phase of his life (and presumably also of his art). He and his friends would drink in the Village, "protected from encounters they perhaps desired with other customers by the glittering moats, inches deep, of their allusive chatter" (*DP,* 3). Protected from encounters—the line seems to be about his poetry as well.[16] Glittering moats, inches deep, of allusive chatter. His early poetry inspired in him a great number of analogies, similes, metaphors. The metaphors are not all retrospective, though—the poems supplied, as he went along, metaphors for themselves. "Dream (Escape from the Sculpture Museum) and Waking" seems to be, in part, about his creative predicament. In his dream, he is locked in a museum with sculptures and statues. Different poets would have different responses to this situation. Pound would turn docent; Frank O'Hara would leap from statue to statue; Lowell would resculpt all of them; Louise Glück would ask to see the archaic torsos. Merrill considers the statues, compares his poise and deportment to theirs, and says, "For a long time now / I have wanted to be more natural / Than they" (*CP,* 115). That is, of course, the way a statue would put it: "For a long time now I have wanted." Certainly, he is not expressing his desire more naturally than a statue would. The title of the poem suggests that he *dreams* he has escaped from the sculpture museum. When he awakens, the poem suggests, he is still there.

His next book is *Water Street,* and the poems in that book suggest that changes have taken place. One can, in this book, feel the poet's pleasure in what has "only now" come into being and what is "already on the point of vanishing." J. D. McClatchy writes, "Though *Water Street* has none of the novelistic coherence of *Life Studies* and certainly none of its anguish, 'An Urban Convalescence' stands in a similar relation to Merrill's previous work. It too signifies a rejection, more by its example than by a declaration, it abjures an earlier belief or mode, in this case the baroque preciosity, the feints and baffles of *First Poems* and *The Country of a Thousand Years of Peace.*" McClatchy adds, "The best of that style— its brio, its lavishness, its fondness for paradox—remains in *Water Street.* Its ornate excesses and riddles do not."[17] Another poet might have felt that naturalness, once achieved, was enough, but sounding "more natural" could never be, for Merrill, the end of the road. What is mysterious to some poets about their creative growth seems from the start to be clear to Merrill. He had to "construct" an everyday voice—it should not be surprising that he is always conscious of it as constructed. Vernon Shetley writes, "What is noteworthy about Merrill's stylistic development is that he has never been tempted to imagine that a more colloquial diction or a freer prosody is any less arbitrary or artificial than any other stylistic choice."[18] He may remark in his memoir,

"No doubt the seedling psyche needed time in the greenhouse," but even that phrase is not quite the self-soothing organic rhetoric to which some poets resort (*DP*, 34). Winning access to an everyday voice, a human voice, a domestic voice did not seem to involve a struggle for Merrill but just "time." And he did not move, did not see himself as moving from the "false" to the "true," the "unreal" to the "real." The voice of ornate excess, the riddling voice—a poet might want to use them. Voices are voices. Why would a poet want to be without any of them? One wants to be able to sound passionate and direct and un-guarded, just as one wants to be able to feint and baffle. Merrill is alert to the uses other people make of these voices. In his memoir he writes of a friend, "To be insufferable was the role of a lifetime, and he played it with style and nerve" (*DP*, 17). And in his essay on Bishop, he praises her for her "instinctive, modest, life-long impersonations of an ordi-nary woman."[19] Merrill is interested in effects. Certain effects can be achieved through varieties of impersonation; other effects seem to re-quire appropriate psychological and emotional growth. Such growth is useless for poetry, though, unless it comes with a mastery of the tones and rhythms we associate with phases of development. The new voice may be a by-product for some people; for some poets the new voice is what they were greedy for, the thing that for a long time they had wanted.

I want to look now at Merrill's efforts to wake from the spell he was under and win access to the everyday voice, the domestic voice, and the human voice. To have access to an everyday voice is to be able to write convincingly about one's ownership of stretches of time during which one led an "everyday" existence. One can look back from some vantage point and be the historian of one's private past, or one can be a chroni-cler of the days as they pass, writing about how it feels to live every day within that stretch of time: what the off days are like (Merrill appoints Maria Mitsotáki as "muse / Of my off-days," which makes her "smile" and "shrug" [*CP*, 236]), what the on days are like, the days that deserve to be called Days of 1964 or 1935 or 1971 or 1941 and '44 (all titles of his poems). When did Merrill begin to be able to write about the everyday this way? Critics have been quick to seize on poems that seem to show some new mastery of the material of the everyday, either monitoring his emotional growth, congratulating him on each milestone, or believ-ing that the only way to write about the extremely playful poems is in an extremely playful critical voice. Ross Labrie writes that Merrill, by the time of *The Country of a Thousand Years of Peace*, is writing poems "about the quotidian details that make up much of his life. The poem 'Three Chores' is a good example, with its mundane subtitles, 'Water Boiling,' 'Night Laundry,' and 'Italian Lessons.' In these poetic sketches Merrill anchors himself in the concreteness of his daily routine and then lets his imagination transform his ostensibly homely subjects."[20] Labrie calls "Night Laundry" (part two of "Three Chores") an "especially successful example":

> Of daily soilure laving
> Fabric of all and sundry
> With no time for believing
> Love might work the wonder
>
> Who among clouded linen
> Has scattered bluing then
> Well over wrist in grieving
> Dismissed all but the doing
>
> May see to clotheslines later
> A week of swans depending
> From wooden beaks take flight
> Flapping at dawn from water's
>
> Jewel of the first water
> And every dismal matter's
> Absorption in its cleansing
> Bring the new day to light.
> (CP, 90–91)

The homely is only "ostensible," here, if that. The imagination swoops down *immediately* to transform. The concreteness of daily routine is exactly what the poet is trying to rescue himself from. Merrill's poem will be, for many readers, an example of not trusting the everyday. In fact, Merrill is never going to write a poem about laundry, though he comes close again in "The Mad Scene," which begins, "Again last night I dreamed the dream called Laundry." (CP, 206). Jorie Graham's poem "The Geese" begins, "Today as I hang out the wash I see them again," and for her too the household task (like the poem about the household task) is only an occasion. In that poem, Graham writes that "the world thickens with texture instead of history / texture instead of place." This is precisely what Merrill is tempted by: texture (of things, of words) as a distraction from and then a substitute for the everyday. It will not always be a substitute. Graham's poem ends by talking about "this astonishing delay, the everyday," and one feels, reading early Merrill, that the everyday is for him really a delay of "texture" and at the same time that "texture" is a delay of the everyday.[21] It is a matter of delay, not impediment; interestingly, it is also a matter of reciprocal delay. For some poets that would be a standoff; for Merrill it suggests that incompatibles are in some kind of relation, and this means that things are going well for him.

For some poets, writing about the everyday means celebrating it, showing off their mastery of, at least their familiarity with, it; for other poets, the everyday means a process of refamiliarizing. In "An Urban Convalescence," Merrill writes about how it feels to refamiliarize oneself with the world. When he lived in Rome as a young man, we are told in his memoir, he "had an apartment, spoke Italian and ate where the Romans themselves did." When friends of his parents visited Rome, they served him American food. This food ("glazed ham with pineapple, rice, sweet potatoes, frozen string beans, biscuits, homemade coleslaw, vanilla ice cream and coconut layer cake") had, he tells us, a "dreamlike familiarity" (*DP*, 82). (It is oddly like Ashbery's lunch in "Grand Galop.") In "An Urban Convalescence," he tells us he has been ill and has spent a week in bed. Going out for a walk,

> I find them tearing up a part of my block
> And chilled through, dazed and lonely, join the dozen
> In meek attitudes, watching a huge crane
> Fumble luxuriously in the filth of years.
>
> (*CP*, 127)

The world we know (or knew) may return to us unchanged, but more and more often it returns to us damaged. The world we are familiar with, Merrill suggests, is more and more often being torn up. The everyday world we call ours is a draft, but it is not we who make the revisions. The revisions take place in our absence, whether that absence is physical or the result of obliviousness. We have to catch up, but we do so in a "daze" and "in meek attitudes." Why are "they" tearing up a part of the block? It is, Merrill writes, as if "the simple fact of having lasted" is a provocation. "Well, that is what life does," he says. It is an everyday thing to live in a city and an everyday thing to tear down the buildings. The everyday is its own worst enemy, in a sense. Again, the everyday is mysterious to us, as if someone else were in charge of it, were running it, putting up and tearing down the buildings, putting out the newspapers. The poet discovers that he cannot remember what building stood there. "Was there a building at all?" Merrill asks and then adds, wonderingly, "I have lived on this same street for a decade."

Stanley Cavell, in *In Quest of the Ordinary*, writes, "The everyday is what we cannot but aspire to since it appears to us as lost to us."[22] Between failures of attention and failures of memory, we are inept curators, remiss guardians of the everyday. "Unwillingly I picture / My walls weathering in the general view." Will they tear down his building next? Can there be a domestic space free from the destructive revisionary energies of the everyday? Even if they spare his building, there is still, *within* houses, what he will call in *Sandover*, "the dim wish of lives to drift apart" (25). He ends the poem with lines about "the dull need to make some kind of house / Out of the life lived, out of the love spent." The word "dull" connects to the word "daze" earlier in the poem. It is difficult to be equal to the everyday. It can be a menacing phenomenon, defamiliarizing itself, presenting itself as lost to us, defying us to remember and recognize it.

These kinds of concerns haunt Merrill's desire to develop a domestic voice. To win access to the domestic voice means, for Merrill, not merely to fill up, to particularize, not merely to crowd but, as I suggested, to domesticate the "sheer space" of his early poems, poems that a critic had called "spaceless and timeless."[23] For Merrill, as for any poet, the domestic means both the life of childhood and adolescence and the life one chooses to live afterward. The family is always the first assignment. Merrill's parents divorced when he was thirteen; he came from a "broken home," a phrase that, because of his poem of that title, seems almost automatically associated with him. They make appearances, at first formally (as if they have been "invited"). In "Five Old Favorites" from *Water Street* we hear about "the mother," "the father," and "the child" gathered "many a cozy evening around the lamp." The poems about his father and mother become more and more confident. In "Scenes of Childhood" in *Water Street* and "The Broken Home" in the next book, *Nights and Days,* he writes memorable and powerful poems about his childhood. In his memoir, he writes about his father: "A half hour alone with him could be all uphill. *His* talk flowed, the pauses companionable, the delivery frank" (*DP,* 33). Merrill adds that he despaired of ever being able to tell his father anything about himself. If he never found it easy to talk to his father, he becomes more and more able to do the next best thing, which is to capture his father's way of talking, his flow, his pauses, his delivery, in his poems. He writes about the family romance with a certain pleasure, without the doom Lowell brings to it, and is able to make fun of the therapeutic value of writing about childhood. "An infantile / Memory promises to uncramp my style." He adds, "I stop in deepening light to jot it down" (*CP,* 178). The juxtaposition of the

words "deepening" and "jot" captures the sense that something is happening in his poetry, something is gathering force and deepening, but
he will be casual about it. Everything in his poems is in motion now: the
light is deepening, he himself is writing.

Merrill is tempted by but sees the danger of imagining the poem as
a house. The poem may be a house, but poems ought to be about
houses as well. Because he comes from a broken home, he never takes
homes for granted. David Kalstone writes, "The particular houses
Merrill writes about in later poems—however real, solidly located and
furnished—are also imagined as vulnerable houses of the spirit. They
are never mere settings. In the details he uses to conjure them up, there
are always reminders of the particular kinds of exposure and emergency against which these domestic arrangements have been con-
trived."[24] Like Lowell, though, Merrill will write poems of what Guy
Rotella calls "settled and unsettled domesticity"; such is his confidence
that he can in some poems take nothing and in other poems everything
for granted.[25] "I'm home, of course," he writes, and adds, "Where
would I be / If not here?" (*CP*, 184). In some ways, the climactic moment in his development of a domestic voice comes in the last line of "A
Tenancy," the last poem in *Water Street*. In the mid-1950s, Merrill and
David Jackson moved to a house on Water Street in Stonington, a sea-
side village in Connecticut. Merrill writes,

> If I am host at last
> It is of little more than my own past.
> May others be at home in it.
>   (*CP*, 170)

He is host of his past—the phrase suggests an increasing mastery of
both the domestic and the everyday.

The word "others" in the phrase "may others be at home in it"
sounds an odd note, of course. Other poets are happy to be at home; for
Merrill the question is, Whom will he be at home to? The question
brings us to the evolution of the "human" in Merrill. What people have
there been in his poems? What does the human mean so far? The
human must be present in his poetry so that the everyday and the domestic will be more than particularized versions of time and space.
There must be someone to whom these abstractions matter, someone to
suffer the everyday and domestic or flourish in it. What kind of people
are there in Merrill's early poetry? He gives us a character named

Charles, a sort of underemployed version of Stevens's Crispin. Charles is not a more ordinary or accessible, that is, "human," version of Merrill, just a more visible one: he allows Merrill to say, in the early "River Poem," "Charles was like that" rather than "I was like that." Charles is for Merrill what Ezra was to Ammons—once all the obvious differences are taken into account. Whatever poetic demands Charles was meant to satisfy do not get placated, though. A recurrent motif in Merrill's poetry is the human being who approaches the poet and, in a sense, the poem itself. Stevens has a short poem called "The Wind Shifts" that is about how the poet's creativity ("the wind") is connected to his sense of the human. The human is always approaching. The question, for Stevens, is how the human approaches the poet and how the kind of approach affects or is affected by the world of the poet's imagination. Because Stevens cannot know how his creative spirit is affected by the approach of the human, he cannot speak in terms of cause and effect. What he can say is that the motion of the human is *like* the motion of his poetry. "The wind shifts like this: / Like humans approaching proudly, / Like humans approaching angrily."[26] The question of how much any one poem needs to do in terms of accommodating or fending off the human is as mysterious for Merrill as it was for Stevens. What is true is that human figures often approach and demand from Merrill not "humane splendor" (the term is used ironically in "The Thousand and Second Night") but humanness.

In "Dream (Escape from the Sculpture Museum) and Waking" the poet tells us that "someone"

> Is stumbling this way. Neither young
>
> Nor old, man nor woman, so
> Propelled by cold, a human figure
> Barely begun, a beggar, no,
> Two by now, and ever nearer, bigger
> Cause me to stiffen in a show
> Of being human also
>
> (*CP*, 116)

If these are compound familiar ghosts, they pass without seeing the poet: he is not familiar to them. Merrill is, though, self-forgiving, optimistic. In an essay, he writes, "Neither Pound nor Eliot promised very much by way of *people* in their poems. You had on the one hand figures like poor Fräulein von Kulp, frozen forever in a single, telling gesture, and on the other, oh, John Adams wound like a mummy in a thousand ticker tape statistics." To be frozen forever in a single telling gesture is a terrible fate in (and for) Merrill's imagination. The gesture may be "telling," but it can tell only the same thing over and over, with nobody to tell it to. The problem with Adams and von Kulp is that they are alone. "To use people as Frost did," Merrill continues, "was something else again. A young poet could easily have been cowed by the sheer human experience needed in order to render 'real life' with even minimal authority. Thanks to the example of Stevens, this pressure could be postponed until the time came." The notion that pressure can be "postponed" is extraordinarily liberating. (One thinks of Ammons, who seems to postpone indefinitely the pressure to include people in his poems.) What Stevens offers Merrill is a certain kind of permission. (There is an appealing perversity about Merrill's using Stevens as a model for how to put people in his poetry, since many critics have felt that for Stevens too the time to include people never came.) Merrill says of Stevens, "His people were unlike any others. Airily emblematic, yet blessed with idiosyncrasy, they fitted snugly into their poems, like figures in Vuillard. Ideas entered and left their minds easily, words came to their lips, giving point to a passage without overwhelming it or reducing it to mere vignette. They served their poet and departed undetained by him. I kept on trying my hand."[27] Other poets might stagger toward the human; Merrill lets the humans, as we saw above, stagger toward him. He will patiently wait for them.

His patience comes in part because he has so many resources. The human can always be displaced. Merrill said in an interview, "I always find when I don't like a poem I'm writing, I don't look any more into the human components. I look more to the *setting*—a room, the objects in it."[28] There are many places to locate the human—or, as Merrill puts it, "the human components"—besides in people. Rooms can be human. In "The Broken Home," he writes, "The green-gold room throbbed like a bruise" (*CP*, 198). Houses can serve for people, suffer like people, endure like people. In "The House," he writes that the house "whose west walls take the sunset like a blow / Will have turned the other cheek by morning, though / The long night falls between" (*CP*, 50), and in "From the Cupola," he writes, "Our orchid stucco house looked on greenshuttered // stoic" (*CP*, 210). Meanwhile, actual people keep approaching, proudly, angrily, mysteriously—sometimes even amiably. In "The Thousand and Second Night," Merrill meets a Greek who

> with time to kill
> Asked me the price of cars in Paradise.
>
> By which he meant my country, for in his
> The stranger is a god in masquerade.
> Failing to act that part, I am afraid
> I was not human either—ah, who is?
>
> (*CP*, 179)

The notion that the divine and the human are both parts to perform will come back in the trilogy. Meanwhile, Merrill confesses that he can't play the human and adds that nobody can. As if to preempt his critics, he calls himself a "vain / Flippant unfeeling monster" (*CP*, 180).

Poets who resist including people in their poetry generally do not (for obvious reasons) write about relationships. Merrill, once again, is the exception. All drama, all comedy for Merrill are in relationship. He likes to say, "I was not human," to *people*. When people outside of familial or romantic relationships appear in his poems, they sometimes seem stranded and do not receive vivid delineation. To get into a Merrill poem it helped to be a family member, a lover, or a contributor to local color. Merrill, in his memoir, writes, slyly, about his "shyness amounting almost to indifference when faced with the treasure of someone else's life" (*DP*, 84). Unsympathetic readers might recognize the fabled incuriosity of the narcissist, but Merrill, as a poet, is infinitely patient. Present in the tone and rhetorical gestures of many of his poems is the sense that for him there is no telling what he will do in the future.

How does Merrill write about relationships? The early poems had often resolved themselves by making gestures toward love. In his memoir, he writes that he "had but to think 'love' and every problem dissolved, light filled him, he knew why he'd been born." Then he adds, "A variety of religious experience? I hadn't yet come across Borges's definition of the lover as founder of a religion with a fallible god, but I was nothing if not devout" (*DP*, 46). He did discover Borges's definition, though, and became in his poetry a devout follower of the religion with the fallible god. What kind of love poems does Merrill write? Judith Moffett describes how love works in the poems of *The Country of a Thousand Years of Peace*, *Water Street*, and *Nights and Days*. "Love matters more than anything else; people are fundamentally unlovable; therefore since I want and need to love you I must contrive not to know you any better than I have to; for what I love is an appearance; a mask you wear or one I project upon you; and we must each do all we can not to

see through each other's masks; kindness, as much as self-interest, requires lover and beloved to guard one another vigilantly from difficult
truths about themselves as long as possible."[29] The poems begin to be
resolved, not surprisingly, less often by allusions to love than to survival. In "Poem of Summer's End," Merrill writes, "For a decade love has
rained down / On our two hearts, instructing them / In a strange bare-
ness, that of weathered stone" (*CP*, 133). In a later poem, he will say that
"nothing either lasts or ends" (*CP*, 313). Younger, enjoying an innocent
view of love, he "knew why he'd been born." But it's clear that he'd
been born for this more "sophisticated" view of love as well. Love neither lasts nor ends: there is material for poems in both of these facts.
Sometimes life will have to be prompted, though. In "Matinées," a
poem about his love for opera, he writes that one would "arrange for
one's / Own chills and fevers, passions and betrayals / Chiefly in order
to make song of them" (*CP*, 269).

If his sentimental education is, in a sense, finished, he has more to
learn about people he is not related to or in love with. People do appear.
Oddly, Merrill cannot always make them last. In "A Vision of the Garden," he writes,

> One winter morning as a child
> Upon the windowpane's thin frost I drew
> Forehead and eyes and mouth the clear and mild
> Features of nobody I knew
>
> (*CP*, 131)

He breathes on the pane, and the face is gone. He keeps drawing people
he doesn't know, as if it were a kind of creative exercise. "The Doodler"
(a poem about telephone pad doodling) is also about the desire to imagine human beings (not lovers, necessarily, and not family) in his
poetry. "This morning's little boy stands (I have learned / To do feet)
gazing down a flight of stairs." Even here, though, a relationship must
be present, making this exercise possible. Is he able to draw these faces
because he is on the phone with someone?

> And when A. calls to tell me he enjoyed
> The evening, I begin again. Again
> Emerge, O sunbursts, garlands, creatures, men,
> Ever more lifelike out of the white void!
>
> (*CP*, 99)

Sunbursts, garlands, creatures, men. But all sequences in Merrill are
reversible—and this keeps critics and Merrill himself from becoming
sentimental about the kind of process I have been describing. The trilogy itself, in a way, reverses this sequence.

Merrill is in the process of developing an "ever more lifelike" sense of the everyday, the domestic, and the human when he decides, in a sense, to test them against other kinds of voices. He could have written about these areas of everyday experience and made a career of doing so, using wit and an irony adapted to each decade's taste to "make it new." Merrill, instead, decides to let the everyday play with what is most threatening to it. (The prophetic takes, for Merrill, the particular form of the supernatural, though I will sometimes refer to "the transcendent" when I want to indicate its resemblance to the prophetic voices in the other chapters.)

Why the supernatural? To use it in a poem is almost to guarantee a feeling of marginality, though not a kind of marginality that will be immediately interesting to most contemporary readers. It seems a mode of uninteresting eccentricity. Merrill himself said in an interview, "Usually the people who write about it have such dreadful style."[30] It isn't useful as a foil to the "small" everyday life because its grandness seems so spurious. It is not "really" grand. The supernatural makes a private life seem as if it has used up its own resources, and it makes a public life (as it did during the Reagan administration) seem lurid, empty. In the interview mentioned above, Merrill went on to say, "The first thing to do is to get rid of that awful vocabulary. It's almost acceptable once it's purged of all those fancy words—'auras' and 'astral bodies.'" Such anxieties seem to belong more to Merrill's readers than to Merrill himself, but that does not make him any the less interested in them.

The modernist period is, for many critics and for Merrill himself, the last great period of the supernatural. Helen Sword writes, "Modernist poets . . . even when they have been tempted by the vatic promise of automatic writing, have frequently been haunted by persistent associations of spiritualist phenomena with faddishness, charlatanism, public naiveté and fraud, widespread impressions heightened by such late-nineteenth and early twentieth-century satires as Robert Browning's *Mr. Sludge, The Medium,* Henry James' *The Bostonians,* and T. S. Eliot's scathing portrayal of Madame Sosostris in *The Waste Land.*"[31] In the trilogy, JM complains to Auden,

> Dear Wystan, VERY BEAUTIFUL all this
> Warmed-up Milton, Dante, Genesis?
> This great tradition that has come to grief
> In volumes by Blavatsky and Gurdjieff.
> (*CLS,* 136)

But it had not come to grief in Yeats, and Yeats is never far from Merrill's mind.[32] The language of the supernatural as "raw material" is (what Yeats called his own vocabulary) "arbitrary, harsh, difficult," but

Yeats had success with it.[33] Still, as Sword points out, "Yeats seldom if ever invoked his spiritualist experience directly in his poetry, nor, indeed, did such modernist contemporaries as H.D. and Rilke."[34] What Merrill will do is what Yeats never did: he will incorporate that language and at the same time make it far more complicated. ("POOR OLD YEATS / STILL SIMPLIFYING," says one of the spirit voices in Merrill's trilogy.) Yeats, according to Richard Ellmann, "remains ambiguous about his symbology" and "lodges it in prose."[35] Merrill lodges it in the poetry. What can it do there? William Dean Howells said of Whitman's work that it was "not poetry, but the materials of poetry."[36] The spirit voices in Merrill's trilogy, though, do not provide even the materials of poetry; instead, they offer centaurs from Atlantis, radioactive bats that are also subatomic particles, UFOs, the Bermuda triangle, a unicorn named Uni. What is more, Merrill enjoys our consternation and shares it. He asks,

> What at this late date
> Can be done with the quaint idiom that slips
> From nowhere to my tongue—or from the parchment
> Of some old scribe of the apocalypse—
>
>   (*CLS*, 274)

And in a prose passage in the poem "From the Cupola," he puts us in the role of one of Psyche's sisters: "'Oh, Psyche,' her sister burst out at length. 'Here you are, surrounded by loving kin, in a house crammed with lovely old things, and what do you crave but the unfamiliar, the "transcendental"?'" (*CP*, 214–15).

In a sense, Merrill couldn't wait to bring on the supernatural. The Ouija board represents, as I said at the outset, an outrageous use of his gifts—but not a misunderstanding of them. Like Lowell, like Ammons, Merrill uses his freedom not simply to explore new avenues of expression but also to celebrate freedom itself. He and DJ moved to Stonington and the second summer they lived there contacted Ephraim on the Ouija board. Before Ephraim arrived, though, they received what Helen Sword calls "a series of rather undistinguished doomsayers" ("James Merrill," 557). We meet them in *The Country of a Thousand Years of Peace* in a poem called "Voices from the Other World." This poem represents Merrill's first attempt to bring the everyday and the supernatural together as voices:

> Presently at our touch the teacup stirred,
> Then circled lazily about
> From A to Z. The first voice heard

(If they are voices, these mute spellers-out)
Was that of an engineer

Originally from Cologne.
Dead in his 22nd year
Of cholera in Cairo, he had KNOWN
NO HAPPINESS. He once met Goethe, though.
Goethe had told him: PERSEVERE.

Our blind hound whined. With that, a horde
Of voices gathered above the Ouija board,
Some childish and, you might say, blurred
By sleep; one little boy
Named Will, reluctant possibly in a ruff

Like a large-lidded page out of El Greco, pulled
Back the arras for that next voice,
Cold and portentous: ALL IS LOST.
FLEE THIS HOUSE. OTTO VON THURN UND TAXIS.
OBEY. YOU HAVE NO CHOICE.

Frightened, we stopped; but tossed
Till sunrise striped the rumpled sheets with gold.
Each night since then, the moon waxes,
Small insects flit round a cold torch
We light, that sends them pattering to the porch . . .

But no real Sign. New voices come,
Dictate addresses, begging us to write;
Some warn of lives misspent, and all of doom
In ways that so exhilarate
We are sleeping sound of late.

Last night the teacup shattered in a rage.
Indeed, we have grown nonchalant
Towards the other world. In the gloom here
Our elbows on the cleared
Table, we talk and smoke, pleased to be stirred

Rather by buzzings in the jasmine, by the drone
Of our own voices and poor blind Rover's wheeze,
Than by those clamoring overhead,
Obsessed or piteous, for a commitment
We still have wit to postpone

Because, once looked at lit
By the cold reflections of the dead
Risen extinct but irresistible,
Our lives have never seemed more full, more real,
Nor the full moon more quick to chill.

(*CP,* 112–13)

The poem begins with the word "presently" as if it were already section P of the poem that waited years in the future. The word also hits a note of pleasant formality, exactly pitched between casual anticipation and attentiveness. Merrill tends to use it just before he is going to say something momentous, as if to absorb the impact. In "Medusa," he wrote, "And presently the word Oblivion / Turns us to one another, as to stone." And he will write in "An Urban Convalescence," "And presently / The massive volume of the world / Closes again." "Presently at our touch the teacup stirred": he does not say "my touch." The Ouija board is usually used by two people and perhaps especially by couples. (Sylvia Plath wrote "Dialogue over a Ouija Board" in 1957, a poem based on the results of the experiments she and Ted Hughes made with the board.)[37] The word "touch" suggests an intimacy between two lovers but an intimacy that has been both put on hold and heightened. (The poem will suggest that their experience with the Ouija board is, among other things, sexually exciting.) The teacup "circled lazily about / From A to Z." One may circle in various ways. In "Medusa," the birds "circled / Delightfully where the white water sparkled." There is a suggestion in the word "circled" both that one is tentatively approaching a space and that that space will be circumscribed. In "From a Notebook," we read of "circles ever / Smaller, smaller." A sense of the predatory is also audible in the word "circling." If this were not a game, there would be even more menace perhaps. One turns to a game such as the Ouija board in part out of boredom in the hope that the game will somehow take one's boredom and transform it. Robert Lowell captures this moment in his translation of a poem by Montale: "Even your ennui is a whirlwind / circling invisibly / the let-ups non-existent."[38] Merrill, sitting down at the Ouija board, is pitched between ennui and excitement; he wants the circling to be signs of a whirlwind and not of his own boredom.

He will do everything he can to invite new energy into his poem. The care is there in the title: some poets might be drawn to writing about "the Other," but Merrill instinctively adds the word "Voices" and the word "World" to the phrase. He wants otherness always to have its greatest possible existence and force, just as the teacup must move from A to Z. The powers too are testing their own range, quietly, sometimes sleepily. The first voice is an engineer, and then there is a space before the next stanza. The space between the stanzas of this poem are full of waiting, expectation, second thoughts as the poem enacts the return of the voices from the other world. One might have scruples, one's boredom might return, but the voices will also return if one wants them.

The engineer is "originally from Cologne. / Dead in his 22nd year." The poet begins to incorporate the peculiarities of style of his "mute spellers-out." His writing "22nd" is a form of politeness; he wants to be receptive to the way the spirit spells on the board. In the next line, we find the first uppercase letters: the engineer had "KNOWN / NO HAPPINESS." This is followed by the sad, witty lines, "He once met Goethe, though. / Goethe had told him: PERSEVERE." A world is opening up— not a strange and terrifying sci-fi world but the world of old Europe. (Goethe will be in the audience when Merrill reads his trilogy to the assembled spirits at the end of *Sandover*.) Is the engineer going to be a figure of pathos, dead before his time like Merrill's friend Hans Lodeizen (who will appear in the trilogy)? One feels expectant: what kind of emotions will this engineer elicit in us? He was told to persevere, and he is persevering by speaking from beyond the grave. There is more. Merrill makes us think (makes us feel he is thinking) about the difference between saying "known no happiness" and "KNOWN NO HAPPINESS." The capital letters suggest either that the engineer's feelings will be granted a sort of arialike grandeur or else that his thoughts will be allowed to find, in the Ouija alphabet, a kind of literal version of the importance the engineer had associated with Goethe. At the same time, the capital letters seem a little embarrassing, standing out in and interrupting the gracefulness and ease of Merrill's poem. The spirits may be delicate in their actions, may make the teacup stir, may make it circle lazily, but when they talk they have no choice but to seem gigantic. What they say, that is, will have to look like the "central gigantic utterance" Grossman referred to and Goethe seemed almost to promise the engineer might come to in his life. I bring up these questions to show how nuanced Merrill is, from the start, in his sense of the supernatural and how immediately interesting such a poem can be both for him and for us.

The notion that there is something crude about the "voices from the other world" is brought up again in the next line. But first, Merrill tells us, "Our blind hound whined"; someone is responding to the weird *intrusion* of these voices, even if the two men are not. Other poets might have been astonished to suspect that there might actually be life after death, but Merrill, it seems, is absorbed by all that is unsaid, not yet said. Merrill writes, "With that, a horde / Of voices gathered above the Ouija board." Why "with that"? The dog, complaining about the voices, seems actually to have encouraged them. The two worlds (not to speak of the canine and the human) are extraordinarily focused on each other. An event in one kind of speech is an event in another.

Nothing (no nuance, anyway) is not registered, not responded to. "Our blind hound whined. With that, a horde / Of voices gathered above the Ouija board." It is only a matter of a teacup moving around a Ouija board, but Merrill, as the host, imagines a place for the spirits "above the Ouija board." The spirits are like party crashers, but the situation is still not menacing: a reader thinks of Jean Stafford's story "An Influx of Poets" rather than of anything scarier. Merrill continues to be the perfect host, showing what Whitman, in "Me Imperturbe," writes of: "aplomb in the midst of irrational things."[39]

Merrill wonders, What are these voices like? How will a new voice be different from the last? Some of them will be "childish and, you might say, blurred / By sleep." The variety is exciting. He begins to visualize them, telling us of "one little boy / Named Will, reluctant possibly in a ruff," who is like a "large-lidded page out of El Greco." Merrill is interested in imagining the relation between the voices, a relation that does not belong to history. What does Goethe have to do with El Greco? There are more voices as Will pulls back the arras: there is a program here, an order of performances, with each performer grander than the last one.

In his memoir, writing about his love of opera, Merrill writes of "the sense [which lasted] all evening, of sheltered communion and psychodrama" (*DP*, 39). This is the appetite Merrill brings, at least at first, to the Ouija board. The next voice is "cold and portentous." The two men are delighted. The voice says "ALL IS LOST. / FLEE THIS HOUSE." Part of the wicked pleasure of this game is the sense that the brief, fleeting narratives may mirror a longer one: the words are like those a panicky lover might say in "household opera" tones to himself at the end of a relationship. That narrative can wait, though; this opera within an opera is too absorbing. Whatever lies behind the sense of emergency expressed by the spirit voice is "no disaster" (to use Bishop's lines) for the two men. In fact, it is just such exciting melodramatic imperatives ("FLEE THIS HOUSE") that make them feel *more* at home. "OBEY. YOU HAVE NO CHOICE." This sounds like psychodrama. Meanwhile, there arises a name from a European aristocratic family, one associated with Rilke. One might hope for a leisurely summer of 1914 atmosphere; instead, the partners are being told to flee and to obey—but this is just as good. The supernatural speaker's lines have the particular pathos of speech that is not quite a speech act; cold and portentous, the voice cannot quite manage to give a context for itself, but, nevertheless, it sounds persuasive as a voice. The voice is real, that is, but only on the level of voice—it is pure voice, in a sense. It is not simply a supernatural voice but almost a prophetic one. "Frightened, we stopped."

They keep going, of course. And "new voices come." Gradually fright and excitement turn to casualness. The partners had sleepless (and possibly amorous) nights at the beginning, but now they are sleeping soundly, although this angers the spirits. Throughout the poem, the two men experience various emotions in response to the other world, and these emotions are mirrored in the other world: reluctance, exhilaration, even the sense of being blurred by sleep. The last stanza of "Voices from the Other World" rings a little false because the poet doesn't know quite what to say about what has happened. What remains most memorable about the poem is the things voices do. They don't start until the third stanza, because this is a poem, in part, about getting under way; once they start, they do not stop. Voices whine, they are cold and portentous, they dictate, they beg, they warn, they exhilarate, they talk, they drone, they wheeze, they clamor. These sounds could be associated with the poets, the spirits, in some cases, the dog. This poem is about voices gathering into a horde, interacting with each other, trying the full range of what they can do. There is even a sense of exchangeability. Both the two men and the spirit voices use portentous language. Both are concerned with knowing (or not knowing) happiness. The teacup is stirred at the start of the poem; they are stirred at the end. The engineer wants to meet great figures, and so do the poets. The spirit voices drone, and the human voices drone.

Merrill puts all this in the poem but does not quite know yet what to think about it, how to proceed with it. "Chill," the last word in the poem, is one of Merrill's most frequently used words: it is there in the poem about convalescence, where he is "chilled through"; it is there in the "mild variation, chilling theme" of his parents downstairs in "The World and the Child"; there are his father's chilled wives in "The Broken Home." He uses the word to talk about the way the world feels when his imagination is not yet ready to go to work on it. The presence of the word in the final stanza of "Voices from the Other World" suggests that Merrill is not yet ready to write his long poem, though he is making transcripts and drafts. Merrill writes that the spirits want "a commitment / We still have wit to postpone." This poem is only ostensibly about the two men finding their own domestic life more real than the domestic life of the spirits. It is about the poet not being ready to orchestrate the voices but wanting to write something he can, in a sense, come back to. Gradually, Merrill does become ready, taking the wit that has been omnipresent in his poetry and giving it ambitions, giving it real work to do.

In my introduction I discussed a fourth term, the ordinary. Ordinariness is never going to be part of Merrill's arsenal as a poet, and some commentators have seized on this as a reason to criticize his poetry. It is true that the ordinary for Merrill will always be subverted by wit. This may make wit seem like a disability—and it is that for some readers of Merrill. Some readers may want a sense of the everyday, the domestic, the human without so much wit, perhaps because they wish to be reverent about it. Yeats said that personality, "no matter how habitual, is a constantly renewed choice."[40] Merrill's own sense of wit is that it is habitual—he is willing to be humorous about the habit, as if to meet some readers halfway, and often calls his punning a bad habit. An unsympathetic reader will respond to Merrill's wit, though, as a constantly renewed choice, and this can make Merrill seem maddening. "The proper word for Merrill's tone is arch," von Hallberg writes. "Archness is the ground note; he cannot silence it, though he can acknowledge and regret, from time to time, its impoliteness or, worse, insensitivity."[41] Von Hallberg wants first of all to assert that there *is* a ground note in Merrill, then wants to imply that Merrill is not in control of it, and then wants to imply both that Merrill is too greatly concerned with manners and that he doesn't have any.

Why such resistance to wit? Wit seems to expose the everyday, open it up to its own language, to other languages. Wit exposes any project that depends on the everyday's being taken with unrelenting earnestness. Sympathetic readers of Merrill will not be able to imagine his (sometimes even their own) version of the everyday, the domestic, the human without the constant accompaniment of the sound of his wit.

I see wit as Merrill's hybrid speech genre, the way in which he is able to be everyday and supernatural at once. Wit is a discourse that allows the supernatural and the everyday to speak to each other and to the reader. The poet (in reference to the poetry of Montale) writes, "Any word can lead you from the kitchen garden into really inhuman depths."[42] (Note the effect of the breezy word "really" on the phrase "inhuman depths.") And there is always the implication that the same word can lead you from really inhuman depths back into the kitchen garden. Wit does a tremendous amount of work in the trilogy. It puts and keeps things in relation. When JM asks Ephraim, "Must everything be witty?" the poem's implication is yes, and therefore everything must be in a kind of relation to everything else. It is as if one were to ask,

Must everything be interconnected? The walls of the dining room at Stonington are witty because they change—now watermelon, now sunburn—and are witty also for being the cause of wit in others. But wit does more for Merrill. Asked in an interview, "Can the joke control that sort of oracular voice of Eliot and Pound, tone it down, make it more human?" Merrill replied, "That is my fond illusion."[43] And wit can make, as I have suggested, the human voice less human, at least less sincere, less unvaryingly earnest. In *The Book of Ephraim*, Merrill will quote Auden's lines:

> The glacier knocks in the cupboard,
> The desert sighs in the bed,
> And the crack in the tea-cup opens
> A lane to the land of the dead.
> (*CLS*, 58)

It is the homiest, what Auden would call the "comfiest," spaces that Merrill focuses on. Wit keeps those places open so that they never become claustrophobic, shut off, homey versions of the spaces of *First Poems*.

Wit can have a strobe-light effect on everyday and domestic space, but, at the same time, it can seem like a defense against any language of transcendence. Wit is supposed to be an impediment to the higher reaches of poetry: Johnson thought it kept the metaphysicals from being sublime. Wit in Blake and in Milton is usually either savage irony or pedantry momentarily conscious of itself. It is not a source of surprise or much pleasure. Wit in Emerson is more aphoristic than witty. Whitman, at first, was uneasy about it. In a note to himself, he wrote,

> Make no puns
> funny remarks
> Double entendres
> 'witty' remarks
> ironies
> Sarcasms.
> Only that which
> is simply earnest,
> meant,—harmless
> to any one's feelings
> —unadorned
> unvarnished
> nothing to
> excite a
> laugh[44]

Transcendental experiences are often communicated in a discontinuous language that nevertheless suggests a world of continuity and
wholeness beyond it. Wit, on the other hand, has no reference beyond
its own discontinuities, nor is it invested in the connections it does
make. The language of transcendence is also interested in correspondences, but its correspondences are supposed to be more permanent
and to have more lasting effect than the correspondences wit distracts
us with. Silent about what it cannot talk about, wit can seem like a language in which it is impossible to talk about anything. And yet wit is, in
Sandover, the language in which one talks about everything. Wit is
Merrill's hybrid speech genre, his act of generosity toward all the parts
of his imagination, his dream of a common language. Although wit is
part of his work from the start, it is his intuition about how *much* wit
can do for him that will make *Sandover* possible.

Merrill not only finds an ambitious use for wit, but finds a use for the
poetic voice as well. *Sandover* contains a great variety of verse forms:
there are *Rubáiyát* quatrains, sonnets, Spenserian stanzas, sestinas, villa-
nelle, terza rima, a canzone. There are many speaking parts in the trilogy, and each part is given its own meter: iambic pentameter for human
characters (living and dead), syllabic fourteeners for the bats. The unicorn speaks in Anglo-Saxon alliterative meter. God, Nature, and the angels are not given any metrical pattern. "The humans," as Judith Moffett writes, "often fall into couplets or stanzas as if for comfort."[45]
Merrill says at one point that he wants to write

> language
> Of such a depth, shimmer and force that, granted
> I could sustain it, it would be above
> Everybody's—even the thinker's—head.
>   (*CLS,* 118)

What relation does this desire have to the encounters between the
human and the supernatural? These poems exhibit the central skills
that humans demonstrate in this poem—not the capacity for feeling but
the capacity for putting feeling into form. It is the one skill that, for example, the archangel Michael wishes he had himself. (Mirabell is con-
gratulated on having "a way with words.") The verse forms show that
JM follows rules as arbitrary and difficult as any the spirits come up
with. But his are not harsh, his give pleasure. Earlier I quoted his remark that his earlier poems "remained verbal artifacts, metered and
rhymed to be sure, shaped and polished and begemmed, but set on the
page with never a thought of their being uttered by a living voice."

Now these shapes, these artifacts are given something to do, something both to represent and to test themselves against. A reader can imagine a living voice speaking them now and have a better sense of what they have to do with life.

Third, Merrill in *Sandover* gives the everyday, domestic, human elements of his poetry something to do. In "Voices from the Other World," he and David Jackson never say anything (in the poem) to the spirits, and they do not say very much to each other. Vendler writes,

> By taking conversation—from lovers' exchange of vows to friends' sentences in intimacy—as the highest form of human expression (in contrast to the rhapsode's hymns, the orator's harangues, or the initiate's hermetic colloquies with the divine) Merrill becomes susceptible to charges of frivolity, at least from readers with a taste only for the solemn. But this espousal of the conversational as the ultimate in linguistic achievement is a moral choice, one which locates value in the human and everyday rather than in the transcendent.[46]

Again, some readers might agree that the espousal of the conversational is moral, but why such relentlessly witty conversation? Why not serious conversation, that of two people being earnestly discursive with each other? Adrienne Rich's hour of talk on a rock or even Bishop's human "hour badly spent" in "One Art"? Lightness ought to belong, according to such readers, only to the human once it is transformed. Such a notion wants to limit the human, though, and to simplify it. Only the usual things can happen to the human, so conceived. Where is the interest for a poet like Merrill? In any event, he wants also to represent conversations between people and spirit voices (and archangels and peacocks et al.). If one has to talk with these sorts of entities, some readers might counter, why not with H.D.'s or Rilke's high seriousness?

I want to return to Vendler's remark about Merrill locating value in the human and everyday rather than in the transcendent. David Lehman, responding to Vendler's observation, writes, "I would argue that Merrill does not choose the human at the expense of the transcendent experience but that he deliberately situates the latter within everyday contexts."[47] It seems to me that Merrill is not deeply interested in choosing either, except as the making of one choice or other might have a particular dramatic value. Certainly, Merrill is, throughout the trilogy, interested in what JM and DJ have to do to keep value located in the human and the everyday and the domestic. When the spirit voices (violating the rules of good conversation) engage in *undramatic* monologues, JM and DJ will, afterward, talk to each other or to W. H. Auden or Maria Mitsotáki. (Merrill's nonchalance is generally played not as in, say, Beckett, against no meaning, but against the threat of too much meaning.) JM and DJ make the moral choice of conversation whenever they can, but they can't always: for much of the second and third volumes of the trilogy, they are trying to make the best of long and extremely monologic monologues. If the spirit voices can babble on about matters that sometimes seem of interest only to them, so can the heroes. JM visits DJ in the hospital and later writes, "I press D's hand. He babbles on. All's well" (*CLS*, 204). Thomas Gardner writes that "on its most direct level, the trilogy asks to be read as a demonstration of the way its two mediums, JM and DJ, receive and render in human terms invisible, otherworldly forces."[48] But they don't receive these forces in entirely human terms, and they can't render them in those terms. Michel de Certeau refers to the conviction that all languages are translatable into "natural everyday language."[49] Merrill's trilogy is about how everyday language must sometimes be put into relation with what *cannot* be translated into everyday language. He puts everyday ways of speaking in constant proximity to this monotony, but this is done for musical as much as for moral effect. The atmosphere of the poem is one of continual surprises: everybody in the poem has the capacity to surprise and be surprised. The everyday is privileged whenever (as in "Voices from the Other World") it would be surprising to privilege it, and the other world is privileged whenever we would expect it not to be. There are musical and shock values in this poem. Merrill locates the ethical in whatever can keep the poem— the conversation—going. (I will have more to say about this question at the end of the chapter.)

In *Sandover*, Merrill also finds an extended use (outside his novels) for his preoccupation with lovers. The fact that there is a relationship at the center of *Sandover* is remarkable, since Merrill could have staged the poem as one in which a prophetic "I" confronts a host of spirits. He could have written a *Book of a Thousand and One Evenings Spent Alone at the Ouija Board*, but instead he wrote of evenings spent "with DJ and our familiar spirit." There is, course, no real "I" in the poem: Merrill mediates everything through a persona called JM, but it is crucial that the experience is shared with DJ. What other long prophetic poem features prophecy delivered to a couple? Yeats collaborated with his wife on *A Vision*, but, as he writes, "My wife [was] bored and fatigued by her almost daily task," and she does not appear in his occult visions in poems.⁵⁰ Nor are there many short lyric poems that feature an experience shared by a couple. A common gesture in the romantic lyric is to turn to the companion, but the mutuality is often either speculative (Wordsworth's "If thou appear untouched by solemn thought, / Thy nature is not therefore less divine") or deferred (Coleridge's "so shalt thou see and hear / The lovely shapes and sounds intelligible / Of that eternal language"). The companions in Merrill's trilogy experience the "eternal language" at the same time. Much of the trilogy must be read as a refusal of certain postures: there is, in this poem, no "solitary figure on the verge of nonentity" as there is in Blake's prophetic poems. Ammons's early prophet figure is, in poems such as "So I Said I Am Ezra" and "Pieces of My Voice" and "Guide," always alone. Allen Grossman creates a persona for whom companionship simply exacerbates the sense of disorientation. Although he is disoriented, he keeps his authority, while Merrill is always working to diminish JM's prophetic authority.

He is quite resourceful at this. Northrop Frye tells us that what Dante says about his own work "has a peculiar interest, but not a peculiar authority."⁵¹ That may be why Merrill has JM and DJ keep up a running commentary: he wants the peculiar interest, not the peculiar authority. (Although, of course, commentary *can* have a peculiar authority, especially if continued over hundreds of pages.) That is another reason why there needs to be, in Merrill's trilogy, *two* people delivering the commentary—more than two, in fact, if dead friends are counted. Wallace Stevens, imagining a world in which imagination has replaced faith, wrote, "How much stature, even vatic stature, this conception gives the poet!"⁵² Merrill doesn't give JM and DJ vatic stature, and he doesn't pretend to have it himself. Stevens's intriguing afterthought ("He need not exercise this dignity in vatic works") might be amended to say that the poet need not exercise this dignity in *unremittingly* prophetic work. He need not identify his voice with the prophetic (or the supernatural); he only has to put himself into relationship with it.

One can feel the creative growth between "Voices from the Other World" and *The Book of Ephraim*, written twenty years later. There is, to use a phrase from the poem, "a new and urgent power":

> The cup twitched in its sleep. "Is someone there?"
> We whispered, fingers light on Willowware,
> When the thing moved. Our breathing stopped. The cup,
> Glazed zombie of itself, was on the prowl
> Moving but dully, incoherently,

Possessed, as we should soon enough be told,
By one or another of the myriads
Who hardly understand, through the compulsive
Reliving of their death, that they have died
—By fire in this case, when a warehouse burned.
HELLP O SAV ME scrawled the cup
As on the very wall flame rippled up,
Hypnotic wave on wave, a lullaby
Of awfulness. I slumped. D: One more try.
Was anybody there? As when a pike
Strikes, and the line singing writes in lakeflesh
Highstrung runes, and reel spins and mind reels
YES a new and urgent power YES
Seized the cup.

                                                         (*CLS*, 6)

I said that the trilogy was continually surprising. The first surprise,
probably, is that the spirit voices are actually interested in the daily life
the two men share. This is not something we encounter in Yeats's *A Vision*. The Instructors "seemed ignorant of our surroundings," Yeats tells
us (10). JM and DJ, in contrast, are told—as the spirits converse about
the installation of a large mirror for their convenience—that they share
with others

A DAILY LIFE WHOSE DEMANDS
LIKE USEFUL PIECES OF furniture fill the living room
& OUR GREAT ORNAMENTAL & BIZARRE OBJECT HARDLY
ABLE TO BE GOT THRU THE DOOR IS IF NOT LAUGHABLE
AT THE LEAST ODD TO HOUSE   YET U HOUSE US FOR ALL THAT WE
DO LITTLE BUT TAKE UP YR ROOM   THIS IS DO U NOT GRANT
RECKLESS? BUT BELIEVE ME MORE RECKLESS OF US TO MOVE IN,
FOR HOUSES OF THE LIVING CHANGE WITH A SPEED WE DO NOT
KNOW

                                                         (*CLS*, 257)

There are precedents for this sort of voice, but not for the voice talking in this informal way. We hear a voice that could not itself be much
stranger commenting on the strangeness of its relationship to the everyday. This theme of the spirits "taking up room," of using the human, is
everywhere in the trilogy. Sometimes this "taking up room" will be a
kind of usurpation, but even usurpation is, in a sense, deftly put into relation with the idea of a more balanced relationship. DJ is hypnotized,
and, in this scene, the voice of Ephraim comes from DJ. Now there is
usurpation, not relation. Merrill is, in this trilogy, less interested in the

idea of possession, in the spirit usurping or taking over the poet or the poem than in the tension—sometimes the struggle—between the human and the supernatural voices in the poem. In the passage quoted at length, the emphasis is on the word "HOUSE." The spirits are not terrifying to internalize or incorporate but rather "ODD TO HOUSE."

Section L of *The Book of Ephraim* contains much that is, for our purposes, surprising about the entire trilogy. "Voices from the Other World" was a kind of test run for this section in particular, and one can feel, comparing the two texts, how much more confident and at the same time adventurous Merrill is now in his sense of the everyday, the domestic, and the human. The first volume of the trilogy covers the period from 1955 to 1974; section L is a meditation on the passage of time, in particular, the kind of everyday time I wrote about earlier in the chapter. The poet is older now, and the stretches of time on which he can meditate are longer. Section L begins with a memory of the midfifties, the period when DJ and JM had first begun to consult the Ouija board. They have just come back from a trip around Asia and are settling back into their house in Stonington.

> Life like the periodical not yet
> Defunct kept hitting the stands. We seldom failed
> To leaf through each new issue—war, election,
> Starlet; write, scratch out; eat steak au poivre,
> Chat with Ephraim. Above Water Street
> Things were advancing in our high retreat.
> We patched where snow and rain had come to call,
> Renewed the flame upon the mildewed wall.
> Unpacked and set in place a bodhisattva
> Green with age—its smile, to which clung crumbs
> Of gold leaf, like traces of a meal,
> Proof against the Eisenhower grin
> Elsewhere so disarming. Tediums
> Ignited into quarrels, each "a scene
> From real life," we concluded as we vowed
> Not to repeat it.
>
> (*CLS*, 40)

Although this passage comes from the middle of the first volume of the trilogy, uppercase lines are, until close to the end of section L, absent. It is remarkable how easily the text repairs itself of these ruptures, remembers its continuities, returns to the rhythms of what the peacock, Mirabell, will call Merrill's "CHRONICLES OF LOVE & LOSS" (*CLS*, 176). R. P. Blackmur, in his discussion of Yeats, writes about "the reality declared when the forms have been removed and the lights taken away."[53] At the end of *The Book of Ephraim,* JM writes, "Let's be downstairs, leave all this, put the light out" (*CLS,* 92). But he cannot then (or now) declare reality, remove the forms, take away the lights, because the entire trilogy has not yet been written. Even after the trilogy had ended, Merrill kept bringing back the forms and removing them, bringing "the lights" back and taking them away. In Book 8 of *Mirabell,* for example, JM says, "Dear Mirabell, words fail us. How banal / Our lives would be, how shrunken, but for you" (*CLS,* 258). Both worlds are praised and blamed throughout. Even in the passage quoted from section L, the lights are not entirely taken away; there is still the phrase "Chat with Ephraim," even if those words have been put at the end of a not very serious list of "Things to Do." Merrill likes to offer the reader "breathers" in this poem, but they work in complicated ways. On one level, they allow the poet to comment at length on what has been happening in the poem. On another level, they are meant (like his use of the word "presently") to put the reader off guard so that the next messenger from the other world will be more alarming. What is surprising here is not so much the supernatural moments themselves as Merrill's relation to them. Knowing exactly what attitudes we want him to take toward this material, he gives those attitudes to JM and keeps himself unpredictable.

He also keeps the locations of the tensions in the poem unpredictable. A return to the everyday will not invariably be the same as waking up or coming alive again. Many readers must think that whatever he has been doing at the Ouija board, he hasn't been living. Wallace Stevens, in one of his essays, condemns "the use of small letters for capitals, eccentric line-endings, too little or too much punctuation and similar aberrations" and asserts, "These have nothing to do with being alive."[54] Frank Bidart's poems suggest that typographic devices can have everything to do with being alive: he uses them, in part, to insist on the untranslatability (in de Certeau's terms) of his anguish into everyday language. Merrill uses his typographic devices as a way of urging the reader not to "discount" this "urgent matter"—matter that might otherwise seem trivial. The question is always implied (and sometimes stated outright): Why wouldn't one feel more alive in the presence of such urgency than in the world of everyday life—and isn't the point to feel alive rather than simply ordinary? Again, the return to a more everyday style, to a lowercase voice, may be for other poets a signal that the poet is coming alive—at least becoming alive *to* whatever had been neglected. Not here. The everyday periodically hits the stands in Merrill's trilogy; it is never quite "defunct." Merrill doesn't have to lie down where all the ladders start because he has been returning there periodically (though he is not always thrilled to return). It has, after all, been his choice—and a constantly renewed one—to leave the ordinary behind.

Section L of *The Book of Ephraim* continues:

> People still unmet
> Had bought the Baptist church for reconversion.
> A slight, silverhaired man in a sarong,
> Noticing us from his tower window, bowed.
> Down at the point, the little beach we'd missed
> Crawled with infantry, and wavelets hissed.
> Wet sand, as pages turned, covered a skull
> Complete with teeth and helmet. Beautiful—
> Or were they?—ash-black poppies filled the lens.
> Delinquency was rising. Maisie made
> Eyes at shadows—time we had her spayed.
> Now from California DJ's parents
> Descended. The nut-brown old maniac
> Strode about town haranguing citizens
> While Mary, puckered pale by slack
> Tucks the years had taken, reminisced,
> Threads snapping at the least attention paid.
> They left no wiser our mysterious East.
> David and I lived on, limbs thickening,
> For better and worse in one another's shade.
>   (CLS, 40–41)

There is a way to read *Sandover* so that all the figures from the spirit world are grand and all the figures from everyday life are diminished. Ephraim described himself, early on, as "blond, sun-kissed, / Honey-eyed, tall." "Real life" supplies a neighbor who is "slight, silverhaired." JM notices this neighbor, bows, and says nothing. At the Ouija board there are hours of garrulousness; in real life people merely nod at each other. Real life offers a gull opening and shutting its beak. What else is diminished? The trilogy is about rhetoric—at one point called "no-proof rhetoric" (*CLS*, 55). It is about the ways in which the spirit voices (sometimes gently, sometimes crudely) persuade the two heroes if not to believe, at least to keep going. Real life requires no acts of persuading, except persuading someone to throw out the magazines. A reader recalls watching the "huge crane / fumble luxuriously in the filth of years" in "An Urban Convalescence (*CP,* 127). There is a similar passage in section Z. "Wait the phone is ringing: / Bad connection; babble of distant talk; / No getting through" (*CLS,* 91). A reader might expect a "bad connection," a "babble of distant talk" to refer to the *other* world, but there the connections have been good, the talk not distant but intimate. The questions that dominate the evenings at the Ouija board—questions about whether JM and DJ will survive this use of them, questions of effacement, of stripping—are remembered dimly in real life in the reference to "our self-effacing neighbor." Other grand themes return diminished. The evenings at the Ouija board are (at times) dominated by the question of composite voices. Maria Mitsotáki, for example, will be revealed to be Plato. Ephraim and the archangel Michael will be revealed to have been one entity. The revelation of composite voices raises the question inevitably suggested by poems that bring the everyday and the transcendent into relation. Where does the one begin and the other end? That problem is represented in section L as the question of whether to "overlap / By winter, somewhere." The erotic too returns diminished. JM and DJ continually flirt with the spirit voices. In section L all this erotic-mystical excitement is moved, like the self-effacing neighbor, to the corner of the poet's eye. It is given to a cat: "Maisie made / Eyes at shadows—time we had her spayed." Diminishment—but also relaxation. Evenings at the Ouija board have produced poems "by" Stevens and Yeats—styles that require Merrill to shift to tones more cerebral, more oracular than he is used to producing without recourse to uppercase.

In the next part of section L, Merrill moves into the 1970s.

> Remembered, is that summer we came back
> Really so unlike the present one?
> The friends who stagger clowning through U.S.
> Customs in a dozen snapshots old
> Enough to vote, so different from us
> Here, now? Oh god, these days . . .
> Thermometer at 90, July haze
> Heavy with infamy from Washington.
> Impeachment ripens round the furrowed stone
> Face of a story-teller who has given
> Fiction a bad name (I at least thank heaven
> For my executive privilege vis-à-vis
> Transcripts of certain private hours with E).
> The whole house needs repairs. Neither can bring
> Himself to say so. Hardly lingering,
> We've reached the point, where the tired Sound just washes

Up to, then avoids our feet. One wishes—
I mean we've got this ton of magazines
Which *someone* might persuade the girl who cleans
To throw out. Sunset. On the tower a gull
Opens and shuts its beak. Ephemeral
Orange lilies grow beneath like wild.
Our self-effacing neighbor long since willed
His dust to them, the church is up for sale.
This evening's dinner: fried soup, jellied sole.
Three more weeks, and the stiff upper lip
Of luggage shuts on us. We'll overlap
By winter, somewhere. Meanwhile, no escape
From Greece for me, then Venice . . . D must cope
With the old people, who are fading fast . . .
But that's life too. A death's head to be faced.

(*CLS*, 41)

So far I have been reading section L as being about diminishment. But the section is complex: it also imagines the relationship between the everyday and the supernatural as competitive. At a symposium in 1982, Merrill said, "I've noticed in my own work, to my horror, writing this trilogy, that suddenly everything was getting much bigger than I thought a life should be."[55] Merrill does here what JM and DJ do: he watches the contest between the everyday and the supernatural impassively; he lets it play itself in front of him. Helen Vendler writes of Elizabeth Bishop: "Elizabeth Bishop's poems in *Geography III* put into relief the continuing vibration of her work between two frequencies—the domestic and the strange. In another poet the alternation might seem a debate, but Bishop drifts rather than divides, gazes rather than chooses."[56] At the same symposium, Merrill remarked, "I kept clinging to the idea of Elizabeth with her sanity and levelheadedness and quirkiness of mind." He drifts, he gazes—and one of the things he gazes at is sheer accumulation. The Ouija board produces (as the trilogy goes on) more and more words, images, ideas, injunctions, explanations. Ordinary life, meanwhile, produces its own accumulation. One metaphorical magazine (*Life*) has become a ton of real ones, and (like the spirits) they take up space in the house. Moments like this can fill some people with despair. Even poets dedicated to teaching others to navigate the everyday can in such moments doubt their own skills. May Sarton writes, "The mail has accumulated in a fearful way, so I have a huge disorderly pile of stuff to be answered on my desk. In the end what kills is not agony (for agony at least asks something of the soul) but everyday life."[57] Merrill, at such moments, cannot choose between the two worlds because both seem like mere accumulation. Instead, he gazes. Allen Ginsberg writes, "The only poetic tradition is the voice out of the burning bush. The rest is trash & will be consumed."[58] The prophetic poet, reading this, will nod agreement. The everyday poet may laugh. Merrill, reading it, might observe that Ginsberg had really named two poetic traditions and note that if the trash really *were* consumed, it wouldn't accumulate so weightily.

Part of the force, the surprise of this section (as of similar sections in the trilogy) is that it is not about the felt dependence of the everyday on the supernatural *only* but also on its felt independence. The spirit voices can use everydayness in one way only: they can make it mean. The spirit voices can, for example, tell JM and DJ the meaning of the thunderstorm or the lost key. When Merrill lodges the spirit world in his poetry, the reader feels the everyday's peculiar resourcefulness in housing the supernatural, in finding a home for it, in its language, whether the future-oriented language of "Things to Do" or the more backward-looking nostalgic language Merrill uses near the end of *The Book of Ephraim* about Ephraim himself. The daily can lodge the supernatural as something that doesn't have to mean anything, as the survival of feeling, as a memory of feeling. "Lodge" suggests hiding or locking away:

> Keys ever remoter
> Lock our friend among the golden things that go
> Without saying, the loves no longer called up
> Or named.
>
> (*CLS*, 85)

"Our friend" here is like "our neighbor" in section L—someone one nods to without speaking, something that goes without saying. Ephraim is (in section L) referred to in the lowercase letters that he himself would never use and is referred to not as Ephraim but E. The move suggests intimacy, but it is also as if Ephraim is himself (for the time being) "tak[ing] up as much emotional space as a snowflake."

In section P of *The Book of Ephraim*, Merrill writes,

> This (1970) was the one extended
> Session with Ephraim in two years.
> (Why? No reason—we'd been busy living,
> Had meant to call, but never quite got round . . .)
> The cup at first moved awkwardly, as after
> An illness or estrangement. Had he missed us?
> YES YES emphatically.
>
> (*CLS*, 55)

This imagined scene is as extraordinary as any of the messages sent by Ephraim or Mirabell. "No reason—we'd been busy living, / Had meant to call, but never quite got round . . ." This is the elegiac tone, conveying and concealing social embarrassment, that Eliot used in "Portrait of a Lady," a poem that Merrill will reinvoke in the last few lines of *The Book of Ephraim*. These lines resemble "An Urban Convalescence" except that here it is Ephraim who is imagined as having had the illness, as sharing the awkwardness. Many poets have asked themselves why they are no longer in touch with some higher voice, but it is hard to think of another poet capable of answering, "No reason—we'd been busy living." It is as if Francis Thompson had said he'd meant to call on "the hound of heaven" but "never quite got round." And near the end of the trilogy Merrill writes something more surprising.

> No, henceforth we'll be more and more alone.
> Uni, our Peacock, Ephraim—each of these
> We have by imperceptible degrees
> . . . What to say? Not tired of. Outgrown?
>
> (*CLS*, 540)

The spirits are often transfiguring themselves (into peacocks, into each other), but only the humans can grow, can outgrow.

There is a kind of excess in passages like this—an excess that answers the excess of the supernatural passages. Dante, at the beginning of Canto 21 of the *Inferno*, writes, "Thus, from bridge to bridge, talking of things of which my Comedy is not concerned to sing, we came on and reached the summit."[59] Merrill deals, in sections like L, with exactly those things of which Dante's Comedy is not concerned to sing. There are many reasons why everyday material might not appear much in long prophetic poems: one reason might be because of its power to take over reality. Philip Fisher, in a discussion of Whitman, writes of those moments when "the common expands so that it fills out the real."[60] Merrill fills his trilogy with moments like that, moments of expanding and filling out. He writes, in section I of *The Book of Ephraim*, of "'languages' / Any one of which, to who could read it, / Lit up the system it conceived" (*CLS*, 31). The language of the everyday can make it seem to be a system of its own, absorbing and totalizing, and like a system to other systems—as the spirit voices suggest when they speak with admiration and a kind of awe about the everyday life the heroes share. The everyday is a reality that houses them but that they can never quite fill out. If the relationship is competitive, though, neither side achieves a permanent victory.

There are moments of truce and expressions, as I have shown, of admiration. Everyday life is a source of admiration for the spirit voices (and for Merrill's readers) because (though it can use tones of exhaustion) it seems much less impoverished than it does in many other poets. This may, in part, be connected to the fact that Merrill's apprenticeship was not as a prophetic poet but as a poet of the everyday. Thom Gunn, in a 1979 review of the first two books of the trilogy, writes,

> One of the triumphs, and it is no minor one . . . is in Merrill's portrayal of the domestic situation in the middle of which it all takes place. It is also, not incidentally, the most convincing description I know of a gay marriage. Much of what makes any marriage successful is the ability to take the importance of one's partner for granted, to *depend* on the other's love without being in a state of continuous erotic or passional tension. Merrill's indication of these abilities is the firmer for being indirect. The men's life together is presented to us in detail which is almost casual: we see them choosing wallpaper, keeping house, traveling, entertaining, and above all sitting at the Ouija board.[61]

Gunn's remarks suggest all that Merrill was not yet ready to do in "Voices from the Other World."

His remarks also underscore Merrill's extraordinary respect for the everyday. It is hard to think of another poem that tests its power as this trilogy does, but the test may be a sign of trust in the everyday, faith in it. Then again, it may not. There are moments in the trilogy when JM and DJ often seem as endangered by the everyday world as by the spirit world. The objects and language of the everyday, that is, seem to be in a contest not just with the objects and language of the supernatural but with the desires of the heroes. The heroes seem, in section L, to engage in actions that are almost but not quite forceful—or if they are forceful, that force is directed against the heroes themselves. JM and DJ do not "scratch" but rather scratch out—and what they scratch out is their own writing: they do not "throw" but throw out (the magazines they've brought home). If there is "hitting," it is a thing, a magazine, hitting the stands; if something advances it is, again, "things": "things were advancing in our high retreat." If something grows wild, it is not JM or DJ or any of the spirit voices, it is the orange lilies beneath the tower. DJ and JM have some active verbs associated with them, but they are not quite agents, and besides, the actions aren't what they desire. Something ignites, but it's a quarrel. The passivity is contagious. All their self-effacing neighbor can will is his own dust to the wild lilies. But this section seems less pallid than other poems about exhaustion because what it shows—"the common expanding until it fills out the real"—has a drama of its own. There is a sense throughout the trilogy that the supernatural is keeping JM and DJ together and that the everyday is endangering their relationship.

What happens next in section L is surprising.

> Meanwhile, no escape
> From Greece for me, then Venice . . . D must cope
> With the old people, who are fading fast . . .
> But that's life too. A death's head to be faced.

This is followed by a space and then the words:

> No, no! Set in our ways
> As in a garden's, glittered
> A whole small globe—our life, our life, our life

Section L could have ended here, with a Hamlet-like repetition of the word with which it began. But it continues for another fifty-three lines. The "whole small globe" turns out to be the mirror they use with the Ouija board. JM is about to relive the death of Rufus Farmetton, his previous incarnation. The section finally does end with the words "Can we stop now please? U DID WELL JM / DEATHS ARE TRAUMATIC FEW REMEMBER THEM." The references in the first part of section L were all backward looking—they were images of diminishment and at the same time of competition. None of them prepare us for what happens in the second half of the section:

> It's sunset next. It's no place that I've been.
> Outside, the veldt stops at a red ravine,
> The bad pain in my chest grown bearable.
> WHO ARE U   A name comes: I'm Rufus . . . Farmer?
> FARMETTON DEC 1925
> December? YES DECEMBER AND   Deceased!
> (*CLS*, 41–42)

Merrill has wanted to show, in the first half of section L, some possible relations between the language of the everyday and the language of the supernatural. Here he wants to represent the terror experienced when they are not in any workable relation with each other. Rilke's famous lines from *Duino Elegies* are always present in Merrill's poem as a kind of counterexample:

> Who, if I cried out, would hear me among the angels'
> hierarchies? and even if one of them pressed me
> suddenly against his heart: I would be consumed
> in that overwhelming existence.[62]

This Rilkean terror is incorporated, assimilated within Merrill's poem. Just as Ammons, in poems like *Garbage,* takes moments that would have been climactic for other poets and hardly pauses for breath before he is on to another thought about a thought, another feeling about a feeling, so Merrill incorporates the terror into the poem and moves on. Readers of Merrill's trilogy may feel that Eliot, in the final section of *The Waste Land,* is wondering which phrase to end on—and might wish for him that he had five hundred pages to work with. Merrill writes like someone who can end as many times as he wants. Angels may be terrifying in Merrill's poem, but Merrill's poem is formidable enough to raise the question of who would be consumed in whose overwhelming existence.

There is a sense in which the entire poem is about a certain kind of competence. Merrill's lines—"I used to / Ask how on earth one got sufficiently / Imbued with otherness. And now I see"—seem, in part, an epiphany about know-how (*CLS,* 89). As Maria Mitsotáki tells JM, "ALL THINGS ARE DONE HERE IF U HAVE TECHNIQUE" (*CLS,* 104). What does Merrill know how to do? He knows how to write two kinds of poetry at once. In order to do this and to show that he is, he needs to distinguish the human voices from each other and from the spirit voices, and he also needs to distinguish the spirit voices from each other. Typography alone will not do it. He is not interested, as a poet, in conflation, in a kind of erasure of difference. He is interested in the composite voice as a revelation but not as an effect in his poetry.

Allen Grossman has written about this desire to merge the two voices, to somehow write as if the two voices were once (and could become again) the same. Grossman wants to remove all the intricacies of relation that Merrill works out in the trilogy. Grossman writes, "If I ever wrote a good poem in a successful style, it would be a poem in which the two voices were so fully hospitable to one another . . . that they would be indistinguishable." He writes, "The most beneficial outcome . . . is, of course, the integration . . . of the voice of the Other *in* the voice of the self: an intimacy which makes the two voices indistinguishable and mutually sustaining."[63] Merrill's voices may be hospitable to one another and mutually sustaining (at times), but they are not indistinguishable. Merrill plays with the boundaries, but he also makes it clear who is speaking: he does not give us the integration of the two voices. The interest of the project for Merrill, as it was for Dante, is to discriminate the living and the dead, the human and the nonhuman. Merrill does not want to merge the voices but instead to imagine the (sometimes very intimate) discursive spaces that can be occupied by both voices; he is interested in simultaneity as well as in the decorums of sequence; he wants to imagine what the voices could learn from each other in their conversations. Rilke, in *Duino Elegies*, wrote,

> Angels (they say) don't know whether it is the living
> they are moving among, or the dead. The eternal torrent
> whirls all ages along in it, through both realms
> forever, and their voices are drowned out in its thunderous roar.[64]

A thunderous roar would be dull. Merrill has a tour de force in which he shows how quickly he can distinguish voices. A spirit voice has just broken in to say, "MYND YOUR WEORK."

> DJ massaged his fingers. Fun was fun.
> The pencil in my writing hand had snapped.
> Like something hurt the cup limped forth again.
> Maya: GEE   THEY PUT THE WHAMMY ON US
> Maria: JUNTA   Stevens: WHERES MY HAT
> E: A DOOR WAS SHUT   THE MIRROR WENT BLACK
> We, no less bowled over than used up,
> By mutual accord left it at that.
>
> (*CLS*, 73)

Yeats, in *A Vision*, writes, "All imaginable relations may arise between a man and his God" (240). Merrill could, making the necessary changes, almost take that observation as the epigraph to his trilogy. He is constantly experimenting with ways in which this intimacy can be represented with language. Stichomythia, the rapid alternation of two voices, is, as in Spenser's *Shephearde's Calender*, a sign of rapport. Lowercase and uppercase lines can rhyme with each other. The humans turn to rhyme for comfort—how much more comforting to be rhymed with? At the beginning of *Mirabell*, when JM and DJ decide to return to the spirit world, Merrill writes, "Our friends / In any case received us as if nothing / Had ever gone, would ever go amiss. / Maria: CHERS ENFANTS   Ephraim: KISS KISS" (*CLS*, 100). A lowercase line can enjamb and shift in the next line into an uppercase line. Sometimes a human voice leads a spirit voice on, sometimes the human voice is led on. Often the human is chastised, brought up short: "YR NONCHALANCE / IS

THE SLEEP OF A VAST TRAVAIL" (*CLS*, 124). JM later says, "Our poem needed those fierce voices" (*CLS*, 175). This is true: the poem needs them, need their resistance. As Maria Mitsotáki (much later in the trilogy) says, quoting the archangel Michael: "'ALL GOOD DISCOURSE MUST, LIKE FORWARD MOTION, / KNOW RESISTANCE'" (*CLS*, 414). The poem sets up a great variety of psychological rhythms, for example, the rhythm of guessing and being proved right. There is something of this in Whitman. "Now I know it is true what I guessed at!" Whitman will cry without ever giving us the earlier guess. Exclamation marks are handed out near the beginning of *Mirabell* (129). They suggest a relationship between the exclamatory (for wonder, disbelief, belief) and the imperative (whose force makes up for its lack of tonal range). If Merrill sometimes uses an exclamation point for a tone of mock command, the spirits begin to use exclamation points in exclamatory ways (*CLS*, 57). DJ and JM are told to "DO NOTHING," and a little later, JM says, "NOTHING is exactly what we do" (*CLS*, 39). Doing NOTHING is, of course, not the same as doing nothing. There is here a characteristic mixture of reverence and irreverence. R. P. Blackmur said of Yeats that he was "never . . . able to retract his system, only to take up different attitudes towards it."[65] Merrill sometimes does retract—but only for the sake of a different attitude. In a poem about attitudes, about tones, one more posture—the retracting or asserting attitude—simply does to the trilogy what he wants continually to do: "complicate / It irretrievably" (*CLS*, 191). A reader begins to take this complexity for granted here, but there is little of it in other supernatural poems and in other poems in which the human and the prophetic are in relationship.

Prophetic poetry is not generally about conversation and not about conversation like this. The human in much prophetic poetry is not envisioned as collaborative but instead as preliminary; the human is something that will have to be fixed and readied. "What in me is dark / Illumine, what is low raise and support," Milton writes in Book I of *Paradise Lost*."[66] Wordsworth thought of *The Prelude* as preliminary to a work that would be less voluble, even grander, not merely about himself. Stevens thought of calling his first book *The Grand Poem: Preliminary Minutiae*. The human may resist this sense of itself as preliminary, but that resistance too is part of the decorum. In much prophetic poetry, including that of the Hebrew Bible, the human voice establishes itself *as* human by expressing reluctance. Isaiah and Ezekiel seem to establish a modest human voice just in time to lose it: they seem to find it almost in order to lose it. Personality is expressed as the act of reluctance. There is reluctance in JM and DJ too, of course:

> But if someone up there thought *we* would edit
> The New Enlarged Edition,
> That maze of inner logic, dogma, dates—
> Ephraim, forget it.
>
> (*CLS*, 14)

The reluctance is real. Merrill did not work out, in poem after poem, a human voice in order to see it merely as preliminary to some other kind of voice. Again, what the reader notices is Merrill's confidence, his capacity to surprise both the reader and himself, and his intimate knowledge of the nature and extent of his gifts.

If the self he presents at the Ouija board is not preliminary, it is oddly *available*. JM and DJ are attractive to the spirits because, as they are told:

> YR ATTENTION, THAT OPULENT FEAST
> HAS NOT BEEN OVERSPICED WITH SELF NOR THE BRIGHT FIELD PITTED
> WITH YR OWN NEEDS LIKE OTHER FIELDS WE HAVE SETTLED INTO
>
> (*CLS*, 258)

Nor is the bright field of self pitted with the needs of others. Later the spirit voices say:

> U'VE ON YR SIDE UTTER NEUTRALITY,
> NO MADE TO ORDER PREJUDICES   NO
> BACKTALK   JUST THE LISTENER'S PURE O!
> NULL ZERO CRYING OUT TO BE FILLED IN
>
> (*CLS*, 328)

Utter neutrality? A null zero, crying out to be filled in? At such moments readers can wonder why a discursive space that other poets might fill with the political is, in the trilogy, here left empty. Politics does not appear in Merrill's poetry in the way it does in that of other contemporary poets. Merrill can seem, to some readers, not to notice political events—or merely to notice them. References to political discourse enter the world of the trilogy without disrupting it. Yeats said his system allowed him to hold in one thought reality and justice. Merrill's system seems to allow him to hold unreality and injustice: the messages from the spirit voices, with their talk of Atlantis and centaurs, seem an anthology of unreality, and the cosmology itself seems built, complacently, on injustices. The trilogy sometimes sees itself as a warning against nuclear disaster. But this passage is typical:

> THE AIR
> ABOVE LOS ALAMOS IS LIKE A BREATH
> SUCKED IN HORROR   TOD MORT MUERTE DEATH

> —Meaning the nearby nuclear research
> Our instinct first is to deplore, and second
> To think no more of.
>
> (*CLS*, 33)

As Moffett says, "Only elect lab souls with sufficient 'densities' prepro-
grammed or cloned in Heaven between lives can do God's work on
earth to build a heavenly paradise."[67] The spirit voices are complacent,
and so, more or less, are JM and DJ. They show little anger either on behalf of or against the message they carry.

The political in the trilogy is located, I think, in Merrill's relationship to his readers. Merrill has, for example, his own distinctive ways
of addressing his readers. Whitman's "you, whoever you are" is nowhere present in the trilogy. It is true that prophetic poets often don't
say *you* to readers: Blake and Crane didn't. Merrill fleetingly imagines
a readership like Milton's ("the few of more than common sense—/
Who but they would be our audience!" [*CLS*, 109]), but the lines are in
the third person and conditional. Merrill does seem at times to be concerned about his readers: sometimes he appropriates them, makes
them characters:

> Years have gone by. How often in their course
> I've "done" for people bits of this story.
> Hoping for what response from each in turn—
> Tom's analytic cool? Alison's shrewd
> Silence?
>
> (*CLS*, 87)

Merrill can never quite imagine who his readership could be. Although
he writes, at the beginning of the trilogy, of reaching "the widest public
in the shortest time" and, later, of his desire to "speak to multitudes and
make it matter," he soon gives up that notion (*CLS*, 82). Sometimes he
imagines his best readers as being not on earth. The archangel Michael
has the face, Auden tells JM and DJ, "OF THE IDEAL / PARENT CONFESSOR
LOVER READER FRIEND" (*CLS*, 286). At one point, Merrill's Auden divides the reader into two categories, one from high culture and the
other from pop culture, but Merrill imagines both kinds of readers as
unsatisfactory, as lacking the precise combination of seriousness and
wit that motivates the poet (*CLS*, 147). Guy Rotella writes, "The terms
of this enchantment are distinctly modern: what is asked of the readers,
as it is exemplified by the poet, is both submersion in and resistance to
the other-worldly revelation of the poem."[68] Most readers either submit
to or resist such material. Some do both, but few want to do both at

such length. This does not matter to the poem, though. Although Whitman is always intent on his "trippers and askers" (they have an effect on the tonalities of his voice, on what happens in the poem), Merrill's occasional anxiety about readership has little effect on his poem. The readers of the trilogy are JM and DJ. They are the ones who are courted, cajoled, chastised, who struggle to be adequate to the material, who wonder if the material is really rewarding their attention. They are as likely to imagine readers as students are likely to imagine their future students. If Merrill does imagine a reader, then it will be, as Vendler puts it, a "listener with whom the only possible wavelength of communication is the assumption of perfect equality." She adds, "In this he is far more democratic than many of our hortatory poets."[69]

This assumption of perfect equality seems connected to Merrill's notion of manners, which has been frequently cited as a poetics but may also be a kind of ethics. Is that where the political is to be found in Merrill? Readers looking for a detachable, perhaps teachable message in the trilogy might decide (and there is much evidence for it) that the poem is really about what Drucilla Cornell, in *The Philosophy of the Limit*, calls "a nonviolative relationship to the Other."[70] We are back to the moral, to the emphasis on conversation and the values of the everyday. According to Lee Zimmerman, the meaning of the trilogy lies in "the increasing importance of conversation, as a narrative strategy and a way of knowing. Conversation, indeed, may model a way of containing the dark forces. As opposed to the narcissistic denial of the Other basic to absolutist world views, in conversation, one voice depends upon its counterpart; the interplay requires both self and other—and *Sandover* locates authority or truth precisely in this interplay. Making sense is revealed as a group effort and an ongoing one."[71]

Any large statement about *The Changing Light at Sandover* would probably have to say something like what these readers say. But one remembers Merrill's comment in an interview, "The poems I most love are so perfectly phrased that they seem to say something extraordinary, whether they do or not."[72] My desire in this chapter has been to imagine that phrases can be a reader's largest unit of sense and to see if I can let larger units, like ideas, take their chances in Merrill's language. The pleasure in this way of reading lies precisely in not summing up. It is true that the poets whom I read in this book are all absorbed— "haunted" is not the word; none of the poets seems haunted—by a conversation that they want the reader to find as endlessly interesting as they do. But time spent moralizing is time spent away from it.

4

"This is what is possible"
Adrienne Rich

Adrienne Rich differs from the other three poets in this study in that her sense of herself as a poet depends on her having given her voice an assignment above and beyond its own creation and elaboration. She actually has a prophetic mission. Merrill writes about the fate of the planet, but his sense of mission in his trilogy is extravagant and seems (deliberately, I think) only intermittently translatable into the terms of any imaginable agenda. Lowell retains a version of the prophetic voice to the end, but he cannot be said, after his first three books, to have any sustained view of prophetic mission. Ammons too can write at length about the fate of the planet, but prophecy for him is one speech genre among several. In *Garbage,* he says he is happy to leave his "unaccomplished mission unaccomplished," adding that "someone somewhere may be at this very moment // dying for the lack of what W. C. Williams says / you could (or somebody could) be giving: yeah?"[1] Ammons is quoting Williams's "Asphodel, That Greeny Flower." What Williams *actually* says is "for lack of what is found there." (By "there," Williams means poetry.) Adrienne Rich had just come out with a collection of "Notebooks on Poetry and Politics" called *What Is Found There.* Both the phrase "what is found there" and Rich herself (who appears only as "someone") are omitted from Ammons's lines. Referring to Rich would complicate the opening of *Garbage* in a way that referring to Williams does not. Her presence complicates this study, as well, which is one reason why I have included her. For Rich, the relationship between the prophetic and the everyday is never merely a relationship between speech genres. The prophetic and the everyday can, for her, represent a lever and a place to stand.

Rich's poetry has had, so far, three phases. The poetry of the first phase (the poetry of the fifties) is technically accomplished but not always memorable. At the beginning of her career she must have hoped that the reward for leading a traditional domestic life might be that one felt fully human. Many of the poems are about the intuition that the world (which usually consists of everything the speaker of the poem understands by domesticity) will have to come to an end. In the poetry of the second phase (the poetry of the sixties and seventies), that world has come to an end. Her poems in this phase are about how the world of her poems looks after it has exploded. No longer organized around elegant intimations of disaster, her poems now employ flat descriptions of fact and plain statements of feeling. She continues to experiment. Imagining private and public space as one great space of floating fragments, she wants her statements and descriptions to appear to be floating as well. She wants to show that *poems*—her poems—have exploded along with everything else.

As the sixties progressed, Rich's poetry became more confident and authoritative, more serious and severe. Poetry may not make anything happen, but it *may*, and a poet must be "responsible for each choice in a poem as if it were an action in the street."[2] In the poems of the sixties and seventies—the poems of *Snapshots of a Daughter-in-Law* (1963), *Necessities of Life* (1966), *Leaflets* (1969), *The Will to Change* (1971), *Diving into the Wreck* (1973), and *The Dream of a Common Language* (1978)—Rich writes about contemporary topics: the women's movement, the civil rights movement, the war in Vietnam. Rich wants, more and more, to imagine herself as an allegorical figure. But what sort of allegorical figure should she be? The proper balance between the prophetic and the domestic is played out in her poetry as the balance between isolation and community. She writes poems in which she imagines herself as a solitary figure in the sky. When that seems limiting, she represents herself as a figure in the city, in the streets. Bringing herself back to earth, she is still tempted to imagine herself as grounded but isolated. Too often, though, she seems not like someone who is leading an everyday life but someone who is walking the earth, and the question of the balance between isolation and community will not go away. If she is going to lead a life of allegory, should it be a life of solitude or a life among— not just among, but with—people? In many of her poems, she longs for solitude, but she is ambivalent about it as well. In *An Atlas of the Diffi-cult World* she will repeatedly ask her readers to picture her in her soli-tude. But again, she cannot escape her sense of her mission. The woman in the desert, the woman on the mountaintop, the woman in the cabin where "the road / in winter is often impassable" is not helping any-one.[3] To help people means to write about them. In "Eastern War Time," she imagines the voice of one of her subjects saying, "I am standing here in your poem unsatisfied" (*ADW*, 44). She feels the pro-phetic and the everyday more and more as a contradiction.

In the poetry of her third phase, the poetry of *A Wild Patience Has Taken Me This Far* (1981), *Your Native Land, Your Life* (1986), *Time's Power* (1989), *An Atlas of the Difficult World* (1991), *Dark Fields of the Republic* (1995), *Midnight Salvage* (1999), and *Fox* (2001) she continues to explore the relation between prophecy and domesticity, between isolation and community. The idea of conversation is helpful in finding what feels like a balance between the contradictions in her life. It is her version of a hybrid speech genre, allowing her to be prophetic and domestic at once. Politics does not work in that way for her (as it does for Lowell) because politics for Rich tends to limit the prophetic and the domestic, tends to make them mean, in any given poem, one thing, both in them-selves and in relation to each other. Conversation, to the extent that it is open-ended, both keeps the two speech genres alive and keeps them in relation with each other. I will have more to say later in this chapter about what conversation means for Rich.

It is important to emphasize at the outset that conversation is help-ful, but it is not a place of rest. Rich, thinking about the power of these two speech genres, begins to speculate about where they came from. How did they come to play such an important part in her poetry? Why, when she was constructing her voice, should the prophetic and the do-mestic have been the materials that seemed at once necessary and there at hand? In the poetry of this period she writes more frequently about her childhood. Remembering it, she recognizes that she has never expe-rienced a domesticity that was free of the prophetic or a prophetic voice that was free of the domestic. The relationship between them is, in a sense, more natural to her than she had thought: they were in conversa-tion from the start.

Adrienne Rich's first book, *A Change of World* (1951), was a critical suc-cess and was chosen by W. H. Auden for publication in the Yale Younger Poet series. Her second book, *The Diamond Cutters* (1955), was also a critical success. Many of the poems in these books are, as I said, about people taking inadequate measures against incipient disaster. Some poets struggle to develop a voice of domesticity; Rich had to begin by making one version of that voice impossible for herself. She begins her career, in effect, by telling us that there are certain kinds of poems she is not going to write. The irony, of course, is that she tells us this in a version of the language those poems themselves use. She tells us politely, in other words, that politeness will be useless against the storm. The poem "Storm Warnings" has the same place in her work as "So I Said I Am Ezra" has in the work of Ammons. It is the first poem in the first book, the first poem in the *Collected Early Poems*. And, like Ammons's poem, it is about the ineffectuality of its speaker. Here is the last stanza of the poem:

> I draw the curtains as the sky goes black
> And set a match to candles sheathed in glass
> Against the keyhole draught, the insistent whine
> Of weather through the unsealed aperture.
> This is our sole defense against the season;
> These are the things that we have learned to do
> Who live in troubled regions.
>
> *(CEP, 3)*

Like the early Ammons, the early Rich never allows her speakers actually to prevent the coming disaster. She shows us things that they "have learned to do," at the same time showing us what *she* has taught herself to do. If she wants us to see her own use of formal pattern and decorous language as a version of the strategies her speakers are taking, she never allows her formal structures to become so elaborate—or her vocabulary to become so exuberant—as to make the poem seem anything more than an allegory about defensiveness. Rich's early poems have a kind of planned obsolescence. The poet's domestic voice sounds frightened. Her voice is prophetic only in the other sense of that word: it predicts the end of exactly this kind of domestic voice. But no version of the domestic or the prophetic voice has any real force in the early poems. Instead, the poet relies on tones of mild irony, though she knows that resorting to irony is in such circumstances itself ironic. Irony will do as little as politeness against the storm. Each poem seems to say that the night is coming when nobody can be either polite or ironic, and each poem says this in a polite, ironic voice. The problem is clear in the title of the first book. "A change of world" has the diminished force of a phrase that is not itself an expression but only echoes one. It sounds like "a change of heart," an expression that is usually used apologetically.

There are memorable poems in both of the first two books; "The Middle-Aged," for example.

> Their faces, safe as an interior
> Of Holland tiles and Oriental carpet,
> Where the fruit-bowl, always filled, stood in a light
> Of placid afternoon—their voices' measure,
> Their figures moving in the Sunday garden
> To lay the tea outdoors or trim the borders,
> Afflicted, haunted us. For to be young
> Was always to live in other peoples' houses
> Whose peace, if we sought it, had been made by others,
> Was ours at second-hand and not for long.
> The custom of the house, not ours, the sun
> Fading the silver-blue Fortuny curtains,
> The reminiscence of a Christmas party
> Of fourteen years ago—all memory,
> Signs of possession and of being possessed,
> We tasted, tense with envy. They were so kind,
> Would have given us anything: the bowl of fruit
> Was filled for us, there was a room upstairs
> We must call ours: but twenty years of living
> They could not give. Nor did they ever speak
> Of the coarse stain on that polished balustrade,
> The crack in the study window, or the letters
> Locked in a drawer and the key destroyed.
> All to be understood by us, returning
> Late, in our own time—how that peace was made,
> Upon what terms, with how much left unsaid.
>
> (*CEP,* 119)

This is a poem about "returning / Late, in our own time." The speaker speaks from a time later than the time of Rich's other early poems. She is not looking anxiously forward to the explosion but, instead, looking back at it. This stance seems more congenial to Rich. Her tone of foreboding sounds derivative (it is hard to break new ground with mild-mannered irony), but looking back she sounds like herself, and the poem itself thematizes that distinction. "The Middle-Aged" is also more memorable than some of the other early poems because the tension is not drawn simply between inadequate measures and approaching disaster. The other poems put the reader, in a sense, at the mercy of their own false placidity. In this poem the speaker places herself in the position of that reader: she is at the mercy of precisely that placidity. If she is "haunted" by the style of these early poems, she is also "afflicted" by it. It is as if Rich is saying that that style, like the house in this poem, is second-hand and will not be hers for long.

The early poems are guarded about everything but their influences: "to be young / Was always to live in other people's houses." Rich seems, in her early poems, to know everything about domestic unhappiness but not to know any unhappy people herself; the people in her poems seem often to come from other poems. She imports them in order to find out what they will say in *her* poems. Her long poem "Autumn Equinox" (which Randall Jarrell called "almost the best Frost-influenced poem I've ever read") is about an unhappy couple.[4]

> Night, and I wept aloud; half in my sleep,
> Half feeling Lyman's wonder as he leaned
> Above to shake me. "Are you ill, unhappy?
> Tell me what I can do."
>   "I'm sick, I guess—
> I thought that life was different than it is."
> "Tell me what's wrong. Why can't you ever say?
> I'm here, you know."
>   Half shamed, I turned to see
> The lines of grievous love upon his face,
> The love that gropes and cannot understand.
> "I must be crazy, Lyman—or a dream
> Has made me babble things I never thought.
> Go back to sleep—I won't be so again."
>   (*CEP*, 98–99)

The poem feels like a pallid version of an original that is itself muted. Once again, she achieves the odd effect she achieved with the phrase "a change of world." If Robert Lowell were writing this poem, the wife would, in fact, have been crazy, and Lyman would have strangled her. (Such an outcome would seem unserious to Rich—not helpful.) "Autumn Equinox" is, like the other early poems, self-consciously about half-measures. The woman in that poem, half-asleep, half-feels her husband's feelings and feels "half shamed." The poem itself occupies a halfway position. Rich cannot quite write the Frost poem and at the same time cannot yet write her own poems. A reader may feel that the poem she wants to write here is her later poem, "Trying to Talk with a Man."

When she tries to sound like a major poet of an earlier generation the result is often that she sounds like an earlier minor poet, sometimes like MacLeish in his 1929 poem "Quite Unexpectedly at Vasserot" or Millay in her sonnets of the twenties and thirties. Sometimes this lightness (which never seems exactly playful) is deliberate. One way to avoid being unintentionally minor is to be deliberately light. Keats, at the beginning of his career, wanted to mix the prophetic and everyday but did not know how. Writing light verse was, for him, a safe way of figuring out how to do it. Rich uses light verse in the same way. She will imitate Auden imitating Cole Porter. A stanza in Rich's poem "The Marriage Portion" reads:

> The telephone is ringing,
> And planes and trains depart,
> The cocktail party's forming,
> The cruise about to start.
> To stay behind is fatal—
> Act now, the time is short.
>   (*CEP*, 120)

Merrill, in "The Summer People" from *The Fire Screen* (1969), can pull this off more successfully because by then he is in full possession of his themes. In other poems, like "The Return of the Evening Grosbeaks," Rich turns to a generic light verse.

> The birds about the house pretend to be
> Penates of our domesticity.
> And when the cardinal wants to play at prophet
> We never tell his eminence to come off it.
>
> The crows, too, in the dawn prognosticate
> Like ministers at a funeral of state.
> The pigeons in their surplices of white
> Assemble for some careful Anglican rite.
>
> Only these guests who rarely come our way
> Dictate no oracles for us while they stay.
> No matter what we try to make them mean
> Their coming lends no answer to our scene.
>
> We scatter seed and call them by their name,
> Remembering what has changed since last they came.
>   (*CEP*, 37)

In this poem Rich combines the prophetic and domestic but without quite knowing why. The poem, though, seems to know more than the poet. (Rich would later write, "Poems are like dreams: in them you put what you don't know you know.")[5] Once again, Rich struggles to find a tone to say the things she will later know exactly how to say. She wants, in "The Return of the Evening Grosbeaks," to say that domesticity is a condition requiring protection and that the end, when it comes, will involve not just this little domestic scene but also "the state." That the personal is political is "news" she wants to put into the poem as well. How can she say things like that in a way that isn't muted, ironic, guarded? Emerson writes, "In genius we recognize our own rejected thoughts: They come back to us with a certain alienated majesty."[6] The evening grosbeaks in this poem seem to represent Rich's own rejected thoughts. Meanwhile, she disguises herself as the kind of poet who puns on the word "cardinal" and who rhymes "prophet" with "come off it." The sonnet doesn't quite work even as light verse, but it is a way of stalling for time. She wants, like Merrill, like many poets at the start of their careers, to stall, to postpone. Merrill could use his extraordinary wit as a way of stalling for time, though of course the wit itself would prove indispensable when the time came. For Rich, though, wit would be a postponing that would ensure that the time never came. Understanding that wit was not going to be her way any more than irony was, she began to trust more and more in what Helen Vendler calls an "unremitting earnestness of tone."[7]

Much of her later work involves repossessing her own rejected thoughts. Sometimes this will mean a taking possession of her own early phrases. For example, she will remember the last line of her early poem "The Wild Sky" thirty years later in the phrase she takes for the title of a book, *Your Native Land, Your Life.* And the phrase "the wild sky" itself will return as *A Wild Patience Has Taken Me This Far.* Here is the poem:

> Here from the corridor of an English train,
> I see the landscape slide through glancing rain,
> A land so personal that every leaf
> Unfolds as if to witness human life,
> And every aging milestone seems to know
> That human hands inscribed it, long ago.
>
> Oasthouse and garden, narrow bridge and hill—
> Landscape with figures, where a change of style
> Comes softened in a water-colour light
> By Constable; and always, shire on shire,
> The low-pitched sky sags like a tent of air
> Beneath its ancient immaterial light.
>
> The weather in these gentle provinces
> Moves like the shift of daylight in a house,
> Subdued by time and custom. Sun and rain
> Are intimate, complaisant to routine,

Guests in the garden. Year on country year
Has worn the edge of wildness from this air.

And I remember that unblunted light
Poured out all day from a prodigious height—
My country, where the blue is miles too high
For minds of men to graze the leaning sky.
The telegraph may rise or timber fall,
That last frontier remains, the vertical.

Men there are beanstalk climbers, all day long
Haunted by stilts they clattered on when young.
Giants no longer, now at mortal size.
They stare into that upward wilderness.
The vertical reminds them where they are,
And I remember I am native there.

(*CEP,* 78)

Wallace Stevens organizes his poem "Notes toward a Supreme Fiction" with the use of three subheadings: "It Must Be Abstract," "It Must Change," and "It Must Give Pleasure." It is as if he is reminding himself what his poem will need to be in order to satisfy him. Rich seems to be telling herself, in this poem, that her poems will need to be "wild." This poem, of course, is not wild. Its borders are as "trim" as the borders of the garden in "The Middle-Aged." Descriptions of the landscape are, as is usual in poems like these, also words for the poem. The poem is itself "subdued by time and custom"; it is itself "complaisant to routine." Many of the lines in the poem begin with strong beats: "Here," "Oasthouse," "Landscape," "Moves," "Guests," "Poured," "Men," "Haunted," "Giants." These beats may suggest the motion of the train moving through the "gentle provinces," but nothing happens to the rhythm when the poet moves, in memory, to the country she was born in. There is no "change of style." The stanzas have been—and they continue to be—like gentle provinces. Stevens brought to the style of his self-consciously American poem, "Anecdote of the Jar," a syntactic strangeness that seemed, so to speak, jarring:

I placed a jar in Tennessee,
And round it was, upon a hill.
It made the slovenly wilderness
Surround that hill.

The wilderness rose up to it,
And sprawled around, no longer wild.

> The jar was round upon the ground
> And tall and of a port in air.
>
> It took dominion everywhere.
> The jar was gray and bare.
> It did not give of bird or bush,
> Like nothing else in Tennessee.[8]

Stevens's tetrameter line, "It took dominion everywhere," is a kind of parody of the elegance and fluidity of lines like Rich's, "And I remember I am native there." Rich's poem looks back at the kind of model Stevens's poem is working against. On page seventy-seven of *The Collected Early Poems,* Rich is still saying things like "We move meticulously, ill at ease / Amid perfections." Stevens's poem moves happily among (grammatical) imperfections.

"The Wild Sky" awakens an appetite for symmetry and then, in one particular, fails to satisfy it. There are five stanzas in the poem, but each has six lines. The poem's asymmetry suggests that it is unfinished, and in a sense it is. At the end of "The Wild Sky," Rich reminds herself that she is native to the country described in the last two stanzas. The poem ends where another poet might begin to describe the experience of being native there. In the middle of "Poem," Bishop's poem about looking at a painting of a landscape, the speaker suddenly recognizes the landscape in the painting: "Heavens, I recognize the place, I know it!"[9] This moment occurs halfway through Bishop's poem, while it is as if Rich had ended her poem with those words.

She ends the poem, I think, because she is not sure where she is. "The vertical reminds them where they are," she writes. The line has a neat ambiguity: the vertical reminds the people in the poem both where they would like to be and where they are. Merrill, perhaps remembering this poem, writes in *The Changing Light at Sandover,* "The mountain / Rippled by heat, scent of green pine, a star / Delicately remind us where we are."[10] In Merrill's lines, it is not quite clear where the speaker is. Rich, too, is not sure where she is. Is the speaker of the poem in the old country, the country of her first two books, or is she already in the country of her next book? Although the poems in general depend for their effects on suppressed longing, suppressed longing does not seem to be Rich's most effective mode. Her poems are most memorable when, as in the case of "The Middle-Aged," they are about suppressed rage. Rich would later describe her poems of this period as those of a woman "almost in touch with her anger." "In those years," she writes, "formalism was part of the strategy—like asbestos gloves, it allowed me to handle materials I couldn't pick up barehanded."[11]

In her next book, she would write "barehanded" poems. Rich's third book is called *Snapshots of a Daughter-in-Law*. Rich's style combines the return of repressed emotions with the return of rejected thoughts. Like Ammons, she is bored with "the self-conscious POEM."[12] She must have felt she had written enough of those to last a lifetime. Her title, *Snapshots of a Daughter-in-Law*, suggests (as Lowell's title, "Life Studies," does) work that is quick, sketchy, preparatory. And exploratory as well. She wants to write about marriage, for example, but she doesn't want to write a poem like "Autumn Equinox." She envisions approaching Frost in a more adventurous spirit. What if she were to write one of his dialogue poems without the dialogue? What if she were to make her poem a series of stage directions? She could also use her own earlier poetry of domesticity as a model, taking what was schematic about it and exaggerating it. Here is her poem "Novella."

> Two people in a room, speaking harshly.
> One gets up, goes out to walk.
> (That is the man.)
> The other goes into the next room
> and washes the dishes, cracking one.
> (That is the woman.)
> It gets dark outside.
> The children quarrel in the attic.
> She has no blood left in her heart.
> The man comes back to a dark house.
> The only light is in the attic.
> He has forgotten his key.
> He rings at his own door
> and hears sobbing on the stairs.
> The lights go on in the house.
> The door closes behind him.
> Outside, separate as minds,
> the stars too come alight.
>
> (*SDL*, 57)

The rhythms of this style come from a children's primer. The primer used by children in the sixties is easily adaptable—in its relentless descriptions of the activities of Dick and Jane—to tales of married life. Rich is drawn to its adaptability and in particular to the way the style enables her to think in abstractions. Younger writers are often told to avoid abstractions, as if particularity were the greatest good and poems mere occasions for it. Abstract language, though, can have enormous force. Jorie Graham writes, "Abstract diction . . . feels especially powerful to me because of its poignancy, the sense of desperation that informs it, the sense of a last avenue being resorted to, a last, bluntest tool." She continues, "It's the urgency (not what teachers often tell us is the laziness) of abstraction that moves me. The sense that it is very late, and we must think fast and hard."[13] We must also be useful, though, unless we want to engage in mere tour-de-force examples of fast and hard thinking. Emerson, in his essay "Nature," writes, "To a sound judgment, the most abstract truth is the most practical."[14] This insight adds the necessary corrective. Rich is making a new style for herself and at the same time developing a faith in it, and the poems she writes will be often also about that faith. In the poems of this period, we watch her constructing the style and the faith.

"Novella" becomes, in its depiction of the couple, more and more abstract. In her next book, Rich will (adapting Browning's title) write a poem called "Any Husband to Any Wife." In part, she wants to illustrate the process whereby a husband and wife become "any husband" and "any wife." But she doesn't leave them there. At the end, the husband and wife have become even more abstract and generalized—they have become "minds." Rich could have said that minds are separate as stars: that would be the sort of poem Matthew Arnold would write. Instead, she tells us that stars are separate as minds, as if minds were the most "separate" things imaginable. The effect of this abstraction is that the husband and wife lose any sense of agency. Rich writes, "The lights go on in the house. / The door closes behind him," not "She turns the lights on in the house. / He closes the door behind him." The wife and husband are each a "zone / Of gray unrest," to borrow a phrase from "Storm Warnings."

Poems that move toward greater generality awaken in their readers (who remember all the poems for whom such a movement is a move from earth to heaven) an appetite for consolation, but Rich's move from one level of abstraction to another offers little consolation. This may be because her poem, in its movement toward greater generality, skips a stage. We go from the house directly to the stars. In an epigraph to *Diving into the Wreck,* Rich will quote George Eliot: "There is no private life which is not determined by a wider public life." Where is the wider public life in "Novella"? Lights go on in the house, and the stars come alight. Writers who work in this style can only say what the style (with its parataxis and its inclination toward non sequitur) allows them to say: that things happen to happen. Like Joan Didion, Rich exaggerates the schematic here in order to suggest that there is no scheme. There are no politics in this poem, no sense of community. Later she will see that the chaos of the world (here represented simply as "night") *is* politics.

Rich wants to connect the world inside the house to the chaos outside it. If she writes only about the world inside the house, she will write poems like the poems in her first two books. She does not want to bring an impoverished domestic voice into relation with the prophetic voice. The problem of what to do at this point is brought to the center of many of the poems in her third book. The people in these poems know that something has happened in the world outside their houses, but they do not know how to let it affect them. Here are three quatrains from "Snapshots of a Daughter-in-Law."

> Banging the coffee-pot into the sink
> she hears the angels chiding, and looks out
> past the raked gardens to the sloppy sky.
> Only a week since They said: *Have no patience.*
>
> The next time it was: *Be insatiable.*
> Then: *Save yourself; others you cannot save.*
> Sometimes she's let the tapstream scald her arm,
> a match burn to her thumbnail,
>
> or held her hand above the kettle's snout
> right in the woolly steam. They are probably angels,
> since nothing hurts her anymore, except
> each morning's grit blowing into her eyes.
>
> *(SDL,* 21)

The phrase "nothing hurts her any more" suggests two things: that the actions do not injure the woman in the poem and that she does not feel the pain they cause. Sylvia Plath, setting a poem in the kitchen, begins it with the words, "What a thrill— / My thumb instead of an onion."[15] If these angels are muses, they are not Sylvia Plath's muses. What the angels want the woman in this poem to feel is ordinary unhappiness— they want her to feel the grit of "each morning" blowing into her eyes.

Pieces of the exploded world have to enter not only the house but also the bodies of the people in the house. Rich returns to this idea in "A Marriage in the 'Sixties."

As solid-seeming as antiquity,
you frown above
the *New York Sunday Times*
where Castro, like a walk-on out of *Carmen,*
mutters into a bearded henchman's ear.

They say the second's getting shorter—
I knew it in my bones—
and pieces of the universe are missing.
I feel the gears of this late afternoon
slip, cog by cog, even as I read.
"I'm old," we both complain,
half-laughing, oftener now.

Time serves you well. That face—
part Roman emperor, part Raimu—
nothing this side of Absence can undo.
Bliss, revulsion, your rare angers can
only carry through what's well begun.

When
I read your letters long ago
in that half-defunct
hotel in Magdalen Street
every word primed my nerves.
A geographical misery
composed of oceans, fogbound planes
and misdelivered cablegrams
lay round me, a Nova Zembla
only your live breath could unfreeze.
Today we stalk
in the raging desert of our thought
whose single drop of mercy is
each knows the other there.
Two strangers, thrust for life upon a rock,
may have at last the perfect hour of talk
that language aches for; still—
two minds, two messages.

Your brows knit into flourishes. Some piece
of mere time has you tangled there.
Some mote of history has flown into your eye.
Will nothing ever be the same,
even our quarrels take a different key,
our dreams exhume new metaphors?
The world breathes underneath our bed.
Don't look. We're at each other's mercy too.

Dear fellow-particle, electric dust
I'm blown with—ancestor
to what euphoric cluster—
see how particularity dissolves
in all that hints of chaos. Let one finger
hover toward you from There
and see this furious grain
suspend its dance to hang
beside you like your twin.

                                            (*SDL*, 45–46)

The poem "Storm Warnings" had been about keeping the storm out of the house. "A Marriage in the 'Sixties" takes place in that storm. It is a storm in which pieces of the world are blown around: a cog, a single drop, a rock, a mote, a particle of dust, a grain. What these tiny units of reality want is what the grit wanted in the other poem: to get into the house, to get into the eye of the poet, to get into the poem. "The world breathes underneath our bed," the poet writes. "Some mote of history has flown into your eye." At the end of the poem, the husband and wife recognize that they are also (to use Stevens's phrase) parts of the world. How are these parts related, the poet wonders. What new kinds of relationships are possible? The Nobel Prize in physics was given to Murray Gell-Mann in 1969 for his explanation of the relationships among the hundreds of subatomic particles that had been discovered during the preceding two decades. The attempt to find relationships among particles is also the subject of this poem.

David Kalstone writes that Rich, "working in a jagged present," is "always pitched toward the future and change," and the optimism of this poem (especially given its setting) is notable.[16] The elaborateness and elegance of Rich's syntax—her *happiness*—recall James Merrill in his scientific mode. Merrill writes, "And on the dimmest shore of consciousness / Polypeptides—in primeval thrall / To what new moon I wonder—rise and fall."[17] Rich writes, "Dear fellow-particle, electric dust / I'm blown with—ancestor / to what euphoric cluster." At the end of the poem, the wife asks the husband to see her not (in Blake's terms) as one of the "blind atoms of Democritus" but instead as a "furious grain." Rich will return to this image later, writing in "An Atlas of the Difficult World" that "each of us [is] now a driven grain" (*ADW*, 22). Rich's use of the word "grain" suggests that some of these "pieces of the universe" might be seeds. In "The Return of the Evening Grosbeaks" she had written, "We scatter seed." Now she is herself one of the scattered seeds.

There is reason for her to be optimistic: she has done part of what she set out to do; she has expanded domestic space to include the world outside the house. She has found her voice—it is the voice of someone who knows what the world looks like and can talk about it in ways that are not monotonously apprehensive but continually responsive, apprehending. New kinds of knowledge become available to her, political knowledge, for one. It is not a completely fresh way of looking at the world. Political knowledge is, for Rich, what poetic knowledge is, the knowledge that the world is in pieces, and political action is what a poem is, the attempt to build a better world from those pieces. Her poems of this period are powerful because she is herself one of the floating pieces. She has not yet acknowledged, though, that the same thing that has happened to the world is happening to language. "The language of past seasons / collapses," Audre Lorde writes.

> Step lightly all around us
> words are cracking
> off we drift
> separate and syllabic
> if we survive at all.[18]

Rich's poems do not yet fully acknowledge this "cracking off." The second is getting shorter, she tells us, and so are her lines—one of the lines in this poem has only one word. But although she has given up her stanza forms, her careful ironies and off rhymes, she hasn't yet found a new form that can represent her new perception of the world. The chaos of the world is entering houses and bodies, but the body of the *poem* is still protected from it.

She may be protecting the poem because she needs a place of rest, of safety. In a poem called "Double Monologue," she says, "I have wanted one thing: to know / simply as I know my name / at any given moment, where I stand" (*SDL*, 33). To write poems that take place inside houses is to write poems about thwarted conversation, emotional frustration. And the utopian houses, as she says in her poem "The Roofwalker," are still only "half- finished." She cannot yet live in them. In "The Roofwalker," she imagines a figure running along rooftops. Elizabeth Bishop in "The Man-Moth" imagines that figure crawling up the wall of a building. Neither of these surrogate figures can live inside buildings, yet both are fascinated by them, both move along the outside of them. Many of Rich's poems of this period are efforts to communicate her intimate knowledge of the inside (and now of the outside) of spaces she cannot occupy.

The title of her next book, *Necessities of Life,* suggests that Rich's poems are going to be characterized in part by their refusals. She wants to be read not just for what she says but for what she does not say and for the kind of language she refuses to use. Later, she worries that these refusals will create not a moral but "a stringent space," but it is imperative now that she create a space for her poems that is free of false speech. False speech, for Rich, means speech that perpetuates or participates in unequal power balances. It is not only a political question but an aesthetic one. It is important that there be a balance—for Rich, a power balance—between the prophetic and the domestic in her poetry. False speech is, in both cases, a form of violence, a threat to the balance that is so important to her work. In poem after poem, she says that she would rather write nothing than use false or "spoiled language." In a poem addressed to Emily Dickinson, she writes that the air

> buzzing with spoiled language
> sang in your ears
> of Perjury
>
> and in your half-cracked way you chose
> silence for entertainment
>   (*NOL,* 33)

The other poets in this study frequently choose spoiled language for entertainment. For the middle-aged Lowell, false speech is just another speech genre; he is curious to see what kind of music it can be made to provide. Ammons, in his folksy mode, exploits the dramatic possibilities of spoiled or false speech. Merrill is fascinated by the dramatic and linguistic possibilities of clichés. He says in an interview, "We *have* all these languages . . . clichés, polite circumlocutions . . . so why not use them?"[19] It is imperative for Rich that she not use them. The space she occupies will be as free of them as she can make it.

Meanwhile, she is certain that she needs only the "bare necessities." All that is necessary (for the making of poems, for the living of a life) is simply that authentic, serious, helpful versions of the prophetic and the domestic are always available to her (and, therefore, to her readers). Constant access to both is crucial, as is protection from false versions. What she wants is to be able to move freely and easily between the domestic and the prophetic. To have access to neither or to have access to one but not the other is to be disempowered both as a poet and as a political activist. In "To a Poet," she writes about the experience of being "with children in a house / where language floats and spins," and it is

a poem that is, like Audre Lorde's poem, about the drift of syllables.
These are the first two stanzas.

> Ice splits   under the metal
> shovel   another day
> hazed light off fogged panes
> cruelty of winter   landlocked   your life
> wrapped around you   in your twenties
> an old bathrobe   dragged down
> with milkstains   tearstains   dust
>
> Scraping eggcrust from the child's
> dried fish   skimming the skin
> from cooled milk   wringing diapers
> Language floats at the vanishing-point
> *incarnate*   breathes the fluorescent bulb
> *primary*   states the scarred grain of the floor
> and on the ceiling in torn plaster laughs   *imago*.
>
> (*DCL*, 15)

The angels chided the woman in "Snapshots of a Daughter-in Law,"
and the floating words seem *"to mock the woman in the kitchen in this
poem. The light bulb says *"incarnate,"* the kitchen floor says *"primary,"*
the ceiling says *"imago."* The adjectives and noun seem to be parts of a
prophetic language, but the words are isolated, about to vanish. Has
prophetic language scattered along with everything else? If so, she will
have to find the fragments and make a new one. Meanwhile, she is
afraid she will never get even *these* words into poems. These prophetic
words have the domestic as their source, but they mock the woman in
the kitchen with their unavailability. A reader has only to think of
Merrill's "Voices from Another World" to feel the heartbreaking difficulty of the task for the woman in the kitchen, to feel the odds against
her and the absurdity of her position. It is worth pointing out, though,
that the absurdity of her position and of theirs is the same absurdity.

In other poems, though, Rich (or her surrogate) does move quickly
and easily between the domestic and the prophetic. Rich refers, in the
course of the poem "Autumn Sequence," "to some burning bush or
maple" (*NOL*, 35). Her ability to move easily between the domestic and
the prophetic enables her to move with the same kind of facility
between her own imaginative space and the space of other writers. Rich
has the confidence now to return to the influences who were so powerful a presence in her first two books. She writes, "The old masters, the
old sources, / haven't a clue what we're about, / shivering here in the
half-dark 'sixties" (*Leaflets*, 15). In a poem called "Pieces," she writes,

> This morning: read Simone Weil
> on the loss of grace
>
> drank a glass of water
>
> remembered the dream that woke me:
>
> some one, some more than one
> battering into my room
> intent to kill me
>
> (*TWC*, 35)

Although she reads Simone Weil, what she really thinks about is the dream she had that morning. Even the austere and serious writing of Simone Weil is of limited use to her. In part, these lines are a belated response to the introduction that Auden wrote to her first book. "So long as the way in which we regard the world and feel about our existence remains in all essentials the same as that of our predecessors," Auden had written, "we must follow in their tradition; it would be just as dishonest for us to pretend that their style is inadequate to our needs as it would have been for them to be content with the style of the Victorians." Rich does not regard the world in the same way anymore, and now the old masters are useful only to the extent that they resemble or prefigure her. She begins to reimagine the prophetic landscapes of other poets, politicizing them. In her first book, she simply reproduced Eliot's prophetic landscape (along with his rhythms): "After the sunlight and the fiery vision / Leading us to a place of running water, / We came into a place by water altered" (*CEP*, 27). Now she does something more daring. Eliot calls the names of doomed cities in *The Waste Land*: "Jerusalem Athens Alexandria / Vienna London / Unreal."[20] Rich counters his litany with her own list: "*Biafra, Bangladesh, Boston, / Atlanta, Soweto, Beirut, Assam*" (*YNL*, 35). She does not add the word "unreal." Here, she shows how close—and how far—Eliot's sense of the prophetic is to her sense of the political. In other poems, she reimagines the playful as political. She calls Wallace Stevens the "Sinner of the Florida keys" and tells him, "you were our poet of revolution all along" (*TWC*, 21). She rewrites a famous poem by e. e. cummings. Here is cummings's poem.

> may i feel said he
> (i'll squeal said she
> just once said he)
> it's fun said she
>
> (may i touch said he
> how much said she

a lot said he)
why not said she

(let's go said he
not too far said she
what's too far said he
where you are said she)

may i stay said he
(which way said she
like this said he
if you kiss said she

may i move said he
is it love said she)
if you're willing said he
(but you're killing said she

but it's life said he
but your wife said she
now said he)
ow said she

(tiptop said he
don't stop said she
oh no said he)
go slow said she

(cccome? said he
ummm said she)
you're divine! said he
(you are Mine said she)[21]

In section 14 of "From an Old House in America," Rich writes,

But can't you see me as a human being
he said

What is a human being
she said

I try to understand
he said

what will you undertake
she said

will you punish me for history
he said

what will you undertake
she said

> *do you believe in collective guilt*
> he said
>
> *let me look in your eyes*
> she said.
>
> (*PSN*, 243)

Rich can move quickly and easily now between domestic and prophetic space and between her own space and the space of other writers. She is always looking for "new combinations, extrapolations." The phrase comes from Audre Lorde, who writes, "Sometimes we drug ourselves with dreams of new ideas. The head will save us. The brain alone will set us free. But there are no new ideas waiting in the wings to save us as women, as humans. There are only old and forgotten ones, new combinations, extrapolations and recognitions from within ourselves—along with the renewed courage to try them out."[22]

There are two spaces, though, between which Rich cannot easily move. The public and the private are both spaces where she is tempted to linger, to rest. This manifests itself in the difficulty she has in reimagining the work of two writers, Emily Dickinson and Robinson Jeffers. They are for her a continual provocation, representing the enormous attractions of solitude, of a mixture of the domestic and prophetic that is divorced from community, divorced from politics. In an essay on Dickinson, Rich writes that she "has increasingly struck me as a practical woman, exercising her gifts as she had to, making choices."[23] Here and elsewhere Rich is able to reimagine Dickinson as more pragmatic, more political than other poets have seen her. Some readers may sense the strain: the word "practical" feels as "off" associated with Dickinson as it does in Emerson's observation, quoted earlier. Readers may feel as well that Dickinson represents a power and occupies a space that is difficult to find words for, particularly when it is a space they want, in a sense, to find words *from*. Robinson Jeffers is a difficult problem as well. He is, Rich writes, "a poet for whose work I have a great deal of troubled and disturbed admiration."[24] It is not surprising that she is often tempted not to reimagine—not always to have to reimagine—but simply to *enter* the poetic space of Dickinson and Jeffers. There she would be protected from false speech. Her dilemma, though, is that she would at the same time be shut off from community, as they were.

Jorie Graham begins her poem "To the Reader" with the words, "I swear to you she wanted back into the shut, the slow."[25] Interpreting

this line in an interview, Graham says, "I think, in a way, the central impulse of each new book involves my wanting to go into a more moral
terrain—a terrain in which one is more accountable, and therefore in
which one has to become increasingly naked."[26] Rich too wants a more
moral terrain, does not want to go "back into the shut, the slow," back
into the houses of her first two books. Her solution is to make her
poetry *more* open, *more* quick. In the poems of this period, she begins to
let the disorder of the world not simply into the house, not simply into
the bodies of the people in her poems, but into the poems themselves.
In loosening the internal cohesion of her poems, she is, in a sense, taking away their last protection from the chaos outside them. In "A Marriage in the 'Sixties," she had written a poem about fellow-particles,
suspending their dance to hang beside each other for a moment. In
"Ghazals: Homage to Ghalib," a poem in *Leaflets*, she shows what that
experience might look like, might feel like. The *ghazal* is an Arabic verse
form that consists of a series of five independent but interconnected
couplets. In a note to the poem, Rich writes that "Each couplet [is] autonomous and independent of the others. The continuity and unity flow
from the associations and images playing back and forth among the
couplets in any single *ghazal*." In one of the sections of the poem, she
adapts the "how long" questions familiar from the Psalms to the constant fear felt by a member of the revolutionary underground. The section is called "7/24/68: ii."

> The friend I can trust is the one who will let me have my death.
> The rest are actors who want me to stay and further the plot.
>
> At the drive-in movie, above the PanaVision,
> beyond the projector beams, you project yourself, great Star.
>
> The eye that used to watch us is dead, but open.
> Sometimes I still have a sense of being followed.
>
> How long will we be waiting for the police?
> How long must I wonder which of my friends would hide me?
>
> Driving at night I feel the Milky Way
> streaming above me like the graph of a cry.
>
> (*Leaflets*, 70)

There are hints of rhymes here in the final words of the last three couplets, but in general the connections in this poem are much looser than
they are in her earlier poems. "The notes for the poem are the only
poem," she writes in "Images for Godard" (*TWC*, 49). What connects

the couplets and the sections of the poem is an instinct for the most extreme version of each of her states of feeling; the excitement of the poem comes from her movement between these states.

In "Shooting Script," a long poem in fourteen sections from *The Will to Change,* she returns to the experiment. The use of couplets in the ghazals implied (as did her lines in "A Marriage in the 'Sixties") a lingering faith in some kind of cohesion. In "Shooting Script" she uses single sentences. This is the first section.

We were bound on the wheel of an endless conversation.

Inside this shell, a tide waiting for someone to enter.

A monologue waiting for you to interrupt it.

A man wading into the surf. The dialogue of the rock with the breaker.

The wave changed instantly by the rock; the rock changed by the wave returning over and over.

The dialogue that lasts all night or a whole lifetime.

A conversation of sounds melting constantly into rhythms.

A shell waiting for you to listen.

A tide that ebbs and flows against a deserted continent.

A cycle whose rhythms begins to change the meanings of words.

A wheel of blinding waves of light, the spokes pulsing out from where we hang together in the turning of an endless conversation.

The meaning that searches for its word like a hermit crab.

A monologue that waits for one listener.

An ear filled with one sound only.

A shell penetrated by meaning.

(TWC, 53)

Although the lines are isolated on the page, Rich, characteristically, complicates the sense of isolation by making conversation the topic of many of the sentences. I will return later in this chapter to the importance of conversation to Rich. Poems like "Ghazals: Homage to Ghalib" and "Shooting Script," which represent the limits of her experiments with form, are still exciting examples of a period sensibility, connected as much to the work of filmmakers like Godard as to the work of poets like Ginsberg and Ammons and Lowell. These poems would influence Jorie Graham as well as the artists Barbara Kruger and Jenny Holzer. At the same time, as Willard Spiegelman points out, "her inheritance from the Blake of *The Marriage of Heaven and Hell,* especially the Proverbs of

Hell, . . . prove[s] how apparently unconnected fragments, in this case epigrams, may embody deeper connections."[27]

Rich's experiments with lineation have made her more conscious of how much her voice has changed since her first two books. She describes that change in "November 1968."

> Stripped
> you're beginning to float free
> up through the smoke of brushfires
> and incinerators
> the unleafed branches won't hold you
> nor the radar aerials
>
> You're what the autumn knew would happen
> after the last collapse
> of primary color
> once the last absolutes were torn to pieces
> you could begin
>
> How you broke open, what sheathed you
> until this moment
> I know nothing about it
> my ignorance of you amazes me
> now that I watch you
> starting to give yourself away
> to the wind.
>
> (*TWC*, 11)

Rich writes, "I watch you / starting to give yourself away / to the wind." Ammons, in "Small Song," writes,

> The reeds give
> way to the
>
> wind and give
> the wind away[28]

Both poets, at the delayed beginnings of their careers, do not know what has happened or what will happen. Their relationship to change, though, is not one of resistance but participation. Rich's poem is optimistic, yet there is, at the same time, something unsettling about it. What is she divesting herself of? "Stripped" is the word Merrill uses in his trilogy for the (irreversible?) process of becoming less human. Rich tends to take terms she has used about herself and (later) use them about her readers. In "An Atlas of the Difficult World," she addresses her reader: "I know you are reading this poem because there is nothing else left to read / there where you have landed, stripped as you are" (*ADW*, 26). By 1991 she will imagine her reader—as she has (by then) imagined herself—as having landed. But in 1971, Rich is floating free, floating upward, and she is no position, as it were, to say if her readers are doing the same. In "The Wild Sky," Rich writes, "that last frontier remains, the vertical." More and more of Rich's poems are (like "November 1968") about that vertical movement. It is significant that when she tries (as she continues to do) to imagine a space to speak from, what she imagines is various levels of elevation. In two poems— "Snapshots of a Daughter-in-Law" and "To the Woods"—she compares herself to a helicopter. In "Orion" she imagines a surrogate figure not racing along the rooftops now but shining in the sky. There too she re- vises the landscape of someone else's poem, Stevens's "Nuances of a Theme by Williams." His poem begins by quoting the Williams poem.

> *It's a strange courage*
> *you give me, ancient star:*
>
> *Shine alone in the sunrise*
> *toward which you lend no part*!
>
> I
>
> Shine alone, shine nakedly, shine like bronze,
> that reflects neither my face nor any inner part
> of my being, shine like fire, that mirrors nothing.
>
> II
>
> Lend no part to any humanity that suffuses
> you in its own light.
> Be not chimera of morning,
> Half-man, half-star.
> Be not an intelligence,
> Like a widow's bird
> Or an old horse.[29]

Rich may feel, at this stage, half-woman, half-star. Here is her poem "Orion."

> Far back when I went zig-zagging
> through tamarack pastures
> you were my genius, you
> my cast-iron Viking, my helmed
> lion-heart king in prison.
> Years later now you're young
>
> my fierce half-brother, staring
> down from that simplified west
> your breast open, your belt dragged down

by an oldfashioned thing, a sword
the last bravado you won't give over
though it weighs you down as you stride

and the stars in it are dim
and maybe have stopped burning.
But you burn, and I know it;
as I throw back my head to take you in
an old transfusion happens again:
divine astronomy is nothing to it.

Indoors I bruise and blunder,
break faith, leave ill enough
alone, a dead child born in the dark.
Night cracks up over the chimney,
pieces of time, frozen geodes
come showering down in the grate.

A man reaches behind my eyes
and finds them empty
a woman's head turns away
from my head in the mirror
children are dying my death
and eating crumbs of my life.

Pity is not your forte.
Calmly you ache up there
pinned aloft in your crow's nest,
my speechless pirate!
You take it all for granted
and when I look you back

it's with a starlike eye
shooting its cold and egotistical spear
where it can do least damage.
Breathe deep! No hurt, no pardon
out here in the cold with you
you with your back to the wall.

(*Leaflets*, 11–12)

This poem, with its six-line stanzas, recalls the orderly early poems, but it is a poem about courage rather than cowardice. "Indoors I bruise and blunder," she writes, echoing H.D.'s lines in "The Walls Do Not Fall":

Our bodies blunder

through doors twisted on hinges,
and the lintels slant

cross-wise[30]

H.D. writes about living through the London blitz. Rich wants to remind the reader of the reality of invisible domestic explosions while at
the same time evoking the courage of the people of that time.

Rich is preoccupied with courage, where it comes from and the uses
to which it can be put. Like Williams and Stevens, she gets a "strange
courage" from her constellation. As she puts it, "an old transfusion
happens again." Rich uses Orion in the way Stevens warned us against
using such figures—as a symbol, as inspiration. Stevens does not want
the star to reflect any inner part of his being, but Orion *does* reflect an
inner part of Rich's being. Orion, with his sword, "an oldfashioned
thing," is an image for Rich of the poet she wants to be, the poet who is,
like Blake, prophetic and political at once ("I will not cease from mental fight / nor let my sword sleep in my hand"). Later, in her poem
"Sources," she writes,

> It's an oldfashioned, an outrageous thing
> to believe one has a "destiny"
>
> —a thought often peculiar to those
> who possess privilege—
>
> (*YNL*, 17)

Anyone, for Rich, may have a destiny. Orion is useful to her because he
(or some version of him) is available to everyone.

"Orion" is not, though, a poem about everyone. She says to Orion
that she is "out here in the cold with you"—that is, not in the house, not
even outside the house but up in the sky with him, her back to the wall.
Rich is unusual among prophetic poets for the frequency with which
she enskies herself. She has, in "Orion," enacted the movement of the
poem "Novella," leaving the house for the star, and she is not interested
in reversing the movement. Although she can move easily between the
prophetic and the domestic, in the poems of the sixties and seventies
she makes the move from the domestic to the prophetic more often
than the reverse. "Night cracks up over the chimney, / pieces of time,
frozen geodes / come showering down in the grate." She knows how
to make use of these pieces now. Her eye, for example, can be like one
of the pieces, it can be "starlike." "*Save yourself; others you cannot save,*"
the angels had told her in "Snapshots of a Daughter-in-Law." Here she
writes,

> A man reaches behind my eyes
> and finds them empty
> a woman's head turns away

from my head in the mirror
children are dying my death
and eating crumbs of my life.

She knows how to make use of these pieces—she can make poems of them—but her children cannot. She gets parts of the world, "pieces of time," and her children gets "crumbs" of her life. Rich has said that some of the phrases in "Orion" come from an essay by Gottfried Benn called "Artists and Old Age." Benn writes, "Don't lose sight of the cold and egotistical element in your mission . . . With your back to the wall, care-worn and weary, in the gray light of the void, read Job and Jeremiah and keep going."[31] Advice to the contemporary prophetic poet.

Rich takes the advice and keeps going, writing more poems about "levitating into the night sky." The phrase is from "Planetarium":

A woman in the shape of a monster
A monster in the shape of a woman
the skies are full of them

A woman   'in the snow
among the Clocks and instruments
or measuring the ground with poles'

in her 98 years to discover
8 comets

she whom the moon ruled
like us
levitating into the night sky
riding the polished lenses

Galaxies of women, there
doing penance for impetuousness
ribs chilled
in those spaces   of the mind

An eye
          'virile, precise and absolutely certain'
          from the mad webs of Uranusborg
                              encountering the Nova

every impulse of light exploding
from the core
as life flies out of us

          Tycho whispering at last
          'Let me not seem to have lived in vain'

What we see, we see
and seeing is changing

the light that shrivels a mountain
and leaves a man alive

Heartbeat of the pulsar
heart sweating through my body

    The radio impulse
    pouring in from Taurus

    I am bombarded   yet I stand

I have been standing all my life in the
direct path of a battery of signals
the most accurately transmitted most
untranslatable language in the universe
I am a galactic cloud so deep   so invo-
luted that a light wave could take 15
years to travel through me   And has
taken   I am an instrument in the shape
of a woman trying to translate pulsations
into images   for the relief of the body
and the reconstruction of the mind.

                                        (*TWC*, 13–14)

The poem begins by suggesting that the skies are full of women. The space of community that might mediate between the house and the stars has been moved up into the sky. By the end of the poem, community has been forgotten. No version of the domestic or of the everyday or of the human or of the ordinary can survive in this kind of space. Rich is, here, a purely prophetic poet. In "Orion," she writes, "Indoors I bruise and blunder, / break faith." Outdoors—up in the sky—she has a strong faith. "Planetarium" ends with one of Rich's most memorable descriptions of her project. She is "an instrument in the shape / of a woman trying to translate pulsations / into images." In "To a Poet," Rich suggests that language "floats at the vanishing point." In this poem she stations herself at that vanishing point, at the place where pulsations become language, become "images." Rich writes, "I am bombarded yet I stand." She adapts a phrase from a song meant to be sung in unison (in this case, a union song, "We Shall Not Be Moved"), but she moves it into the first person; it is a song for herself alone. There are some precedents for this moment. H.D. compared herself to a telegraph receiving station, a switchboard, a radio.[32] But the strangeness of Rich's poem can be emphasized by comparing it to the moment in *The Changing Light at Sandover* when Merrill gives us the actual voice of God.

May we ask questions? HUSH   WE STRAIN TO HEAR
Now, ripple within ripple on black water,
O O O O O O O O O O
Pulse of the galactic radio
Tuned then to mortal wavelength in mid-phrase:

IVE BROTHERS HEAR ME BROTHERS SIGNAL ME
ALONE IN MY NIGHT BROTHERS DO YOU WELL
I AND MINE HOLD IT BACK BROTHERS I AND
MINE SURVIVE BROTHERS HEAR ME SIGNAL ME
DO YOU WELL I AND MINE HOLD IT BACK I
ALONE IN MY NIGHT BROTHERS I AND MINE
SURVIVE BROTHERS DO YOU WELL I ALONE
IN MY NIGHT I HOLD IT BACK I AND MINE
SURVIVE BROTHERS SIGNAL ME IN MY NIGHT
I AND MINE HOLD IT BACK AND WE SURVIVE.[33]

Merrill imagines God describing himself as "ALONE IN MY NIGHT." Rich is alone in hers. There are no fellow-particles with her. Although the sky is full of women, there is only the prophetic figure at the end of the poem. There are "brothers" in Merrill's passage and sisters in Rich's poem, but they are not actually present. In Merrill's lines there is a sense of isolation and endurance, the tone of the doomed Arctic explorer. Yenser calls this a "proud lonely survivor's message."[34] This voice too might say, "I am bombarded yet I stand." Rich hopes to be a useful example here, but her isolation is apparent too, and with that isolation comes the deep strangeness of this prophetic voice. We use "prophet" now often to mean that someone has a passionate political agenda. Rich is that kind of prophet, certainly, but she is this kind, too. In poems like "Planetarium," she reminds us of what Heschel means when he says that the "we and the prophet have no language in common" and that the prophet "employs notes one octave too high for our ears."[35] After hearing the voice of God, JM says, "Life itself speaking. Song of the blue whale / Alone in Space? Bravery, vertigo, / Frontier austerities . . ."

Rich continues in the seventies to write poems of frontier austerities. And she continues to write poems of "bravery" and "vertigo." She imagines herself—in two poems—enskied in an airplane and looking down at the earth.

Sometimes, gliding at night
in a plane over New York City
I have felt like some messenger

> called to enter, called to engage
> this field of light and darkness.
>   (*YNL*, 36)

"A grandiose idea," she adds, "born of flying." In *Diving into the Wreck*, she has a poem called "Merced," the Spanish word for "grace." There too she imagines herself on a plane. In "Planetarium," she writes about the "reconstruction of the mind." In "Merced," she worries that the pieces are getting put back together in the wrong way.

> Taking off in a plane
> I look down at the city
> which meant life to me, not death
> and think that somewhere there
> a cold center, composed
> of pieces of human beings
> metabolized, restructured
> by a process they do not feel
> is spreading in our midst
> and taking over our minds
> a thing that feels neither guilt
> nor rage: that is unable
> to hate, therefore to love.
>   (*DITW*, 36–37)

She writes, "I wish there were somewhere actual we could stand." She is "weary," to use Gottfried Benn's language, of "the gray light of the void" and wants to imagine herself on an elevation on the *earth*. What about a mountain? Keats (in his poems from the Scotland trip) imagined climbing a mountain as a comic act. Rich does not want to be playful, but she also does not want to be "grandiose." The idea of a communal enterprise is useful as a strategy to avoid the grandiose. "Phantasia for Elvira Shatayev" is written, as she tells us, "in the voice of the leader of a women's climbing team, all of whom died in a storm on Lenin Peak, August 1974." The poem ends with these words:

> In the diary as the wind   began to tear
> at the tents over us   I wrote:
> *We know now we have always been in danger*
> *down in our separateness*
> *and now up here together   but till now*
> *we had not touched our strength*
>
> In the diary torn from my fingers I had written:
> *What does love mean*
> *what does it mean   "to survive"*

> *A cable of blue fire ropes our bodies*
> *burning together in the snow   We will not live*
> *to settle for less   We have dreamed of this*
> *all of our lives.*
>
> (DCL, 4–6)

There is a less anxious relationship here between the "I" and the "we." Still, Rich calls the poem a "phantasia," and her readers may feel that she is setting too many poems on the heights. She does write poems set in the street (part of "Merced" is set in the street), and other poems are set in other ordinary places. Writing about America in "An Atlas of the Difficult World," she writes, "Where do we see it from is the question" (*ADW*, 6). The problem, she comes to see, may be her elevated language. Lowell, in *The Dolphin*, refers to his own "perfunctory all-service rhythms."[36] Rich is beginning to feel that her own rhythms may be "all-service" and "perfunctory." The flat statements of her poems of the midsixties have become heightened, part of a dream language rather than a common language. In "Transcendental Etude," she writes,

> But there come times—perhaps this is one of them—
> when we have to take ourselves more seriously or die;
> when we have to pull back from the incantations,
> rhythms we've moved to thoughtlessly,
> and disenthrall ourselves, bestow
> ourselves to silence, or a severer listening, cleansed
> of oratory, formulas, choruses, laments, static
> crowding the wires.
>
> (DCL, 74–75)

Like the other poets in this study, she wants to be "the speaker who also listens" (*ADW*, 11). In "Shooting Script," there was "an ear filled with one sound only"—that is surely a fate to be avoided. Another poet might feel that the way to disenthrall herself would be to allow more colloquial rhythms, more lightness, more verbal exuberance into her poetry, but, as the references to "silence" and "severer listening" suggest, Rich suspects that she has not been taking her domestic life, her everyday life, seriously enough.

She is making corrections, changing "I" to "we," trying to stay out of the sky, as congenial a space as that might be. "Nothing could keep him / off the mountains," Ammons writes in "He Held Radical Light." Rich begins to write poems in which, though she is no longer in the sky, she is still a solitary figure. When she says "we" in the passage from "Transcendental Etude" ("we have to take ourselves more seriously or die"), the "we" sounds strained. I referred earlier to the section of her poem "Merced" in which she describes herself walking down the street. She wants, in that poem, to face ordinary people, but she can hardly bear it. The notion that the American poem in particular has to include "other people" was given force by Whitman and has frequently, since then, found expression in unexpected places. There is a powerful version of it, for example, at the beginning of Wallace Stevens's poem "Of Modern Poetry":

> The poem of the mind in the act of finding
> What will suffice. It has not always had
> To find: the scene was set; it repeated what
> Was in the script.
>   Then the theater was changed
> To something else. Its past was a souvenir.
> It has to be living, to learn the speech of the place.
> It has to face the men of the time and to meet
> The women of the time.[37]

In this passage from "Merced," Rich tries to face the men of the time and to meet the women of the time. It is not pleasant or easy.

> For weeks now a rage
> has possessed my body, driving
> now out upon men and women
> now inward upon myself
> Walking Amsterdam Avenue
> I find myself in tears
> without knowing which thought
> forced water to my eyes
> To speak to another human
> becomes a risk
>   (*DITW*, 36)

Why can't she, like Jeffers, simply learn to hate people? Or, like Ammons, learn to ignore them? Many of her poems are about her desire to "float free" of all the other parts of the world, her desire simply to *be* "cold and egotistical." In "Orion," she said she wanted to go where she could "do least damage." The problem—it is a problem that haunts her—is that she would not, in such a place, be able to do any good. There might be a lever and a place to stand, but there wouldn't be any people, there would be no world to move. Too much austerity, too much isolation may not, in fact, be a kind of "severer listening" but, instead, mere theatricality. May Sarton, in her journals, particularly in *Journal of a Solitude*, writes about these questions, though she does so in a manner that can strike readers as histrionic. The theatrical, the self-dramatizing is the version of "false speech" to which Rich feels most susceptible.

> The longer I live the more I mistrust
> theatricality, the false glamour cast
> by performance, the more I know its poverty beside
> the truths we are salvaging from
> the splitting-open of our lives.
>
> (*DCL*, 74)

Many of her poems in the seventies are about the movement toward and then the turning back from theatrical spaces of "silence" and "severer listening." At the end of a long poem called "Turning the Wheel," she writes about deciding not to drive to the Grand Canyon.

> Today I turned the wheel   refused that journey
> I was feeling too alone on the open plateau
> of piñon juniper   world beyond time
> of rockflank spread around me   too alone
> and too filled with you   with whom I talked for hours
> driving up from the desert   though you were far away
> as I talk to you all day   whatever day
>
> (*AWP*, 59)

Instead, the poem is about a memory of conversation. Rich has a poem in *A Wild Patience Has Taken Me This Far* called "What Is Possible":

> A clear night   if the mind were clear
>
> If the mind were simple, if the mind were bare
> of all but the most classic necessities:
> wooden spoon   knife   mirror
> cup   lamp   chisel
> a comb passing through hair beside a window
> a sheet
>   thrown back by the sleeper.
>
> (*AWP*, 23)

Stevens's poem "Of Modern Poetry" ends with the lines:

> It must
> Be the finding of a satisfaction, and may
> Be of a man skating, a woman dancing, a woman
> Combing. The poem of the act of the mind.

Rich gives us, at the beginning of her poem, the woman combing. It is one of the things that is supposed to suffice, and it would suffice, Rich writes, "if the mind were simple." The poem continues:

> A clear night in which two planets
> seem to clasp each other   in which the earthly grasses
> shift like silk in starlight
>   If the mind were clear
> and if the mind were simple   you could take this mind
> this particular state   and say
> *This is how I would live if I could choose:*
> *this is what is possible*
>
>   (*AWP*, 23)

She can imagine (as she did in her early poem "For the Conjunction of Two Planets") that planets are clasping each other. But this is an odd, almost metaphysical way to represent relatedness. And where is she standing that she can call the grass "earthly"? ("Where do we see it from is the question.") Whitman has many odd adjectives for grass in "Song of Myself" but none as odd as Rich's. In another poem, Rich writes, "Writing these words in the woods, / I feel like a traitor to my friends, / even to my enemies" (*NOL*, 11). In the poem "Incipience," she writes about lying awake in the middle of the night "at an hour when nothing can be done / to further any decision" (*DITW*, 11). The poem "What Is Possible" is about a *place* where nothing can be done to further any decision. The poem begins again:

> A clear night.   But the mind
> of the woman imagining all this   the mind
> that allows all this to be possible
> is not clear as the night
> is never simple   cannot clasp
> its truths as the transiting planets clasp each other
> does not so easily
>   work free from remorse
> does not so easily
>   manage the miracle
> for which mind is famous
>   or used to be famous
> does not at will become abstract and pure
>
> this woman's mind
>
> does not even will that miracle
> having a different mission
>   in the universe

If the mind were simple   if the mind were bare
it might resemble a room   a swept interior
but how could this now be possible

given the voices of the ghost-towns
their tiny and vast configurations
needing to be deciphered
       the oracular night
with its densely working sounds

If it could ever come down to anything like
a comb passing through hair beside a window

no more than that
     a sheet
     thrown back by the sleeper
but the mind
of the woman thinking this   is wrapped in battle
is on another mission
a stalk of grass   dried feathery weed   rooted in snow
in frozen air stirring   a fierce wand graphing

Her finger also tracing
pages of a book
knowing better than the poem she reads
knowing through the poem
       through ice-feathered panes
the winter
    flexing its talons
the hawk-wind
     poised to kill.

             (*AWP*, 23–25)

She is one of the "separate minds" now, but that mind is not simple and clear. It is less and less easy, she says, to become "abstract and pure." This is one of the poems that marks a move away from the severe abstraction that had marked her poems since her third book.

I said at the outset that conversation would act as a kind of hybrid speech genre for her. It is not politics (as it is for Lowell) because politics for Rich limits the prophetic and the domestic and makes them mean, in any given poem, one thing, both in themselves and in relation to each other. What she most misses in these abstract, pure spaces is conversation. At the end of "Turning the Wheel," she pulled back from the Grand Canyon because of her memory of an ongoing conversation. In *Day by Day*, Lowell writes, "My thinking is talking to you"; there is the same sense of the connection between thinking and relationship in

Rich's poetry.[38] Muriel Rukeyser, whom Rich admires, has a (once much anthologized) poem called "Effort at Speech Between Two People." And Rich often represents conversation in her poetry as effortful. One of her most famous poems is called "Trying to Talk with a Man." Conversation is the place, though, from which Rich expects most of her happiness. In "A Marriage in the 'Sixties," she had imagined "the perfect hour of talk / that language aches for." At the end of "Cartographies of Silence," she writes, "what in fact I keep choosing // are these words, these whispers, conversations / from which time after time the truth breaks moist and green" (*DCL*, 20). She knows, as she writes in "Cartographies of Silence," that "Language cannot do everything," but no other kind of language in her poems can do as much as conversation. In a prose passage of a poem for her husband (who had killed himself), she writes, "no person, trying to take responsibility for her or his identity, should have to be so alone" (*YNL*, 25). Rich shares Bunyan's sense of conversation as a way for pilgrims to "brake their hearts" to each other and to guide and correct each other.

Conversation can be valued so intensely because it is, apart from everything else, a way of being useful. Rich imagines, for example, that she is having an ongoing conversation with her readers. Many poets have phrases they characteristically use when addressing their readers. Whitman says, "Whoever you are, to you endless announcements!"[39] Rich says, "I wanted to choose words that even you / would have to be changed by" (*Leaflets*, 42). There are readers who have heard all the news from all the poets and have come away disappointed—those are the readers she wants. In "An Atlas of the Difficult World," she writes, "I know you are reading this poem because there is nothing else left to read" (*ADW*, 26). Because success came to her early, she never imagines herself as someone who is not heard. Audre Lorde writes:

> there is a timbre of voice
> that comes from not being heard
> and knowing you are not being
> heard.[40]

That tone is absent from Rich's poetry. In an early poem, "The Lag," she says, "With you it is still the middle of the night," and she ends the poem with the words,

> My words
> reach you as through a telephone

> where some submarine echo of my voice
> blurts knowledge you can't use.
>
> (*CEP*, 190)

Rich's greatest fear, again, is that she will not be useful. Conversations are useful to her because they give her—momentarily—a space to stand. She is in relation to another person; she is standing in relation to that person in a space that is not theatrical but intimate. What she wants to avoid, as I said, is condescension. Aaron Kramer, in a book about nineteenth-century American prophetic poets, offers one version of the prophetic poet: "No matter how high and aloof his tower, the Truest Prophet is he who loves his fellows, who peers more deeply into their memories and dreams than they themselves do."[41] Rich has been tempted by this mode but understands the dangers of it. There is also the sense more and more in her work that she would like her readers to have access to their *own* prophetic language. Each of us is a driven grain, each of us has a task. This fact helps to keep the idea of conversation unpredictable. What she is listening to when she listens to people may be prophetic speech. Thomas Couser writes, "The ultimate ideal toward which the [prophetic] tradition points is . . . like that of the Old Testament prophets, a community in which prophecy is no longer necessary because each individual is his own prophet."[42] Anybody who has thought about the relationship between solitude and community will have imagined *this* kind of community as a possible solution.

But to conclude by invoking "conversation" would be sentimental, a humanist, comforting gesture, and not faithful to Rich's sense of her mission. She is interested in conversation most of all because it is a way of bringing the prophetic into relation with the everyday, the domestic, the human, the ordinary where it is not predictable which voice the poet will take on. Many poets, many people, might give up the prophetic voice as too scary, too estranging. But neither Rich's politics nor her aesthetic instincts will allow her to abandon that voice. Like Ammons, she might say (though we can hear the different resonance it must have in her voice), "I would give up nothing / if I had my way."

She senses that the prophetic voice in some way belongs to her. But how? In what sense? It becomes important to her to find out. Rich, in her poems of the eighties, is increasingly aware that she will not completely trust their usefulness until she knows the source of both her prophetic and domestic voices. "Poetry never stood a chance / of standing outside history," she writes (*YNL*, 33). She does not want to stand outside her own history either but to enter it. Are there sources of her authority within that history? In her early poem, "The Kursaal at Interlaaken," she had written about "days where we speak all languages but our own" (*CEP*, 8). To be eclectic, to move randomly among sources of authority, obliviously, hoping to be useful— that would be unserious. She wants, after all, to be useful to other poets as well who might be engaged with similar problems. Her early work showed an unguarded approach to her influences, and in her later work she had often taken an experimental or parodic approach. Now she wants to take a more serious approach. In *A Wild Patience Has Taken Me This Far,* she has a poem called "Integrity." The dictionary definition she uses as an epigraph ("the quality or state of being complete; unbroken condition; entirety") suggests, with its three incomplete sentences, that even a definition of integrity cannot come in an "unbroken condition." Integrity is, nevertheless, an idea that is more and more important to her. In her poetry of the sixties and seventies Rich was content to be one of the floating parts of the world. She might hide from the other parts, she might float higher than the other parts, but she was still just a floating fragment. Now she asks herself, What was she a fragment of? In her poem "Sources" from *Your Native Land, Your Life,* she explicitly questions the source of her own authority.

> *From where?*   The voice asks coldly.
>
> This is the voice in cold morning air
> that pierces dreams.   *From where does your strength come?*
>
> Old things . . .
>
>   (*YNL,* 5)

This is a self-mystifying, a theatrical answer. She is having recourse to an antiquity that, as she writes in "A Marriage in the 'Sixties," is only "solid-seeming." The voice keeps repeating the question. As "Sources," which is twenty-four pages long and divided into twenty-three sections, continues, she begins to try to answer the question seriously. Possible sources are imagined. She does not look, at first, inside her own private history but into New England history, the history of the Puritans.

> Why has my imagination stayed
> northeast with the ones who stayed
>
> Are there spirits in me, diaspora-driven
> that wanted to lodge somewhere
>
> hooked into the "New" Englanders who hung on
> here in this stringent space
>
> believing their Biblical language
> their harping on righteousness?
>
> (*YNL*, 11)

This "stringent space" is not hers. She is not actually a seventeenth-century Puritan preacher. What about other possible sources of her authority? She wonders about the Native Americans in New England.

> is the passion I connect with in this air
> trace of the original
>
> existences that knew this place
> is the region still trying to speak with them
>
> is this light a language
> the shudder of this aspen-grove a way
>
> of sending messages
> the white mind barely intercepts.
>
> (*YNL*, 14)

These messages cannot be intercepted by her; she is not standing in the direct line of them. In other poems, she offers other possible sources of authority, showing the reader "figures of ecstatic women striding / to the sibyl's den or the Eleusinian cave" (*DCL*, 28). In another poem, a voice comes over the radio: "a woman's voice singing old songs / with new words, with a quiet bass, a flute / plucked and fingered by women outside the law" (*DCL*, 31). But she can only catch—can only offer— tantalizing glimpses of these figures. What about the feminists of the nineteenth century? In the poem "Heroines," she addresses them. (The "you" is plural.)

> Your mind burns
> not like the harbor beacon
> but like a fire
> of fiercer origin
> you begin speaking out
> and a great gust of freedom

<pre>
                              rushes in with your words
            yet still you speak
                        in the shattered language
                                    of a partial vision
            You draw your long skirts
                          deviant
                                    across the nineteenth century
            registering injustice
                          failing to make it whole
            How can I fail to love
                          your clarity and fury
            how can I give you
                        all your due
                                    take courage from your courage
            honor your exact
                        legacy as it is
            recognizing
                    as well
                        that it is not enough?
</pre>

                                                        (*AWP*, 35–36)

The visual difference between this poem and "Storm Warnings" is striking. But this poem, too, is about a kind of ineffectuality. "Heroines" is, in part, about the drama of the lines sometimes making it all the way to the edge of the page and sometimes falling short. It is as if Rich wants them to go the distance and they can't. She tells the heroines of the nineteenth century that their minds "burn." It is what she told Orion: "you burn, and I know it." She knows that she herself burns, that she has a mission. Worried that her voice will lose power if she does not discover its source, she returns to the moment when she first experienced a sense of mission. Now, at last, she is inside her own personal history. In section 20 of "Sources," she writes,

> The faithful drudging child
> the child at the oak desk whose penmanship,
> hard work, style will win her prizes
> becomes the woman with a mission, not to win prizes
> but to change the laws of history.
> How she gets this mission
> is not clear, how the boundaries of perfection
> explode, leaving her cheekbone grey with smoke
> a piece of her hair singed off, her shirt
> spattered with earth . . . Say that she grew up in a house
> with talk of books, ideal societies—
> she is gripped by a blue, a foreign air,

> a desert absolute: dragged by the roots of her own will
> into another scene of choices.
>
> (*YNL*, 23)

This is the story of her career: the style of her early work won her prizes, and then she became "the woman with a mission, not to win prizes / but to change the laws of history."

But the question returns. How did she get the mission? In "November 1968," she writes,

> How you broke open, what sheathed you
> until this moment
> I know nothing about it
> my ignorance of you amazes me

In section 20 of "Sources" she is, at one moment, in a house and, in the next moment, in "a desert absolute." Rich still does not know how to put these scenes into relation; she does not know how they are connected. The reader remembers the voice of the angels in the sound of the coffeepot banging into the sink and the prophetic language floating at the vanishing point in the kitchen. What the poet remembers, what her readers remember, is that the prophetic and the domestic are always already in conversation in life. The conversations between people in her poems are often, in a sense, underwritten by that other conversation. Rich wants to tell the readers what she has heard when she has listened in. The task of the poet is to make those conversations audible to us.

In a poem in *Leaflets*, Rich had written, "I am thinking how we can use what we have / to invent what we need" (56). She now begins to write more about her father and mother. Almost every time she has mentioned her father in her work she has associated him with versions of a biblical voice: "in the booklined room / . . . the Jewish father reads and smokes and teaches / Ecclesiastes, Proverbs, the Song of Songs" (*TP*, 4). She had avoided thinking of her father as a "source" because he seemed like one of the patriarchs. How can Rich get what she needs from him? Helen Sword writes, "Male prophetic poets, even when making unconventional visionary claims, can draw upon established prophetic traditions for authority and justification, whether by echoing biblical cadences, by employing images associated with classical prophecy, or simply by introducing a thematics of privilege. Female poets, however, are likely to regard tradition and authority more as dangerous adversaries than as appropriate allies."[43] The fact that Rich's father has an ambivalent relation to his Judaism gives the poet,

in a sense, something to do. She realizes that her father, too, is a floating fragment. She refers to her father's world as a "floating world of
the assimilated." Her strength comes in part from something that will
never be fully available to her. At the same time, she can have her own
imaginative relationship to her father's world. She does not have to
think of Judaism as an ideology that she must either accept or reject; instead, she can think of Judaism—and, specifically, the prophetic books
of the Bible—as a poetic resource she can increasingly make use of.
This does not mean she begins to imagine herself in the biblical landscapes she had undermined in her early parodies and revisions. In fact,
she continues to revise them. In "The Desert as Garden of Paradise,"
she writes,

> Where it all stands clear you come to love
> the place you are:
> *the bundle of bare sticks soaked*
> *with resin*
> always, and never, a bush on fire
> *the blue sky without tale or text*
> *and without meaning*
> *the great swing of the horizontal circle*
> Miriam, Aaron, Moses
> are somewhere else, marching
> You learn to live without prophets
> without legends
> to live just where you are
> your burning bush, your seven-branched candlestick
> the ocotillo in bloom
>
> (*TP*, 30)

"You learn to live without prophets," she writes. She means that if you
have never learned to live or to write *without* using prophetic speech,
then you are going to sound inhuman and therefore unhelpful when
you do use it. Knowing this, she begins to use the voices of the biblical
prophets more and more freely in her work.

What are the sources of the domestic component of her voice? She remembers her mother now. In "Solfeggietto," a poem in *Time's Power*,
she remembers the piano lessons her mother gave her. Although the
daughter was, as usual, "faithful and drudging," she never learned to
play the piano in the way her mother wanted her to. She addresses her
mother:

> what I remember isn't lessons
> not Bach or Brahms or Mozart
> but the rented upright in the summer rental

> *One Hundred Best-Loved Songs* on the piano rack
> And so you played, evenings   and so we sang
> "Steal Away" and "Swanee River,"
> "Swing Low," and most of all
> "Mine Eyes Have Seen the Glory of the Coming of the Lord"
> How we sang out the chorus   how I loved
> *the watchfires of the hundred circling camps*
> and *truth is marching on* and *let us die to make men free.*
>   (*TP*, 4)

She wants, as she said in "Heroines," to "honor your exact / legacy as it is." The poem begins by evoking the singing of familiar songs in a domestic situation, though the situation is undermined by the fact that both piano and house are rented. Then the songs shift: they are singing "Mine Eyes Have Seen the Glory of the Coming of the Lord." Mother and daughter have moved into prophetic language. The poem "The Middle-Aged" ended with the words, "with how much left unsaid." In this poem, she writes, "How we sang out the chorus how I loved / *the watchfires of the hundred circling camps.*" If much is left unsaid, nothing is left unsung. And the prophetic songs are full of resonance. The *"circling camps"* recall the tents in "Fantasia for Elvira Shatayev." The *"watchfires"* are like the starlike eye in "Orion" and the "harbor beacon" and the "fire / of fiercer origin" in "Heroines."

When she remembers singing choruses with her mother she also remembers the fears she expressed in "Transcendental Etude." These songs are rhythms she is (then and now) moving to thoughtlessly. She has not "cleansed" her poetry of "oratory, formulas, choruses, laments, static / crowding the wires." To cleanse them of such static would be to cleanse them of relation with other people. She is tired, as she says in section 9 of "Sources," of the Puritans' "endless / purifications of self" (*YNL*, 11). This singing with her mother is theatrical in its way, but because she trusts the relationality behind it (it is a kind of conversation), she doesn't mind the theatricality. Here, again, is a mixture of the prophetic and the domestic that is grounded in the poet's own early life. Her father and mother were unable to pass on Judaism or the desire to play the piano, but she can nevertheless use what she has to invent what she needs.

Rich's sense of who she is as a poet has been strengthened by this return to these first versions of prophecy and domesticity. In *Your Native Land, Your Life,* she writes about leaving the East Coast and moving to California. (She is going to occupy the moral terrain of Robinson Jeffers.) In her poem "An Atlas of the Difficult World," she emphasizes the continuity: "this is where I live now. If you had known me / once, you'd still know me now though in a different / light and life." She is conscious of her readers' need to know where she is, to picture her.

> This is no place you ever knew me.
> But it would not surprise you
> to find me here, walking in fog, the sweep of the great ocean
> eluding me, even the curve of the bay, because as always
> I fix on the land.   I am stuck to earth.
>
> (*ADW*, 4–5)

Her emphasis on continuity here leads her to imagine that she has always fixed on the land, always stuck to earth.

Her four-page poem, "Yom Kippur 1984," is a meditation on solitude and the experience of feeling cut off from one's own people and from people in general. It begins with an epigraph from Robinson Jeffers: "I drew solitude over me, on the lone shore." Rich quotes him in the body of the poem as well. She writes, "I find the hatred in the poet's heart: . . . *the hateful-eyed / and human-bodied are all about me: you that love multitude may have them*" (*YNL*, 75–76). Rich takes the "headland," which is central to Jeffers's landscape, and reimagines it as a place for what Stevens calls "the intensest rendezvous." In a poem called "To Judith, Taking Leave" the headland is a place where "two women can meet" (*CEP*, 271). She also makes a prophetic landscape of her own. In an essay on "Yom Kippur 1984," she writes, "In the course of those months I was reading a lot in the Bible . . . When I came back and looked at the poem, I looked at the line-lengths, which were fairly short, and broken up with blank spaces. I realized that this technique, which I do use a lot, was altogether wrong for this poem. And something about living close to the edge of the ocean made the whole rhythm of the poem become clearer to me, what it had to be. It was that, it was also reading in the Hebrew Bible, the Old Testament."[44] At the end of the poem she writes,

> What is a Jew in solitude?
> What is a woman in solitude, a queer woman or man?
> When the winter flood-tides wrench the tower from the rock,
>   crumble the prophet's headland, and the farms slide
>   into the sea
> when leviathan is endangered and Jonah becomes revenger
> when center and edges are crushed together, the extremities
>   crushed together on which the world was founded
> when our souls crash together, Arab and Jew, howling our
>   loneliness within the tribes

when the refugee child and the exile's child re-open the blasted and
        forbidden city
when we who refuse to be women and men as women and men are
        chartered, tell our stories of solitude spent in
        multitude
in that world as it may be, newborn and haunted, what will
        solitude mean?

                                              (*YNL*, 78)

Rich's poems still take place at an elevation—this one takes place on a cliff. But it is a place to stand, a place she feels is free from false speech. Her poems about childhood have strengthened her in her sense of the source of her power. It is almost as if everything has been in place from the start. In her early poems, she had created domestic spaces that were, in a sense, to small for her, while in the poems of her second phase, she began filtering the tones of biblical prophecy through the tones of a Puritan sensibility, creating a "stringent space." More and more, she had tried to open up that space—opening it up so much that it began to seem, in a sense, too big. The space was Space itself. She had begun to see herself as only a spokeswoman, "an instrument in the shape / of a woman." In her third phase she begins to take from her mother a new interest in the communal, the relational. From her father she takes the voice and rhythms of biblical prophecy. She begins to write poems that explore these new possibilities, poems in which the voices are open to each other, accessible to each other, in conversation with each other.

Conclusion
Louise Glück and Jorie Graham

In this book, I have tried to show that the relationship between the prophetic voice and the everyday voice is central to an understanding of postwar poetry. A focus on the relationship between these voices can illuminate not only the larger themes of a poet's work but also the smallest decisions in the writing of the poem—decisions having to do with tonal coloration, phrasing, rhythm, juxtaposition of words, lineation, and the shape of stanzas. It can also illuminate the shape of a poet's career. It has been my concern throughout to avoid forcing any of the poets I consider into rigid categories. It is true, in any event, that the most interesting poets break free of expectations, make surprising choices. Although they may stop and wait for readers, they are happiest in motion.

The careers of the poets I have discussed exhibit some clear similarities. For Lowell, the first voice was a prophetic voice, and it worked wonders for him. For Ammons, the prophetic voice at first would hardly work at all. Merrill's first voice was too exquisite, in a sense, too "written." He began to develop an everyday voice, but that voice could not, all alone, offer him the kinds of pleasure and power he looked for in poetry. For Rich, the first prophetic voice did what she wanted it to do, but she needed it to change in the ways in which her life was changing. All these poets grew impatient with their first voice, experiencing it as limiting. All of them became more and more aware of aspects of experience about which they had no way to talk. And all four poets seemed to sense that the voice they had chosen (or that had chosen them) was intimately related to another voice. Readers may think of this voice as the opposite voice or even as a completely independent one, but to these poets it began to seem as if the move from one voice to another was not arbitrary, that the voices were deeply implicated in each other. One voice seemed, somehow, to accompany the other, even if inaudibly; one voice seemed to be, in poem after poem, exactly what was not there. To use only one was, then, more and more to feel that the poet was using only half of what was available to the poem. All four poets experimented with the other voice, understanding that it was not a matter of rejecting the first voice, and found, gradually, that they could take on not only more of their private experience but a wider experience as well. The decision to experiment with the other voice, though, was only the beginning of a long series of experiments. To read the poems of these authors is, in part, to watch a series of adjustments, corrections. These are different for each poet, though in each case the reward was the same. All four poets *kept writing*.

It seems to me that poets who find success in bringing the prophetic and the everyday together have won something as well for the culture. Against an American culture of coercive, sentimental versions of prophetic and everyday language, of exhausted narratives about what the prophetic and the everyday can mean to us, of prophetic and everyday voices that are both deaf to themselves and to each other, these poets offer poems with tremendous restorative and liberating properties. Certainly, they have already acted as liberating figures for the next generation of poets, although not for all of them, of course. Some poets will feel no tension between speech genres, while some will experiment with other speech genres and look with benign indifference at these two. But there are poets who have already read the careers of these four poets as if the careers were themselves poems, taking, perhaps uneasily, what they could use, rejecting, sometimes reluctantly, what they could not use—or not use yet. In other words, just as there are many ways for poets to read other poets' poems, so there are many ways they might read other poets' careers. A later poet's own career might seem to readers to represent a commentary on—even a series of corrections of—an earlier career.

Louise Glück offers a compelling example of a poet who chooses to remain inside the conditions in which other poets have found it difficult to keep writing interesting poetry. The early poems of Lowell, for example, are filled with disgust; those of Ammons, with paralysis. Merrill's early poems seem, in their way, to turn away from an uncontrollable external world. Glück shows us that it may be sentimental to

believe that we can—or ought—simply to "get over" paralysis and revulsion. Readers of poetry are not, Glück suggests, meant to conclude
that poets are people who keep liberating themselves, nor should readers expect all poets to express an openhearted acceptance of the imperfect world. Glück, in her eight books of poetry, from *Firstborn* (1968) to
The Seven Ages (2001), shows a continuing preoccupation with the relationship between the prophetic and the everyday. Her concern in
many of her most powerful poems is simply to show the ways in
which a poetic consciousness of extraordinary alertness and resourcefulness sees the continually shifting relationship between these two
ways of looking at the world.

    Disgust is Glück's first note. She announces its presence in the first
poem in her first book—"The Chicago Train." Her disgust is not preliminary, not staged so as to be corrected. Nor can it be disowned: it is
not deflected onto a speaker in a dramatic monologue. The speaker is
confident that we will feel, that we already feel, what she feels, even
though her disgust is directed against subjects (a family on a train, in
some sense "the family of man") toward whom most readers do not
like to feel they could experience revulsion. What Glück does in this
poem is not something many poets risk. Robinson Jeffers may feel disgust, but he has usually, in his poems, already turned away from the
world, and so he is not compelled to offer this kind of detail. In the introduction, I discussed a poem by Mark Halliday in which he cheerfully imagined moving the scene of his poem to Chicago, expecting to
be impressed, to be challenged by whatever he might find there. By
contrast, this is what Glück sees in Chicago:

> Across from me the whole ride
> Hardly stirred: just Mister with his barren
> Skull across the arm-rest while the kid
> Got his head between his mama's legs and slept. The poison
> That replaces air took over.
> And they sat—as though paralysis preceding death
> Had nailed them there. The track bent south.
> I saw her pulsing crotch . . . the lice rooted in that baby's hair.[1]

Glück's first line suggests a tone of self-pitying complaint: I had to
watch them the *whole* ride. The phrase "the whole ride" sounds childlike, but this is not a child speaking; and if the speaker can sound like a
child, it does not tempt her to identify with "the kid" opposite her. She
tells us that the family "hardly stirred," and the reader feels oddly
grateful on the speaker's behalf, sensing that their motion would have

been unbearable to her. (The "pulsing" in the last line is hardly to be endured, and, in fact, the poem does stop just afterward.) The poem continues, "just Mister with his barren / Skull across the arm-rest." When e. e. cummings uses a word like "mister," the reader feels his excitement that there are such common words and that he can put them in poems. But there is no exuberance in Glück's use of the word. One thinks of all the directions in which other poets—Karl Shapiro and Philip Levine, for example—could have taken this poem. The speaker of this poem, though, refuses the generosity of supplying the family with an imagined narrative. Narratives, like people, are, to this speaker, dreadful: families are dreadful, bodies are dreadful, but all of this could be withstood if we didn't have to *see*. In later poems, Glück will let escape the full horror, which is that we have to have our own families and have to have bodies ourselves. Now she simply reports that "the poison / That replaces air took over." The poet represents herself here as a sort of connoisseur of poisons ("now *this* is the kind of poison that replaces air"), but it is the connoisseurship not of a poisoner but of someone who is always being poisoned. This family is not as badly off as I am, she seems to say, because they can actually breathe this air. They are oblivious—to themselves, to the poet. Other people seem never to have heard that they are what hell is.

The poem continues, though it is a miracle that it does: "And they sat—as though paralysis preceding death / Had nailed them there." Paralysis is a word readers may associate with *Dubliners,* but Joyce's epiphanies about paralysis tend to include the narrator in the paralysis and at least sometimes to provoke some tentative sense of fellow feeling. There is no epiphany in this poem, just a series of observations; there is no sense of compassion. She writes of the family that it is as if paralysis "had nailed them there" but does not make them Christ-like. For Glück, the imagined nails are just another detail in the grotesque picture. The poem ends with one more look at the family. "I saw her pulsing crotch . . . the lice rooted in that baby's hair." We realize that Glück was saving the baby, and the lice, so that we could feel at the end of her poem as estranged as her speaker is. (Not that we would join her in her estrangement or feel a fellowship based on it.) The speaker does not suggest that paralysis of the people on the train is an allegory of her life. She does not see herself in the family, not even to the extent of wanting to be (to adapt what Merrill said of the statues in the museum) more graceful, more energetic than they. Paralysis in the poems of Lowell and Rich and Lowell and Ammons is always the paralysis preceding

extraordinary energy, but Glück rejects any such notion of what paralysis might be, offering us instead "paralysis preceding death." In fact,
her refusals, all of them, have a kind of grim almost-humor to them.
This poem has—or almost has—something of the horrified comic vision of John Kennedy Toole's *A Confederacy of Dunces,* but what is memorable about Glück's early poems lies not just in her refusal of compassion but in her refusal even of black humor. She comes close to both
modes but only, it seems, so that we can feel more sharply her swerve
away from them.

Memorable too is the bracing confidence of her rejections. Although
Lowell waited until his third book, *The Mills of the Kavanaughs,* to bring
in the everyday subjects that Glück introduces in *Firstborn,* Glück is
ready for them at the start. Family holidays are for Glück, as they were
for Lowell, full of dread, and the dread can locate itself anywhere. In
her poem "Thanksgiving," she offers us the wonderfully straight-faced
line: "Yet on and on the preparation of that vast consoling meal /
Edged toward the stove," and adds, "My mother / Had the skewers in
her hands."[2] And in another poem she tells us, "All day I smell the
roasts / Like presences."[3] In fact, Lowell's example seems always to be
present for her in her early poems; much of what she does or refuses to
do in bringing the prophetic to bear on the everyday seems related to
what she takes or rejects from Lowell's experience. What is crucial,
though, is that the everyday world is admitted to Glück's early poems
solely on her terms.

Glück's poems about domesticity remind us that Rich was rescued
from an unsurvivable domesticity by politics, and Glück has a poem
called "World Breaking Apart" (from her third book, *Descending Figure*
[1980]) that seems to be a kind of answer to Rich. Writing about "incoherent particles that went on / shining forever," Glück argues that such
particles cannot be used to make a new and just world for every person.
"Pain," Glück says,

> changes almost nothing.
> Like the winter wind, it leaves
> settled forms in the snow. Known, identifiable—
> except there are no uses for them.[4]

Political art cannot change lives.

Here is another poem from Glück's first book. It is called "Grandmother in the Garden," and, again, it brings disgust to what has usually
been thought inoffensive.

The grass below the willow
Of my daughter's wash is curled
With earthworms, and the world
Is measured into row on row
Of unspiced houses, painted to seem real.
The drugged Long Island summer sun drains
Pattern from those empty sleeves, beyond my grandson
Squealing in his pen. I have survived my life.
The yellow daylight lines the oak leaf
And the wire vines melt with the unchanged changes
Of the baby. My children have their husbands' hands.
My husband's framed, propped bald as a baby on their pianos,
My tremendous man. I close my eyes. And all the clothes
I have thrown out come back to me, the hollows
Of my daughters' slips . . . they drift; I see the sheer
Summer cottons drift, equivalent to air.[5]

The first line of "Grandmother in the Garden" suggests a vision of pastoral but—and here the speaker stages her own disappointment for us—it turns out to be suburban pastoral. Many poets would feel "at home" in the poem now and would know what to do next. Glück does too. The wash is curled with earthworms. A tone—it seems fresh each time—of disgust enters the poem and takes it over. Weariness too, though the weariness has a kind of volatile energy. For the speaker, "the world / Is measured into row on row / Of unspiced houses, painted to seem real." She is like the grandmother in Williams's "The Last Words of My English Grandmother," with the important difference that she is not dying and that her disgust cannot be attributed to failing powers or to approaching death. This grandmother is not medicated, losing her powers of concentration, feeling forgetful. Instead, it is the sun that is drugged, the sleeves that are losing the pattern, the sleeves that are empty. The speaker in this poem is a prophetic figure for whom the fault lies always with the world. The speaker in a James Wright poem may say, "I have wasted my life," but for the woman here the failure lies not with her (she did not waste her life) but with her life, which ran out too soon. "I have survived my life," she tells us. The poem has something of the savagery of "The Chicago Train" in its refusal of guilt or complicity in the scene and in the speaker's refusal of any prophetic vision but her own. Rilke's "Archaic Torso of Apollo" ends with the words: "You must change your life." "I must change my life?" the grandmother seems to ask. No, it is the *baby* who must be changed, she answers, calling our attention to "the unchanged changes / Of the baby."

Now the grandmother closes her eyes and has a vision in which all the aspects of experience that seem to disgust her (what Glück will, in a later poem, call "the rejected world") return to her in a version that is acceptable to her. "And all the clothes / I have thrown out come back to me, the hollows / Of my daughters' slips." The clothes are "equivalent to air." This is a world she can breathe in. (Some such disembodied elements are what was needed on the train.) There are no earthworms curling on these clothes. Like the empty sleeves mentioned earlier, they are empty of pattern; they are like ghosts but with the happy difference that they have nothing to tell her. There are no people wearing them and certainly no babies: they are not wet like diapers. The grandmother—again, there is something grim and almost funny here—has found, at the end of the poem, a way to love the things of this world. Glück does not judge or satirize her speakers. She does not reject *them.* Instead, she demonstrates loyalty to them, a kind of protectiveness of their revulsions.

In her third book, *Descending Figure,* she writes a poem in parts (a favorite style of hers) called "Tango" in which we can see everyday pleasures affirmed, then destroyed. Here is part 1:

> On evenings like this
> twenty years ago:
>
> We sit under the table,
> the adults' hands
> drum on our heads. Outside,
> the street,
> the contagious vernacular.
>
> Remember
> how we used to dance? Inseparable,
> back and forth across the living room,
> *Adios Muchachos,* like an insect
> moving on a mirror: envy
> is a dance, too; the need to hurt
> binds you to your partner.[6]

Possibilities of happiness are everywhere in the poem, though the scene described is somewhat mysterious. Why (to ask the sort of question Bishop asked when she wrote Lowell about his early poems) are the adults drumming on the heads of the children? The family is listening, enraptured, to music. At the 1913 premiere of Stravinsky's *The Rite of Spring,* audience members drummed on the heads of those seated in front of them. Something of that high culture atmosphere of riot seems to be fleetingly evoked here but domesticated, made safe, and shifted into the world of popular culture. It is a *family's* popular culture, though, which is not the same as the world's or the street's. She writes, "Outside, / the street, / the contagious vernacular." Contagious, but not to the poem. Ammons and Lowell work to catch the contagion, but Glück does not: she keeps it outside the house, outside the poem. The phrase itself (outside, the street, the contagious vernacular) seems wary of interruption, particularly in comparison to the sentences of Lowell or Ammons, which seem hungry for interruption. Lee Upton writes that Glück "seldom qualifies statements even when discussing doubt itself. For their impact, her poems rely on tone, and her own tone is one—for all her emphasis on the promise uncertainty holds—of extreme knowledge, even of fatedness."[7] In one of her essays, Glück offers a kind of explanation for her impulse to write the kinds of sentences she writes. "I was born into an environment in which the right of any family member to complete the sentence of another was assumed. Like most of the people in that family, I had a strong desire to speak, but that desire was regularly frustrated: my sentences were, in being cut off, radically changed—transformed, not paraphrased."[8] Her sentences seem to move as if they fear that someone will tamper with them; at the same time, they seem to erase, as they progress, any suggestion that she herself has tinkered with them.

Whatever has made it possible, the fact is that she is remembering and telling us about family happiness. There is drumming and dancing. The adults respond to the music, and now the two sisters dance: they have moved out from under the table and taken over the living room. The mood for most of the first part of the poem is celebratory, excited. The grandmother in the earlier poem wants her losses restored to her in memories emptied of the human. The speaker of this poem wants the human too—more specifically, she wants her sister. "Remember / how we used to dance? Inseparable, / back and forth across the living room." The speaker remembers a phrase from the song they dance to: "Adios Muchachos." But the introduction of the phrase (which means "good-bye, children") changes the poem: it exerts a contagion that the vernacular in English was not permitted to do. Representations of "family dancing" may often have an undertone of violence. The father in Roethke's "My Papa's Waltz" beats time, as the grownups do here, on his child's head. And that poem too suggests that the dancing may enact what it purports to be relief from. In Glück's poem, the meaning of the dancing shifts. She and her sister now resemble an insect and its mirror image. This is a different kind of inseparability and a different kind of motion from the one we just heard about. The idea of the small and contemptible is entering the poem, as are ideas of narcissism and envy. Before we have heard much about what the tango feels like, we are reminded that envy is a dance too and that what binds the two sisters together might be a "need to hurt." Glück has delayed this shift and has allowed everyday pleasures their moment. Still, that moment has not been even as long as the first part of a poem. This family has ultimately been observed as coldly as the family on the train.

In her fifth book, *Ararat,* Glück focuses almost exclusively on the dynamics within a family, and she refers explicitly, for the first time, to psychiatry. Psychiatry cannot liberate the speakers of her poems; it simply allows them to speak with clarity of a lifelong bitterness while at the same time making it clear how much of that bitterness is still repressed. The unhappiness is everywhere by now. Earlier she had written,

> It doesn't matter
> who the witness is,
> for whom you are suffering,
> for whom you are standing still.[9]

Something of that atmosphere of indifference to both cause and spectators, remarkably, prevails in the poems that directly address the family. In the unexamined life, families are grotesque; examined, they are still grotesque, but the narratives surrounding them make a little more sense to the reader. Nobody is freed by this sense. Helen Vendler writes of Robert Lowell, "Now that it is his ongoing personal history that concerns him in *Life Studies,* he must find some vantage point from which to tell it, and he must discover, as well, a level of utterance suitable to his new persona, the analysand, rather than to the denunciatory prophet. One of his discoveries is a detached mildness of tone."[10] Glück identifies with both the analysand and the analyst. There is little detached mildness of tone for her, though there is detachment, and there is little of the garrulousness that one might associate with the analysand. There is not much looseness anywhere in this book: the characters speak to each other in charged and highly controlled phrases. Still, though they use the tones we might associate with truth telling, they cannot be trusted. In "The Untrustworthy Speaker," Glück writes, "I know myself; I've learned to hear like a psychiatrist. / When I speak passionately, / that's when I'm least to be trusted."[11] She hears like a psychiatrist and sometimes speaks like one. The psychiatrist is lofty, detached, seeming to speak from an unassailable, unanswerable space: he or she is a version of the prophetic figure. The analysand is confused, untrustworthy, speaking from a space that is constantly assailed, continually vulnerable to new versions of itself: he or she is a version of the everyday figure.

To merge the voices, to imagine oneself as both analysand and analyst, is to come tentatively toward a hybrid speech genre. Glück is drawn toward the hybrid speech genre (however tentative she may be in her arrival at it) because of her increasing sense of loyalty to contrasting ways of speaking. In a revealing essay on Eliot, she writes, "The charges against him, cumulatively, make him out to be the enemy of the life force. What characterizes the life force appears to be improvisation, variety, frankness, vigor, personality, some version of the common touch, some sense of communal affiliation. Or, alternatively, the kind of linguistic inventiveness which can be taken as the thriving organism's throwing off of constraints." Observing that some readers associate these qualities with Williams, she turns to the question of having to choose between Eliot and Williams. "I find what seem to be manifestations of a pressure to choose very interesting, since an advantage of literature over life is that the heart of the reader can be given wholly and simultaneously, even to writers who detested each other." She adds, "I love both these poets, all the time."[12] Many poets, like many people, have evolved further as readers than as people; certainly, many poets can admire in other people's poems results that they cannot yet bring about in their own. In a poem from *Descending Figure*, Glück writes, "A child draws the outline of a body. / She draws what she can, but it is white all through, / she cannot fill in what she knows is there."[13] A poet may never want to do more than draw outlines, and an outline can have as much dramatic or even explanatory power in a good poem as a figure entirely filled in. Glück's bringing together of the prophetic and the everyday here (and in her later books) always reflects exactly how far she is willing to go, how much she can believe in their coexistence in her own work.

Glück's is a different sort of hybrid speech genre from those we have seen in the other four poets. She has not, until recently, been drawn to the representation of conversation, for instance. When there is conversation in Glück's poetry, it is often hushed and mysterious, overheard by the speaker and never explained, either to the speaker or by her. In her recent books, she has experimented in writing conversation poems that retain their mystery while at the same time telling a story, telling two stories, in the case of the poems from *Meadowlands,* which counter-point the story of Penelope and her husband and son with the story of the speaker's husband and son. These poems do not, however, represent any celebratory sense of multivocality. Nor has she opened her poetry up to political rhetoric or to the rhetoric of large social movements. Nor does she use science, say, as Ammons or Merrill does. Her hybrid speech genre—one can call it her first one—is not an exuberant opening out to the world. Glück admires, in Williams's poems, his improvisation, variety, frankness, vigor, personality, common touch, and sense of communal affiliation, but she recognizes that those qualities may seem (in life, in poems) coercive sometimes or uninteresting, and she leaves them, for the most part, out of her poems. Ammons found his early prophetic spaces uninhabitable, but Glück stays in those spaces. Merrill found his early poems too still, too motionless, but Glück prolongs and protects that stillness. Lowell found the voice of his early poems too filled with disgust—Glück holds onto her disgust. Rich found the domestic arrangements she saw around her impossible and therefore precarious; Glück finds them impossible too but does not imagine that they are therefore precarious or more precarious than anything else. Glück seems to have asked herself a question that Allen Grossman, for example, never quite seems to have phrased in exactly this way to himself. What if the prophetic figure *were* already human, what if a disgusted turning away were a *way* of being human, a way of living an everyday life? There are indications in her recent work of a deep shift away from disgust, and it will be fascinating to see what happens to the relationship between the prophetic and the everyday in the poems Glück will write next. In many of her poems, though, she has shown us that, though a prophetic poet may have to become, to some extent, a poet of the everyday, this is not the same as falling in love with the world.

There are younger poets who begin their careers in the thick of the tension between the prophetic and the everyday. They have already in their first book a sense of what it might mean to be able to do justice to both kinds of experience, a sense of the difficulty and also of the necessity of it. Jorie Graham, for example, begins her career as a kind of prophetic poet, but her prophetic voice is already at the start more flexible, more nuanced than Lowell's. That is, she is aware from her very first poem that the prophetic voice is a speech genre. Such poets may never come to a satisfactory hybrid speech genre—their minds are too restless to see the finding of a hybrid as anything but a dubious place of rest.

From the beginning, Graham has been writing poems in which she risks recording the almost unrecordable shifts and turns in the relationship between the everyday and the prophetic. This relationship has been a continuing preoccupation from her first book, *Hybrids of Plants and of Ghosts* (1980), to her most recent book, *Never* (2002). Her dedication to tracing the vicissitudes of that relationship leads her to thinking of her own self as describable—perhaps *only* describable—in terms of it. (She calls a poem in her third book "Self-Portrait as the Gesture between Them.") She cannot offer the self an autonomous space—whatever space opens up seems immediately to divide or close or else turns out to be previously occupied. But she can give the self work to do. She can invent the gestures between the prophetic and the everyday (engineering, choreographing them); she can make them audible, visible in her poems. Because her poetry comes more and more to doubt not only any place for the self but a place of rest for any kind of energy, she depends for a sense of her own reality on the reality, the value, of the gestures she records. The title of Graham's first book, *Hybrids of Plants and of Ghosts*, suggests, in and of itself, a version of the tension I have described in my book. I want to turn here to a poem from that book, a poem glanced at in my chapter on James Merrill. It is called "The Geese" and describes both the openings and crossings of space:

> Today as I hang out the wash I see them again, a code
> as urgent as elegant
> tapering with goals.
> For days they have been crossing. We live beneath these geese
>
> as if beneath the passage of time, or a most perfect heading.
> Sometimes I fear their relevance.
> Closest at hand,
> between the lines,
>
> the spiders imitate the paths the geese won't stray from,
> imitate them endlessly to no avail:
> things will not remain connected,
> will not heal,
>
> and the world thickens with texture instead of history,
> texture instead of place.
> Yet the small fear of the spiders
> binds and binds

the pins to the lines, the lines to the eaves, to the pincushion bush,
as if, at any time, things could fall further apart
and nothing could help them
recover their meaning. And if these spiders had their way,

chainlink over the visible world,
would we be in or out? I turn to go back in.
There is a feeling the body gives the mind
of having missed something, a bedrock poverty, like falling

without the sense that you are passing through one world,
that you could reach another
anytime. Instead the real
is crossing you,

your body an arrival
you know is false but can't outrun. And somewhere in between
these geese forever entering and
these spiders turning back,

this astonishing delay, the everyday, takes place.[14]

This poem is freer, more exploratory, more adventurous than a poem written in the forties and fifties—even the sixties—would have been. Space for Graham—whether it is the space of the sky above her back yard or the entire "visible world" or what is "closest at hand" or (even closer) the space of the body—can be located but not compartmentalized. The poem is full of spaces; the poet tries to account for them and the crossings between them, the fallings between them. She tries to describe attempts to connect or bind these spaces, attempts to prevent them from falling farther apart, attempts to divide the world into only two spaces, in and out. Within the poet too there is the space of the body and the space of the mind. Another poet (Frost, perhaps) doing household chores would have noticed the geese and the spiders and perhaps concluded that we work together even if we work apart. For Graham, the everyday world is extraordinarily complicated and strange: it feels that way simply as a presence around her, not intensely attended to, because it is already—even in her first book—a mixture of prophetic and everyday space. She lives in both worlds at once, trying to do justice to each, but it is not always easy to know which is which.

"Today as I hang out the wash I see them again." The opening of the poem is casual: because Graham has seen them on a previous day, their reappearance suggests they are an occasion to which she must in some way rise. "For days they have been crossing," but today she will say something. But what should one say about geese? They occupy, at least they cross, the same space occupied by the everyday activity of hanging out the wash. This suggests that that space is larger than she thought: something has been trying to recontextualize her activities, and she is now taking notice. What she notices is that "the wash" itself is not recontextualized. Nothing happens to it in the poem. Another poet— Merrill, for example—would have made the laundry dreamlike. Glück saw the laundry covered with earthworms. Graham leaves it as it is. It is as real as the geese. Whatever space they both occupy is hospitable to various kinds of phenomena. Again, her casualness is important. She is not, like Yeats, going out to the hazel wood. She is simply out in her own back yard, not watching but happening to see.

The flight of the birds seems like a code, though, as she says, and that is a temptation of a kind. She could have staged the movement between the everyday and the prophetic in that tempting way: "I am hanging out the wash like one kind of poet, but when I see something like geese crossing I turn into another kind of poet, I become as urgent, as elegant as possible, a reader of codes." Her phrase "tapering with goals" is in part a refusal to read the code. Like Stevens in "Sunday Morning," who sees "at evening" that "casual flocks of pigeons make / Ambiguous undulations as they sink, / Downward to darkness on extended wings," she leaves the undulations of the birds ambiguous.[15] By contrast, Adrienne Rich writes, "I have been standing all my life in the / direct path of a battery of signals," and what she says *is* offered as an interpretation of those signals, just as Merrill too—once one has made all the adjustments required by the tone he takes—interprets codes.[16] Graham does not imagine herself as someone who can offer us special wisdom: her poem takes place in a space of mental action prior to speech. The poem enacts silent, swift occupations of and departures from various kinds of space, including temporal space.

Graham allows the geese to be the prophetic figures. They seem to know what they know, and she can only guess what it is; she will not try to read their code. Still, some large statement seems required. It will seem a little obvious, it will have the air of statements that expose their rhetorical ambitions without quite satisfying them: "We live beneath these geese // as if beneath the passage of time, or a most perfect heading." Everyday tasks are not urgent, are not elegant, they are imperfect or at least are about imperfection, but the geese remind us of what *is* urgent, elegant, perfect. Now the poet has made her large philosophical statement, but it seems inadequate. High language ought to elevate its speaker; large statements ought to have some force in the world,

perhaps a protective force. The speaker, having made her generalization about all of us, now makes a statement about herself. It does not
seem to add to what she said before; if anything, it contradicts it. Its
tone, certainly, seems corrective.

"Sometimes I fear their relevance," she says. The word "sometimes"
suggests that her intensity has a kind of intermittency (anyway, a lack
of urgency), and this is part of what she fears the geese are telling her.
Although she is drawn to generalization, she realizes that generalization alone will not suffice—there is a higher, more urgent seriousness,
and the geese seem to embody it. The language has intensified somewhat to try to match that intensity: we live not under a perfect heading
but "a most perfect heading," and the spiders, we will see, are not close
at hand but "closest at hand." The geese, as prophetic figures, now correspond to a prophetic voice in the poet without being an occasion for
its release. She wants to remind herself of the reality of what they correspond to, even if she often feels unequal to it or fears it.

The speaker tells us she is afraid. Of what? She cuts off that line of
response, of feeling and looks at the world again. Looking has become
more urgent now, as if her first act of noticing the geese has committed her to further acts of seeing that might help to connect or to heal
what she has seen. What she sees are the spiders: "Closest at hand, /
between the lines, // the spiders imitate the paths the geese won't
stray from." In Graham's poem, all the urgency, the sense of purpose,
the drama are given to the geese and spiders. She is merely hanging out
the wash.

Although she gives herself statements, they tend to sound inadequate to her. At least, she does not continue far along the lines of spec-
ulation they introduce. It might help to hear her voice more clearly if
we compare this early Graham poem to an early Lowell poem, "Mr.
Edwards and the Spider," which begins: "I saw the spiders marching
through the air, / Swimming from tree to tree that mildewed day."[17]
Lowell is bold in observation as well as in generalization. And he is full
of certainties: that the spiders are marching, that they are swimming,
that the day is mildewed, that he can withstand whatever fear these
facts might fill him with. Lowell is not interested in establishing a
"human" tone or even an alibi for seeing the spiders: he does not try to
hide the fact that he is stalking the natural world in search of allegorical
material. Graham's, on the other hand, is a voice that wants to *register*
rather than seek out; she is a poet who wants to see how many spaces
she can keep in relation. Allegory, even the most tentative of allegorical

impulses, is interesting to her only insofar as it shifts one's sense of what it is like to stand in one's own back yard.

She writes, "between the lines, // the spiders imitate the paths the geese won't stray from, / imitate them endlessly to no avail." Where Lowell and Rich had to learn to complicate their poems, Graham's early poem complicates itself further with every new line. Graham, writing the poem, making lines, is, like the spiders, imitating the geese but also, like the spiders imitating the geese, "endlessly to no avail." The poet began by talking about "today" and then used the word "days" and is now using the word "endlessly." She is trying to suggest that there are different kinds of time just as there are different kinds of space in the poem. The prophetic voice has entered—it is, she suggests at the end of the poem, "forever entering." The poet's fear does not go away but attaches itself to the prophetic voice, finding in it a way of expressing if not solacing itself.

The poet began the poem as a poet of the everyday, writing about hanging out the wash. The geese alarmed her. Thinking to ground herself, to bring herself back down to earth, she considered the spiders. To identify with them might be a corrective to thinking about herself in terms of the geese. But the spiders are simply doing what the geese are doing, and she is doing it too, endlessly to no avail. What she knows now (though not with the chilling self-satisfaction of Lowell's speaker in "Mr. Edwards and the Spider") is that the everyday and the prophetic are intimately involved with each other, are constantly entering and exiting each other's time and space. When she makes large statements now she does not try to ground herself afterward (by looking at the worms, say) but lets the statements have their effect in the poem. And she knows more. The spiders are close at hand, occupying an intimate space of proximity (they ought to represent safety of a kind), yet what they do they do "endlessly" and "to no avail." The poet's attention to the world and to her own responses never falters. The reader feels her care in every line, perhaps especially when the predominant sensation is fear.

Everyday and prophetic experience are both present in this poem. For a mystical poet, this would mean incipient union, but although Graham does not doubt that odd moments of union are possible, she knows that some connections are false and also that "things will not remain connected." She immediately adds—in the same spirit in which, earlier in the poem, she followed an impersonal statement with a more personal one—that things also "will not heal." The poet has been, all along, performing operations involving connection: attaching the clothes to the clothesline, connecting the geese to philosophical concepts, connecting those concepts to us ("We live . . . "), connecting them to her own fears ("Sometimes I fear . . . "), but still, "things will not remain connected." Part of the excitement of this poem is that one cannot say how it will end. She is not heading, as Bishop's speaker in "At the Fishhouses" is, toward any visible depth. Graham's poems often have no faith in their beginnings. She has been trying to write, had thought to write, a poem in which she says that design seems to govern in the flight of geese, in the binding of the spiders, that design can seem urgent, elegant, perfect, and that imitation of it can seem futile in spiders and in this poem. But where can she go from here? Although the prophetic poet can talk about design, the experience of the prophetic is cold and uncomforting. What good does it do to know what the prophet knows? How does it help us to live? How does it help us even to think?

The thoughts of the prophetic voice do not seem to go on very long in Graham's first book. (She will discover ways in her later poems to elongate them.) The voice of the everyday in this early poem seems equally cold, uncomforting: natural processes are limited in their ability to console. The geese belong to both the prophetic and the everyday world, but they do not do much for the speaker in either capacity. Stevens's poem, after all, was called "Evening without Angels" and not "Evening without Geese." Where can Graham go in this poem? There are no other people here. Glück's poem about the grandmother in the garden is full of people, even if none of them matters much. But here there are no people even to reject.

Graham has imagined a space where it doesn't seem possible to survive for very long. She is not doing badly. The speaker in one of Ammons's early poems would have decided by this point in the poem to join the things that will not remain connected. Graham, on the other hand, becomes herself urgent and elegant. How else to describe the lines "things will not remain connected, / will not heal"? And there is the same obstinacy I noted in Glück: these are the conditions, and she will stay in them. She will not use any "trick" to get herself out of the poem or out of this way of writing poems. Another poet, seeing the geese, would describe them as memorably as possible, then, having earned the right, begin to generalize about how we discover patterns, then move to a tour de force of spider description, telling us how we make our own patterns. Other images would be introduced to assist us in realizing that we live both in history and in our own social lives, both in the world and in a local social habitation. One needs to compare Graham's poem to other possible versions of it to feel the absence of escape hatches in her work.

Meanwhile, all she can see is smaller versions of her own fear everywhere. She refers to the "small fear" of the spiders. When the speaker in Lowell's "Skunk Hour" "stand[ing] on top / of our back steps" saw the skunks, he was struck by the fact that the mother skunk would "not scare."[18] Readers have disagreed about whether the fact that the skunk could not be scared made the poem itself more scary or less. What would it be like if every living thing in that poem were afraid? In this poem, it is only the spiders and the speaker who are scared—but then they are the only living things on the earth in the poem. Although Lowell reveals his skunks only at the end of his poem, Graham, halfway through her poem, has already brought out her geese and spiders. They have already done their work, and her isolation seems deeper than Lowell's as she continues.

What now? Graham does not bring a new kind of being into the poem in the middle of the poem but, instead, a new way of experiencing the world. She writes that "the world thickens with texture instead of history, / texture instead of place." She will, as I suggested above, reject the consolations of both history and place in this poem, though she will later return to both subjects, writing a number of poem with "History" as the title. To refer to texture, to say that *that* is what the world is thickening with, is a way for her to keep open, to maintain a space (she senses she will need one) for her own perceptions. At the same time, she wants to suggest that to take an interest in texture is to ally oneself somehow with "the world." To call such a momentary world "the world" and to identify it with texture rather than history or place suggests that it is texture, rather than time, say, that might heal all wounds. It should be said that "texture" here is not something one arrives at through acts of close observation. The poet does not describe the spiders' lines, just as she does not describe the geese. For her, texture is not limited to sensuous apprehension but can also refer to emotional and intellectual apprehension; it includes the other sense of apprehension that suggests fear. These are all she has, she seems to say, but at least she has something.

The next word is "yet," and we are back with the spiders and their fear:

> Yet the small fear of the spiders
> binds and binds
>
> the pins to the lines, the lines to the eaves, to the pincushion bush,
> as if, at any time, things could fall further apart
> and nothing could help them
> recover their meaning.

The spiders are not interested in the poet's hopeful recourse to the still-unelaborated idea of texture; they have their own elaborations to perform, as urgent as hers. If the spiders covered the "visible world," the poet asks, would we be in or out? How much do their activities involve us? How much can we learn from watching them? What is complex enough adequately to allegorize the operations of our minds? At this point in the poem, she seems almost to be asking also, What else besides the human has as little space in the world it can call its own?

Graham writes poems that are self-portraits as a gesture between various kinds of energies. At this point, the poem is a self-portrait as a gesture between geese and spiders, between the prophetic and the everyday, between history and place and texture. It cannot be a self-portrait as a self because she is herself divided. Conscious of her own body in space, she writes not "I go back in" but "I turn to go back in." But the body is not a place where she can simply *be*. She writes, "There is a feeling the body gives the mind / of having missed something." There is no self; there is, instead, "the body" and "the mind." The poem could only be a self-portrait as a gesture between body and mind. To speak of the body and the mind as two separate kinds of energy, like the geese and the spiders, is to multiply divisions, to suggest that there is nothing in the world of this poem that does not need binding.

Interestingly, Graham does not use "you" in this poem (a pronoun she uses frequently in the other poems) until the end. This is a poem about an "I" who talks about "them" and who sometimes allows herself to use the word "we." She cannot say "you" to the spiders or to the geese or to the readers. The mental actions of this poem seem preliminary to that: the urgency of the poem lies in demonstrating how much work is involved in keeping the world together, that to say "you" would bring in a sense of dramatic address that the poet cannot yet afford. The theater of the world is in danger of flying apart. But she does call herself "you" at the end ("Instead the real / is crossing you"), and then it seems as if this address is a way of relieving pressure on a self hoping to continue to imagine itself as an I.

What is the something that has been missed? Is it an experience of the body and the mind as one? Is it the sense of having lived a "real" life? Graham refers to a bedrock poverty. There, connections become tenuous, and this, in a poem about connections, seems dire. Meanwhile, the sense that things are falling apart has shifted to a sense that one is, oneself, falling. Stevens has a poem called "The Men That Are Falling" in which he mocks himself for "speaking the speech // of absolutes, bodiless."[19] Falling, for both poets, is a state in which one cannot speechify, a kind of punishment for grand rhetoric or for any certainty at all. Is what is happening in the poem now a result of, a response to, what the poet said about texture? It can seem as if the body is telling her that to live in a world of perceptions is to have no bedrock on which to stand. The speaker has said originally that we live beneath the geese. Now she is beneath nothing—she keeps falling, and to fall is to be like the failed prophetic figure in Ammons's early poems. The speaker has privileged texture over history and place, and now nothing seems "real" (a word she is about to use), yet, without texture, history and place can seem unreal to us as well. Everyday space and prophetic space are both potentially terrifying. They do not seem to heal each other, they simply show up each other's inadequacies. But it seems, in this poem, even more dangerous to presume to choose one over the other.

The poem continues. "Instead the real / is crossing you." The line echoes (or binds itself to) the line at the beginning of the poem about the geese. "For days they have been crossing." "You" are a space like any other space, not privileged as a self. She is not the end point of the real, she is not what the real is heading toward; instead, the real is simply crossing her on the way to some other space. What is happening here is that the everyday, the human, the domestic (she was heading indoors when she began to fall) are being shown up. Now the poem—which shifts, alters, corrects itself moment by moment, word by word almost— changes again. She discovers where the real is actually heading. She writes, "Your body an arrival / you know is false but can't outrun." The real is crossing her to get to her body. Why? The body here is a space at which the truth arrives; the body does not have to go out in search of it. It does not have to distinguish between texture and history and place, knowing that whatever is real will arrive eventually at the body. Some poets would end the poem here. The body is, for some poets (Sharon Olds, for example), a space of authority and privilege. For Graham, though, this arrival is false; the connection between the body and the reality is only one of many connections and not necessarily the

most reliable. (She will return to the idea of the false arrival in "Self-Portrait as Apollo and Daphne," in which she writes, "She stopped she
turned, / she would not be the end towards which he was ceaselessly
tending, / she would not give shape to his hurry by being its destination.")[20] Graham is a poet, however, who is always very close, especially in her first book, to the language not of belief but of wanting to believe. In "The Way Things Work," the first poem of her first book, she
writes "I believe" three times in a short poem. Now, as she writes "your
body an arrival / you know is false," one can hear in the lines her wish
that she could believe the arrival to be true. But the poem (which is the
one space in which she must believe) does not feel this "arrival" as its
own arrival. The body does, nevertheless, have a "real" authority in the
poem. Its reality—it is born and dies—is irrefutable. That is, she can't go
faster than it, she cannot get ahead of it.

Now the poet sees a way to end this poem. There is, I think, something in the phrase "can't outrun" that opens up a line of thought. If one
cannot outrun, cannot escape any of the conditions the poem immerses
us in, what can one do? One can choose the best possible space (Graham calls it "somewhere in between") and the best possible time (she
calls it "delay").

> And somewhere in between
> these geese forever entering and
> these spiders turning back,
>
> this astonishing delay, the everyday, takes place.

Although things could fall farther apart at any time, they have not yet.
The speaker, nevertheless, has no space with which to counter or survive the everyday and the prophetic; there is no third space of the self.
Body and mind simply get swept up into the debate, where the mind's
experience is sometime prophetic, sometimes everyday, and the body's
experience is sometimes prophetic, sometimes everyday. The poem
might be a third space, but only, the poet seems to say, if it makes itself
available to the prophetic and everyday, if it stages their crossings, their
fallings, their entrances and turnings back.

At the end of the poem, trying to think what she does have, given all
she does not have, Graham finds a version of time and place that is "relevant" to her but not something she has to fear. She does not have to
specify the space (to do so might be to stage a false arrival) but only has
to say it is "somewhere in between." What she is between is the prophetic and the everyday: the poem itself has been a gesture between

them, a gesture or gestures the poet has observed but also a gesture the poet has made. She finds as well a version of time in which she can live, calling it "delay." What is delayed is death, of course, but other acts are delayed: falling farther apart, a final belief in some unalterable relation between the prophetic and the everyday that would weave a "chainlink over the visible world." Texture finds a place in the poem in Graham's use of the word "astonishing." In using that word she reminds us and herself that she has the right to say at every moment what the "delay" feels like to her. The everyday is privileged at the end not because of any ethical commitment to domesticity—like Lowell in "Skunk Hour," she does not go back inside the house—but instead because it has become textured space. In prophetic space there would be no clotheslines, no spiders, no bushes, no houses, no people—only crossings and fallings, elegant but not urgent. There would be nothing to impede, nowhere to arrive, nothing to interrupt. In "Still Life with Window and Fish," a poem from her second book, *Erosion,* Graham will write about "the beautiful interruptions, the things of this world, twigs / and powerlines."[21] In "The Geese," she shows us how we do not have to choose either the everyday or the prophetic but can consciously station ourselves (where, in any event, we are) *between* them. The poem, like many of the most interesting contemporary poems, becomes, at the end, a self-portrait as the gesture between them.

Looking back at the earlier poets from the vantage point of these new departures, readers may see them somewhat differently. In the light of the earnestness of Glück and Graham, readers may prize more highly Merrill's gift for lightness, wit, the unemphatic. We may feel more strongly—in the light of the tendency to the symbolic and the allegorical in Glück and Graham—Ammons's firm commitment to a promiscuously heterogeneous version of the everyday. We can see what Rich's earnestness becomes once it is depoliticized; we long, perhaps, for a poet with Lowell's topical and historical urgency. In this way, we not only see the younger poets in the shadows of their precursors in this hybrid genre, but we also reread and see more clearly the outline of antecedent poets as we come upon their most original followers. Poems still unwritten will show us fresh and surprising ways of bringing these voices together, and the poets who produce them will remind future readers how much is at stake in taking the work seriously and getting it right.

Notes

Bibliography

Index

_____

Notes

Introduction

1. Grossman, *The Sighted Singer,* 68. Grossman discusses the tension between selfhood and personhood, which can be seen as analogous to the tension between the everyday poet and the prophetic poet.
2. Glück, "Education of the Poet," in *Proofs and Theories,* 17.
3. Wittreich, *Visionary Poetics,* 34.
4. Wittgenstein, *Philosophical Investigations,* 32.
5. Sword, *Engendering Inspiration,* 4.
6. For general discussions of the relation between poetry and biblical prophecy, see Heschel, *The Prophets;* Alter, *The Art of Biblical Prophecy;* Kugel, ed., *Poetry and Prophecy;* Fisch, *Poetry with a Purpose;* von Rad, *The Message of the Prophets;* Wojcik and Frontain, *Poetic Prophecy in Western Literature;* and Marks, "On Prophetic Stammering." For interesting feminist readings of the prophets, see Swatos Jr., ed., *Gender and Religion,* and Tribe, *God and the Rhetoric of Sexuality.*
7. Du musst dein Leben ändern (Rainer Maria Rilke, "Archaic Torso of Apollo," in Rilke, *Poetry,* 180).
8. James Merrill, "Bronze," in Merrill, *Collected Poems,* 454–55.
9. M. M. Bakhtin, "The Problem of Speech Genres," in Bakhtin, *Speech Genres,* 79, 86n. Hereafter cited in text.
10. Heschel, *The Prophets,* xi, xiii.
11. James, *The Varieties of Religious Experience,* 414. Hereafter cited in text.
12. Sword, *Engendering Inspiration,* 4.
13. Sarton, *Journal of a Solitude,* 99.
14. Altieri, *Self and Sensibility,* 14.
15. Nelson, *Kenneth Patchen,* xiv.
16. Bentley, ed., *Blake Records,* 294.
17. Merrill, *The Changing Light at Sandover,* 217.
18. Walker, *Bardic Ethos,* 241. Hereafter cited in text.
19. Allen Grossman, "Hart Crane and Poetry: A Consideration of Crane's Intense Poetics with Reference to 'The Return,'" in Grossman, *The Long Schoolroom,* 113.

20. Des Pres, *Praises and Dispraises,* 23.

21. For valuable accounts of the relationships between prophecy and radical politics, see Cohn, *The Pursuit of the Millennium;* Norbrook, *Poetry and Politics;* Hill, *Milton;* Hill, *A Tinker;* Erdman, *Blake;* Hopkins, *A Woman to Deliver Her People;* and Thomas, *The Lunar Light.*

22. Heidegger used the term *weltarm* in the 1929–30 Freiburg Lectures. Quoted in Derrida, *Of Spirit,* 48.

23. Ammons, *Garbage,* 93.

24. Wallace Stevens, "Notes toward a Supreme Fiction," in Stevens, *The Collected Poems,* 389.

25. T. S. Eliot, *The Waste Land,* in Eliot, *The Complete Poems and Plays,* 38; Hart Crane, "Atlantis," *The Bridge,* in Crane, *The Complete Poems,* 116; H.D., "The Walls Do Not Fall," in H.D., *Trilogy,* 58–59; Robert Penn Warren, "Terror," in Warren, *The Collected Poems,* 77; Allen Ginsberg, *Howl,* in Ginsberg, *Collected Poems 1947–1980,* 129; Robert Lowell, "As a Plane Tree by the Water," in Lowell, *Lord Weary's Castle,* 53; Adrienne Rich, "Planetarium," in Rich, *The Will to Change,* 14; Allen Grossman, "In My Observatory Withdrawn," in Grossman, *Of the Great House,* 77; Allen Grossman, "Of the Great House," in Grossman, *Of the Great House,* 10.

26. Allen Grossman, "Hart Crane and Poetry," in Grossman, *The Long Schoolroom,* 126n.

27. Ezra Pound, Canto 81, in Pound, *The Cantos,* 535.

28. Hart Crane, "The Broken Tower," in Crane, *The Complete Poems,* 193; A. R. Ammons, "Guide," in Ammons, *Collected Poems, 1951–1971,* 80; Allen Grossman, "The Lecture," in Grossman, *The Woman on the Bridge,* 79.

29. Wallace Stevens, "The Comedian as the Letter C," in Stevens, *The Collected Poems,* 36.

30. Hart Crane, "Atlantis," *The Bridge,* in Crane, *The Complete Poems,* 116; William Carlos Williams, "The Sea Elephant," in Williams, *The Collected Poems 1909–1939,* 341; John Ashbery, "Grand Galop," in Ashbery, *Self-Portrait,* 15; Philip Larkin, "Sad Steps," in Larkin, *Collected Poems,* 160; W. H. Auden, "Bucolics," in Auden, *The Collected Poems,* 563; William Carlos Williams, "Danse Russe," in Williams, *The Collected Poems 1909–1939,* 87.

31. Mary Oliver, "The Summer Day," in Oliver, *New and Selected Poems,* 94.

32. William Carlos Williams, "Pastoral," in Williams, *Selected Poems,* 15; Langston Hughes, "Theme for English B," in Hughes, *The Collected Poems,* 409–10; Frank O'Hara, "My Heart," in O'Hara, *The Collected Poems,* 231; Elizabeth Bishop, "Five Flights Up," in Bishop, *The Complete Poems 1927–1979,* 181; Randall Jarrell, "Next Day," in Jarrell, *The Complete Poems,* 280; John Ashbery, "Soonest Mended," in Ashbery, *Selected Poems,* 87.

33. David Kalstone writes, "Jarrell's 'women' always rankled [Bishop]. She disliked even more than Lowell did those poems addressed to or spoken by women ('Next Day' in the final book, was an example—a *memento mori* spoken by a suburban housewife). She wonders 'where he *gets* these women—they seem to be like none I—or you—know'" (*Becoming a Poet,* 226).

34. William Blake, "Auguries of Innocence," in Blake, *The Complete Poetry and Prose,* 493.

35. Jorie Graham, "Some Notes on Silence," in Dow, ed., *19 New American Poets*, 411.

36. The phrase comes from the original title of an essay by Merrill that was later published as "Acoustical Chambers" in McClatchy, ed., *Recitative*, 3–7.

37. T. S. Eliot, *The Waste Land*, in Eliot, *The Complete Poems and Plays*, 39.

38. Heschel, *The Prophets*, 9.

39. Brad Leithauser, "Two Summer Jobs," in Leithauser, *Hundreds of Fire-flies*, 31.

40. Kaplan and Ross, eds., *Yale French Studies*, 3. See also Lefebvre, *Critique of Everyday Life*; de Certeau, *The Practice of Everyday Life*. Laurie Langbauer, in her discussion of the importance of the term *everyday* in cultural studies, observes the frequency with which cultural critics accuse each other of having pinned their hopes on the wrong version of the everyday ("Introduction," in Langbauer, *Novels of Everyday Life*).

41. Sarton, *Journal of a Solitude*, 101.

42. The phrase comes from Merrill's answer to an interviewer's question about the messages he received from the Ouija board. "One didn't want to be merely skeptical or merely credulous. Either way would have left us in reduced circumstances." The phrase can be useful as well in evoking what the everyday means for Merrill (James Merrill, "Interview with Fred Bornhauser," in McClatchy, ed., *Recitative*, 53).

43. Michel de Certeau, "Quotations of Voices" and "A Common Place: Ordinary Language," in de Certeau, *The Practice of Everyday Life*, 160, 12.

44. Ezra Pound, "I Gather the Limbs of Osiris," in Pound, *Selected Prose 1909–1965*, 41.

45. Frank O'Hara, "Personism: A Manifesto," in O'Hara, *The Collected Poems*, 498.

46. Grossman, *The Sighted Singer*, 85.

47. Poirier, *Poetry and Pragmatism*, 14.

48. Bryson, *Looking at the Overlooked*, 84.

49. Donna Haraway, "Ecce Homo, Ain't (Ar'n't) I a Woman, and Inappropriate/d Others: The Human in a Post–Humanist Landscape," in Butler and Scott, eds., *Feminists Theorize the Political*, 96. The term *strategic essentialism* has been suggested to sum up the ways in which subjects can assert a voice while leaving the question of essentialism under erasure. See, for example, Spivak, *In Other Worlds* and *The Post-Colonial Critic*.

50. Elizabeth Bishop, "The End of March," in Bishop, *The Complete Poems*, 179.

51. Bishop, *One Art*, 597.

52. Robert Duncan, "Pages from a Notebook," in Duncan, *A Selected Prose*, 15.

53. Allen Grossman, "Mary Snorak the Cook, Skermo the Gardener, and Jack the Parts Man Provide Dinner for a Wandering Stranger," in Grossman, *The Sighted Singer*, 175–76.

54. Auerbach, *Mimesis*, 22, 151, 154, 184, 554.

55. Wallace Stevens, "Chocorua to Its Neighbor," in Stevens, *The Collected Poems*, 300.

56. Yeats, *A Vision*, 22.

57. Theodore Roethke in Wagoner, ed., *Straw for the Fire*, 174.

58. Robert Duncan, "Pages from a Notebook," in Duncan, *A Selected Prose*, 18.
59. Pinsky, *Poetry and the World*, 58, 55.
60. Robert Lowell, "The Drunken Boat," in Lowell, *Imitations*, 81.
61. John Berryman, "So Long? Stevens," in Berryman, *The Dream Songs*, 238.
62. Wallace Stevens, "Negation," in Stevens, *The Collected Poems*, 97.
63. Sind wir vielleicht *hier,* um zu sagen: Haus, / Brücke, Brunnen, Tor, Krug, Obstbaum, Fenster,—/ höchstens: Säule, Turm . . . (Rilke, *Duino Elegies,* trans. Mitchell, 199–200).
64. Robert Duncan, "The Quotidian," in Duncan, *Ground Work II,* 10.
65. Wallace Stevens, "Large Red Man Reading," in Stevens, *The Collected Poems,* 423–24. Charles Berger has a valuable reading of this poem in his essay on Merrill's trilogy. He writes, "The dead in Stevens' poem are compelled to return in order to hear the poet read from the earthly Book of Life, as if the heavenly volume were found wanting. The dead long for the domestic as well as the vatic, both perhaps being present in the notion of '*Poesis, poesis,* the literal characters.' The dead are spent and need the tones of the living, while the somewhat inhuman author needs them as his truly appreciative audience" (Berger, "Mirabell: Conservative Epic," in Bloom, ed., *Modern Critical Views: James Merrill,* 188).
66. Bryson, *Looking at the Overlooked,* 13–14.
67. Quoted in Kalstone, *Becoming a Poet,* 16.
68. D. H. Lawrence, "The Song of a Man Who Has Come Through," in Lawrence, *The Complete Poems,* 250.
69. There can be a certain satisfaction in restoring some human agency to projects that have disowned it. James E. B. Breslin writes, "The Allen Ginsberg Archives at Columbia University contain about forty pages of worksheets for Part II of 'Howl' and the earliest of these sheets reveal that Ginsberg used the speed of a typewriter as a means to invent, freely, variant epithets for his repeated base word 'Moloch '. . . and that at some point he went back and underlined those phrases that struck him as most effective; many, but not all, of these turn up in the completed poem" (Breslin, *From Modern to Contemporary,* 65). For a historical discussion of the tension between the idea of *furor poeticus* and the idea of revision, see Kerrigan, *The Prophetic Milton.*
70. Cavell, *In Quest of the Ordinary,* 161.
71. Quoted in Grossman, *The Sighted Singer,* 137–38.
72. Pinsky, *The Situation of Poetry,* 140.
73. Scott, *Visions of Presence,* 2, 7.
74. The phrase comes from Robert Duncan's poem "The Ballad of the Enamord Mage," in Duncan, *Selected Poems,* 49.
75. Waggoner, *American Visionary Poetry,* 2, 22.
76. Grossman, *The Sighted Singer.* Hereafter cited in text.
77. Neil Hertz, "The Notion of Blockage in the Literature of the Sublime," in Hertz, *The End of the Line,* 40.
78. Altieri, *Self and Sensibility,* 82, 10–11.
79. Pinsky, *The Situation of Poetry,* 134. Hereafter cited in text.
80. Wordsworth, Preface to *Lyrical Ballads* (1800), in Wordsworth, *The Prose Works,* 1:122.

81. Wallace Stevens, "Effects of Analogy," in Stevens, *The Necessary Angel*, 122.

82. Pinsky, *The Situation of Poetry*, 6.

83. Von Hallberg, *American Poetry and Culture*, 18.

84. Pinsky, *The Situation of Poetry*, 30, 38.

85. Longenbach, *Modern Poetry*, 17.

86. Ammons, *Tape for the Turn of the Year*, 9.

87. Randall Jarrell, "The Age of Criticism," in Jarrell, *Poetry and the Age*, 85.

88. Moffett, *James Merrill*, 174.

Chapter 1. "I felt my guides no longer carried me"

1. T. S. Eliot, *Four Quartets*, in *The Complete Poems and Plays: 1909–1950*, 124–25.

2. "As a Plane Tree by the Water," in Lowell, *Lord Weary's Castle*, 53. Hereafter cited in text as *LWC* (I use the edition that includes *The Mills of the Kavanaughs*). Lowell's other volumes will be cited as follows: *The Mills of the Kavanaughs* as *Mills; Life Studies* as *LS; For the Union Dead* as *FTUD; Imitations; Near the Ocean* as *NTO; Notebook; History; For Lizzie and Harriet* as *FLH; The Dolphin* as *Dolphin; Day by Day* as *DBD*.

3. Von Hallberg, *American Poetry and Culture*, 158.

4. Elizabeth Bishop to Robert Lowell, January 21, 1949, in Bishop, *One Art*, 180 (emphasis in original).

5. Marius Bewley, "The Complex Fate," in London and Boyers, eds., *Robert Lowell*, 6–7.

6. Adrienne Rich, "North American Time," in *Your Native Land*, 33.

7. Merrill, *The Changing Light at Sandover*, 217.

8. Bunyan, *Grace Abounding*, 5.

9. Wallace Stevens, "Academic Discourse at Havana," in Stevens, *The Collected Poems*, 144.

10. John Berryman, "Robert Lowell and Others," in Lowell, *The Freedom of the Poet*, 290, 286.

11. Adrienne Rich, "Sources," in Rich, *Your Native Land*, 16.

12. Wallace Stevens, "The Comedian as the Letter C," in Stevens, *The Collected Poems*, 34.

13. Eliot quoted in Seamus Heaney, "Lowell's Command," in Heaney, *The Government of the Tongue*, 145. In later years, Lowell would simply have rewritten the poem (even if it had already been published) and inserted the "personal reminiscence."

14. Bloom, *Ruin the Sacred Truths*, 54.

15. Letter to Robert Lowell, December 3, 1947, in Bishop, *One Art*, 152.

16. Adrienne Rich, "When We Dead Awaken: Writing as Revision," in Gelpi and Gelpi, eds., *Adrienne Rich's Poetry and Prose*, 171.

17. The word "uncle" is there in part, of course, as a way of preventing the lines from sounding too Yeatsian. Words like "uncle" or "cousin" can change any line of Yeats into a line of early Lowell: "A shudder, Uncle, in the loins engenders there, / the broken wall, the burning roof and tower" or "How can those terrified vague fingers, Cousin, push, / The feathered glory from her loosening thighs?"

18. Wittgenstein, *Philosophical Investigations*, 8.

19. Allen Ginsberg, *Howl*, in Ginsberg, *Collected Poems 1947–1980*, 126.

20. Philip Larkin, "Talking in Bed," in Larkin, *The Whitsun Weddings*, 29.

21. Merrill, *The Changing Light at Sandover*, 25.

22. Adrienne Rich, "Twenty-One Love Poems," in Rich, *The Dream of a Common Language*, 34. (Anne Sexton brings her own kind of wit to the subject, writing a poem called "For My Lover, Returning to His Wife.")

23. The arc of Lowell's career can be seen in the decreasing intensity with which he writes about his grandfather. In *The Dolphin*, he writes,

> This night and the last, I cannot play or sleep,
> thinking of Grandfather in his last poor days.
> Caroline, he had such naked nights,
> and brought his *tortures of the damned* to breakfast—
>
> (57)

By the time he writes *Day by Day*, he can write about his grandfather this way: "My grandfather towered above me, / 'You damned little fool,' / nothing to quote, but for him original" (85).

24. Merrill, *The Changing Light at Sandover*, 14.

25. Longenbach, *Modern Poetry*, 17.

26. James Merrill, interview with J. D. McClatchy, in McClatchy, ed., *Recitative*, 79–80. Merrill's comments come in the context of a discussion of meter:

> Just as I love multiple meanings, I try for contrasts and disruptions of tone. Am I wrong—in the old days didn't the various meters imply different modes or situations, like madness, love, war? It's too late, in any event, to rely very much on meter— look at those gorgeous but imbecile antistrophes and semichoruses in Swinburne or Shelley or whoever. I'm talking from a reader's point of view, you understand. Poets will rediscover as many techniques as they need in order to help them write better. But for a reader who can hardly be trusted to hear the iambics when he opens *The Rape of the Lock*, if anything can fill the void left by these obsolete resources, I'd imagine it would have to be diction or "voice." Voice in its fullest tonal range—not just bel canto or passionate speech.

27. Robert Lowell, "William Carlos Williams," in Lowell, *Collected Prose*, 40.

28. John Ashbery, "Soonest Mended," in Ashbery, *Selected Poems*, 87.

29. Blackmur, *Language as Gesture*, 362.

30. Adrienne Rich, "Ghost of a Chance," in Rich, *Snapshots of a Daughter-in-Law*, 55.

31. Longenbach, *Modern Poetry*, 5. Longenbach writes, "But in the 'Age of Lowell,' as Irvin Ehrenpreis dubbed it, readers found a similar aesthetic 'breakthrough' (often accompanied by a psychological 'breakdown') in the careers of many of Lowell's contemporaries, especially John Berryman and Theodore

Roethke: a poet's status was often measured by the strength of what one reviewer called, apropos of Roethke, 'the famous "breakthrough" that it is the custom to talk about.'"

32. Allen Ginsberg, *Howl*, in Ginsberg, *Collected Poems 1947–1980*, 127.

33. Wallace Stevens, "The Man with the Blue Guitar," in Stevens, *The Collected Poems*, 183.

34. Frank Bidart, in an interview in Hamilton, *Robert Lowell*, 420.

35. Such sentences seem now very much of that time. R. D. Laing, the psychologist, published a book of poetry in 1970 that consists entirely of such sentences. Part of one poem reads:

> Jack realizes that he knows
> Jill does not know
> Jack knows
> he doesn't know
> what she thinks
> he does
> but that this is not what she thinks he knows
>
> Moreover Jack sees that Jill herself knows what Jill
> thinks Jack knows, but that Jill does not realize
> she knows it.
>
> *(Knots, 72)*

36. Adrienne Rich, "After Dark," in Rich, *Necessities of Life*, 29.

37. Adrienne Rich, "For Memory," in Rich, *A Wild Patience*, 21.

38. Quoted in Jonathan Raban, "Introduction," in Raban, *Robert Lowell's Poems*, 13.

39. Bell, *Robert Lowell*, 153.

40. M. M. Bakhtin, "The Problem of Speech Genres," in Bakhtin, *Speech Genres*, 66.

41. Merrill, *The Changing Light at Sandover*, 414.

42. Ibid., 70. This distrust is present in many prophetic poets. Emily Dickinson writes, "Because my Brook is fluent / I know 'tis dry" (*The Complete Poems*, 530).

43. A. R. Ammons, "So I Said I Am Ezra," in Ammons, *Collected Poems 1951–1971*, 1. Jorie Graham, "Self-Portrait as Demeter and Persephone," in Graham, *The End of Beauty*, 59.

44. T. S. Eliot, *Four Quartets*, in Eliot, *The Complete Poems and Plays: 1909–1950*, 144.

45. Theodore Roethke, "In a Dark Time," in Roethke, *The Collected Poems*, 231.

46. See Wordsworth's note to "Ode: Intimations of Immortality from Recollections of Early Childhood," quoted in Wordsworth, *Selected Poems and Prefaces*, 537.

47. Whitman, *Leaves of Grass*, 103.

48. Beckett, *Waiting for Godot*, 20.

49. Vendler, *Part of Nature*, 133.

50. Robert Bly, "Robert Lowell's 'For the Union Dead,'" in London and Boyers, eds., *Robert Lowell*, 76.

51. Theodore Roethke, "In a Dark Time," in Roethke, *The Collected Poems*, 231. Roethke told friends that he wrote this poem in part to outdo the early Lowell.

52. Lowell has his own strategies for dealing with "the recurrent." Poets who write about recurrent events tend to adopt predictable tones. Lowell avoids these "hackneyed" tones because he is drawn to writing about things that happen to happen—they might occur once or thousands of times, but their occurrences are not predictable. "Man and Wife," for example, is about what it feels like to have "a fourth time faced the kingdom of the mad."

53. Seamus Heaney, "Lowell's Command," in Heaney, *The Government of the Tongue*, 145, 137, emphasis added.

54. Heaney, *Station Island*, 93.

55. Bell, *Robert Lowell*, 155.

56. Heaney, "Lowell's Command," *The Government of the Tongue*, 142.

57. Von Hallberg, *American Poetry and Culture*, 149, 150.

58. Wallace Stevens, "Girl in a Nightgown," in Stevens, *The Collected Poems*, 214.

59. Bunyan, *Grace Abounding*, 42.

60. Allen Grossman, "The Poetry of Robert Lowell," in Grossman, *The Long Schoolroom*, 144.

61. Adrienne Rich, "Shooting Script," in Rich, *The Will to Change*, 53.

62. Heaney, *Station Island*, 94.

63. James Merrill, "Interview with Donald Sheehan," in McClatchy, ed., *Recitative*, 33. Merrill is discussing Herbert's poem "Love (III)."

64. Allen Grossman, "The Poetry of Robert Lowell," in Grossman, *The Long Schoolroom*, 144.

65. Robert Lowell, "Interview with Frederick Seidel," in Parkinson, ed., *Robert Lowell*, 31.

66. Wallace Stevens, "Notes towards a Supreme Fiction," in Stevens, *The Collected Poems*, 392.

67. Letter to Stanley Kunitz, April 14, 1972, quoted in Mariani, *Lost Puritan*, 411.

68. Hardwick, in her essay "Jane Carlyle," suggests at first that the marriage with Thomas Carlyle was a kind of marriage between the prophetic and the domestic: "The center of the marriage was Carlyle's life-long, unremitting agony of literary creation, done at home, every pain and despair and hope underfoot. Her genius, in her letters and in her character, was to turn his gigantism into a sort of domestic comedy, made out of bedbugs, carpets, soundproof rooms, and drunken serving girls. Just as the form and style of Carlyle's works set no limits upon themselves, so she sets limits upon everything. His grandiosities are accomplished in the midst of her minute particulars." She then proceeds wonderfully to complicate the picture (*Seduction and Betrayal*, 165).

69. A. R. Ammons, "Gravelly Run," in Ammons, *Collected Poems 1951–1971*, 55.

70. Bunyan, *The Pilgrim's Progress*, 9–10. The pilgrim cannot talk to his family because his family has one relation to time and he has another. There are two ways of imagining the relationship between conversation and time. One is an edenic relationship, in which time does not matter. Milton imagines Eve saying to Adam, "With thee conversing I forget all time." In the fallen version of conversation, time does matter. Fallen accounts of conversation may, however, by specifying a certain amount of time, gesture toward the unfallen version. Yeats, in "A Prayer for My Daughter," brooding about his hopes for his daughter, tells the reader that "for an hour I have walked and prayed." Herbert imagines conversation with God as "the six-day's world transposing in an hour." The notion of "an hour" of talk haunts twentieth-century versions of happiness. The notion becomes, as the century progresses, more and more sardonic in its expression. T. S. Eliot writes, in *The Waste Land*, "We stopped in the colonnade, / And went on in the sunlight, into the Hofgarten, / And drank coffee, and talked for an hour." Adrienne Rich, in her poem "A Marriage in the 'Sixties," writes, "Two strangers, thrust for life upon a rock, / may have at last the perfect hour of talk / that language aches for" (*Snapshots of a Daughter-in-Law*, 46). The dream of "an hour" of conversation survives, outside poetry, in the psychoanalytic session. Lowell will have none of it. He doesn't believe in the very rich hours of other poets. "We haggle at cross-purposes an hour," he writes (*Dolphin*, 22). His unit of secular time is the day, not the hour. The poetic hour implies an hour of what is sometimes called "quality time" and twenty-three hours of neglect. Furthermore, the notion of "an hour" seems dishonest. In one of the poems in *The Dolphin*, Lowell listens to someone saying, "W. B. Yeats was not a gent, / he didn't tell the truth: *and for an hour, / I've walked and prayed*—who prays exactly an hour?" (67).

71. Merrill, *The Changing Light at Sandover*, 51.

72. Emily Dickinson, "The Only News I know," no. 827 in Dickinson, *The Collected Poems*, 401.

73. Robert Lowell, "Interview with Frederick Seidel," in Parkinson, ed., *Robert Lowell*, 25.

74. Adrienne Rich also writes frequently about the relationship between the physical and the political. But for her the relationship can be graceful, epiphanic. In "The Blue Ghazals," she writes, "*The moment when a feeling enters the body* / is political. This touch is political" (*The Will to Change*, 24). See Joanne Fiet Diehl, "'Of Woman Born': Adrienne Rich and the Feminist Sublime," in Gelpi and Gelpi, eds., *Adrienne Rich's Poetry and Prose*, 419.

75. Lyotard, *The Inhuman*, 7.

76. Some poets—particularly prophetic poets—will offer an aesthetics of clumsiness triumphantly as if here at last the human might be discoverable. They sentimentalize clumsiness. Lowell has, instead, Yeats's vision, in "A Dialogue of Self and Soul," of being "Brought face to face with his own clumsiness." In a poem called "The Book of Wisdom," Lowell is someone "destroying what I lurch against, / not with anger, but unwieldy feet" (*Notebook*, 97). When he writes, at the end of *The Dolphin*, "my eyes have seen what my hand did," the reader feels that the missing adverb might be "clumsily."

77. Vendler, *Part of Nature*, 138.

78. Allen Grossman, "The Poetry of Robert Lowell," in Grossman, *The Long Schoolroom*, 148–49.
79. Adrienne Rich "Transcendental Etude," in Rich, *The Dream of a Common Language*, 74.

Chapter 2. "Both ways is the only way I want it"

1. Ammons, *Tape for the Turn of the Year*, 161. Hereafter cited in text as *TT*. Other Ammons poems (unless otherwise indicated) will be taken from *Collected Poems 1951–1971*, cited as *CP*.
2. Wallace Stevens, "The Comedian as the Letter C," in Stevens, *The Collected Poems*, 30.
3. Walker, *Bardic Ethos*, 173. The phrase comes from his discussion of Williams's *Paterson*.
4. Quoted in Pinsky, *Poetry and the World*, 55.
5. Roland Barthes, "The Grain of the Voice," in Barthes, *Image—Music—Text*, 181.
6. Allen Grossman, "Of the Great House," in Grossman, *Of the Great House*, 6.
7. R. S. Thomas, "Night and Morning," in Thomas, *Selected Poems*, 12.
8. Geoffrey Hill, "Genesis," in Hill, *New and Collected Poems*, 3. "Genesis" is the first poem in his first book. The poem continues:

> And first I brought the sea to bear
> Upon the dead weight of the land;
> And the waves flourished at my prayer,
> The rivers spawned their sand.

Sometimes the poet sends out another figure, a surrogate for the prophetic figure. Hopkins's windhover, for example, "rebuff[s] the big wind."
9. William Blake, "Preludium" to *America a Prophecy*, in *William Blake, The Complete Poetry and Prose*, 52.
10. Helen Vendler, "Ammons Berryman Cummings," in Vendler, *Part of Nature*, 330.
11. John Hollander, "On the Calendar," in Hollander, *Spectral Emanations*, 43. Probably the most famous contemporary poem about refusing to dominate a landscape is Mark Strand's "Keeping Things Whole." Strand's poem, with its "reasons for moving," is less anguished about, more reconciled to, those reasons than Ammons's poems on the same subject.
12. Allen Grossman, "The Lecture," in Grossman, *The Woman on the Bridge*, 79.
13. In the later poems, we hear about the unremarkable things the prophetic figure does, the "long uninteresting walks" he takes. By the time Ammons returns to the mannerism of the suspended "I," he has a sense of humor about it; he knows we recognize it: "Momentous and trivial, I / walk along the lake cliff" (*Lake Effect Country*, 10).
14. John Keats, "Endymion," in Keats, *The Complete Poems*, 124, emphasis added.
15. Elizabeth Bishop, "At the Fishhouses," in Bishop, *The Complete Poems*, 65, emphasis added.
16. A. R. Ammons, *Pray without Ceasing*, in Ammons, *Selected Longer Poems*, 1.

17. John Ashbery, "In the American Grain," in Bloom, ed., *Modern Critical Views: A. R. Ammons*, 58.

18. Blanchot, *The Space of Literature*, 24.

19. Robert Frost, "The Most of It," in Frost, *Collected Poems, Prose and Plays*, 307.

20. Ammons's phrase must come, in some sense, from William Carlos Williams's lines:

> All along the road the reddish
> purplish, forked, upstanding, twiggy
> stuff of bushes and small trees
> with dead, brown leaves under them
> leafless vines—
> ("Spring and All," in Williams,
> *Selected Poems*, 39)

21. Rilke, *Duino Elegies*, trans. Leishman and Spender, 73.

22. Dante Gabriel Rossetti, "The Woodspurge," in Rossetti, *The Poetical Works*, 297–98.

23. Elizabeth Bishop quoted in Kalstone, *Becoming a Poet*, 16.

24. Whitman, "Salut au Monde!" in Whitman, *Leaves of Grass*, 293.

25. John Ruskin, *Modern Painters*, in Ruskin, *The Works of John Ruskin*, 134.

26. Elizabeth Bishop quoted in Kalstone, *Becoming a Poet*, 16.

27. A. R. Ammons, *Essay on Poetics*, in Ammons, *Selected Longer Poems*, 33.

28. Blanchot, *The Space of Literature*, 29.

29. T. S. Eliot, *Four Quartets*, in Eliot, *The Complete Poems and Plays*, 126.

30. For a fascinating discussion of the uses of humility as a poetic strategy, see Merrin, *An Enabling Humility*. Moore's essay is quoted on page 8.

31. A. R. Ammons, "Ridge Farm," in Ammons, *Sumerian Vistas*, 4.

32. A. R. Ammons, "The Constant," in Ammons, *Northfield Poems*, 9.

33. Rilke, *Duino Elegies*, trans. Leishman and Spender, 73.

34. Theodore Roethke, "In a Dark Time," in Roethke, *The Collected Poems*, 231.

35. Grossman, *The Bright Nails*, 73.

36. Wallace Stevens, "Notes toward a Supreme Fiction," in Stevens, *The Collected Poems*, 387.

37. T. S. Eliot, "Tradition and the Individual Talent," in Eliot, *Selected Prose*, 40.

38. John Milton, "Lycidas," in Milton, *Complete Poems and Major Prose*, 125.

39. Frank O'Hara, "Poem," in O'Hara, *The Collected Poems*, 282.

40. The sense that one might be redeemed by the complexity and richness of these phrases finds one of its most powerful expressions outside of poetry in Tobias Wolff's short story "Bullet in the Brain," in which the hero, at the moment of his death, remembers a moment of pure pleasure from his childhood. He and some friends are playing baseball. Someone asks a boy from Mississippi what position he wants to play: "'Short stop,' the boy says. 'Short's the best position they is.' Anders turns and looks at him. He wants to hear Coyle's cousin repeat what he's just said, but he knows better than to ask. The others will think he's being a jerk, ragging the kid for his grammar. But that isn't it, not at all—it's that Anders is strangely roused, elated, by those final two words, their pure unexpectedness and their music. He takes the field in a trance, repeating them to himself." Anders's final memory is of

himself as a boy chanting "They is, they is, they is" (in Wolff, *The Night in Question*, 205–6).

41. T. S. Eliot, *The Waste Land*, in Eliot, *The Complete Poems and Plays*, 41.
42. Hart Crane, *The Bridge*, in Crane, *The Complete Poems*, 109.
43. T. S. Eliot, "Ash-Wednesday," in Eliot, *The Complete Poems and Plays*, 61.
44. A. R. Ammons, *Essay on Poetics*, in Ammons, *Selected Longer Poems*, 44.
45. T. S. Eliot, "Ash-Wednesday," in Eliot, *The Complete Poems and Plays*, 60.
46. Ibid., 63.
47. David Bromwich, "Elizabeth Bishop's Dream-Houses," in Bloom, ed., *Modern Critical Views: Elizabeth Bishop*, 160.
48. Robert Lowell, "The Severed Head," in Lowell, *For the Union Dead*, 52.
49. De Certeau, *The Practice of Everyday Life*, xxii.
50. Robinson Jeffers, "Continent's End," in Jeffers, *Selected Poems*, 4.
51. In a later poem, Ammons (for whom "scope" is an important word) uses the word "scopy." This *y*-ending playfulness is also found in Whitman, who, in "Song of Myself," writes, "The laughing-gull scoots by the slappy shore" (*Leaves of Grass*, 61). This playfulness may be more American than British. Tennyson's *y* endings come from the Augustans ("the finny tribe," etc.). But British poets seem less willing to use it in a comic way; they may be less able to be *momentarily* whimsical: whimsy seems to exert more of a tug on their work. A poet like Stevie Smith seems, in some of her poems, to want to be less whimsical than she is. It may be because of the force of this pull that poets who foreground a terminology (like Yeats) resist trying out, even for a moment, a playful, slangy version of that vocabulary. It is as if there were no safe place between "perne in a gyre" and "gyre and gimble in the wabe." Ammons can be playful because he has, I think, no deep commitment to his vocabulary; he doesn't really identify himself with its fortunes. As one critic points out, "Ammons can flourish a vocabulary of 'saliences' and 'suasions,' motions, forces and forms in mountain, wind, brook, and tree, with no missionary intent to substitute his vocabulary for ours" (R. S. Flint, "The Natural Man," in Bloom, ed., *Modern Critical Views: A. R. Ammons*, 181). Sometimes he even shares with us his decision-making process. In "The Ridge Farm," he writes, "minutiae is a fussy word / matrix is too perfect" (in Ammons, *Sumerian Vistas*, 36).
52. T. S. Eliot, *Four Quartets*, in Eliot, *The Complete Poems and Plays*, 125, 128.
53. John Ashbery, "Soonest Mended," in Ashbery, *Selected Poems*, 87.
54. Spiegelman, *The Didactic Muse*, 116.
55. A. R. Ammons, "Weight," in Ammons, *Diversifications*, 39.
56. A. R. Ammons, *Extremes and Moderations*, in Ammons, *Selected Longer Poems*, 54.
57. Blanchot, *The Space of Literature*, 25.
58. Wagoner, ed., *Straw for the Fire*, 84.
59. Wallace Stevens, "The Comedian as the Letter C," in Stevens, *The Collected Poems*, 36.
60. A. R. Ammons, *Essay on Poetics*, in Ammons, *Selected Longer Poems*, 39.
61. William Wordsworth, "Ode to Duty," in Wordsworth, *Selected Poems and Prefaces*, 185.
62. Koestenbaum, "Logorrhea," 102–7.

63. Blanchot, *The Space of Literature*, 27.

64. A. R. Ammons, "Event: Corrective: Cure," 1983 interview with *Poetry Miscellany*, reprinted in Bloom, ed., *Modern Critical Views: A. R. Ammons*, 219.

65. A. R. Ammons, "Ridge Farm," in Ammons, *Sumerian Vistas*, 15–16.

Chapter 3. "Some kind of workable relation"

1. Merrill, *The Changing Light at Sandover*, 20. Hereafter cited in text as *CLS*. References to Merrill's other books will be cited in text as follows: *Collected Poems* as *CP*, and *A Different Person* as *DP*.

2. Merrill, *A Different Person*, 128–29.

3. Helen Sword refers to "the kind of rushing, eruptive intensity that is perhaps most frequently associated with prophetic discourse." See also her statement that "prophetic utterances can come in many forms; generally, however, one expects some show of physical or emotional intensity, a booming or a raving" (*Engendering Inspiration*, 14, 146).

4. For a complete discussion of this cosmology of the poem, see Moffett, *James Merrill*; Yenser, *The Consuming Myth*; and Polito, *A Reader's Guide*.

5. Moffett, *James Merrill*, 179.

6. Yenser, *The Consuming Myth*, 317.

7. Poss, "'What Underlies,'" 354–58; Stitt, "Knowledge, Belief, and Bubblegum," 699–700, 704–7; Donoghue, "What the Ouija Board Said," 11, 20; Harmon, "The Metaphors," 29–41; Bedient, "Books Considered," 22–23. For an overview of the critical reaction to the trilogy, see Guy Rotella, "Introduction," in Rotella, ed., *Critical Essays*. The reviews to which I refer are garnered from Rotella's introduction.

8. For a valuable discussion of interruption in the trilogy, see "The Sacred Books of James Merrill," in Spiegelman, *The Didactic Muse*.

9. Moffett, *James Merrill*, 26.

10. Richard Howard, "James Merrill," in Bloom, ed., *Modern Critical Views: James Merrill*, 10.

11. Helen Vendler, "James Merrill," in Vendler, *The Music of What Happens*, 353.

12. Robert Duncan, "Among My Friends Love Is a Great Sorrow," in Duncan, *Selected Poems*, 5.

13. Duncan's example is fascinating in this context because of his sense that he had given the poetry of everydayness a fair try but had it rejected—by William Carlos Williams himself. Duncan's *Domestic Scenes* contained poems with such titles as "No ideas but in things," "Breakfast," "Bus Fare," and "Lunch with Buns." The poem "Breakfast" begins with the line "I shall awake to the ennui of breakfast foods." In a 1969 interview with George Bowering and Robert Hogg, he remembered,

> When I wrote *Domestic Scenes* I kept making these poems I could send to Williams as a little homage or something; they were filled with domestic scenes, filled with things around like buses, and paraphernalia of the contemporary world. I sent them off to Williams and, oh, what a blast back I got back about it; there was

no American language in there. Of course I have never written
in American language, nor did I ever in my whole life. But that
letter was in itself an inspiration, because then with vengeance I
wrote *Medieval Scenes*. I mean I just decided to write: okay, no
American language.

Duncan's version of the kind of "idling" found in Ammons and Merrill
might be found in his line "We move as dragons in the lethargy." He is a poet, I
think, who never broke free of this "lethargy," and that may be in part because
the "medieval" or the "mystical" does not offer the poet any opportunities for
creating a tension with the everyday. Duncan turned his back on the everyday
and never developed a way of writing with which he could return to the everyday and strike some sparks. See Robert Duncan, "The Albigenses," *Medieval
Scenes*, in Duncan, *Selected Poems*, 20.

14. James Merrill, "An Interview with Donald Sheehan," in McClatchy, ed.,
Recitative, 26.

15. Von Hallberg, *American Poetry and Culture*, 104.

16. Yenser, in an interesting discussion, connects Merrill's patience to
Rilke's example (*The Consuming Myth*, 19).

17. J. D. McClatchy, "On Water Street," in Lehman and Berger, eds., *James
Merrill*, 66.

18. Shetley, *After the Death of Poetry*, 22.

19. James Merrill, "Elizabeth Bishop (1911–1979)," in McClatchy, ed., *Recitative*, 121.

20. Labrie, *James Merrill*, 62.

21. Jorie Graham, "The Geese," in Graham, *Hybrids of Plants and of Ghosts*, 38.

22. The sentence comes in a discussion of Thoreau and Emerson. Cavell
writes, "There is nothing beyond the succession of each and every day; and
grasping a day, accepting the everyday, the ordinary, is not a given but a task.
This is also why Emerson says, 'Give me insight into today, and you may have
the antique and future worlds.' His words have the rhetoric of a bargain, or a
prayer, as in 'Give us this day our daily bread'; it is not something to take for
granted" (*In Quest of the Ordinary*, 171).

23. Labrie, *James Merrill*, 53.

24. Kalstone, *Five Temperaments*, 89.

25. Guy Rotella, "Introduction," in Rotella, ed., *Critical Essays*, 2.

26. Wallace Stevens, "The Wind Shifts," in Stevens, *The Collected Poems of
Wallace Stevens*, 83.

27. James Merrill, "On Wallace Stevens' Centenary," in McClatchy, ed., *Recitative*, 118–19.

28. James Merrill, "An Interview with Ashley Brown," in McClatchy, ed.,
Recitative, 44.

29. Moffett, *James Merrill*, 16.

30. James Merrill, "An Interview with J. D. McClatchy," in McClatchy, ed.,
Recitative, 70.

31. Sword, "James Merrill, Sylvia Plath and the Poetics of Ouija," 554. Hereafter cited in text as "James Merrill."

32. See Leslie Brisman, "Merrill's Yeats," in Bloom, ed., *Modern Critical Views: James Merrill*, 189–98.

33. Yeats, *A Vision*, 23.

34. H.D., according to Sword, "conversed by means of a tapping table with a group of slain RAF pilots who spelled out dire predictions of nuclear disasters." Sword cites Friedman, *Psyche Reborn*, 173–75.

35. Ellmann, *The Identity of Yeats*, xi.

36. William Dean Howells, quoted in Kaplan, *Walt Whitman*, 27.

37. Sword offers an interesting comparison of Plath's and Merrill's experiments with the Ouija board. I disagree, however, with her conclusion that Plath and Merrill "transport the age-old prophetic mode toward the cynical, subversive, ludic realm of the postmodern" ("James Merrill, Sylvia Plath and the Poetics of Ouija," 570).

38. Robert Lowell, "Dora Markus," in Lowell, *Imitations*, 107.

39. Walt Whitman, "Me Imperturbe," in Whitman, *Leaves of Grass*, 173.

40. Yeats, *A Vision*, 84.

41. Von Hallberg, *American Poetry and Culture*, 106.

42. James Merrill, "An Interview with Donald Sheehan," in McClatchy, ed., *Recitative*, 28.

43. Ibid.

44. Blodgett, ed., *An 1855–56 Notebook*, 5–7, quoted in Kaplan, *Walt Whitman*, 206. Thoreau also wrote, "In thy journals let there never be a jest!" (Torrey and Hallen, eds., *The Journal of Henry D. Thoreau*, quoted in Buell, *Literary Transcendentalism*, 275).

45. Moffett, *James Merrill*, 159.

46. Helen Vendler, "James Merrill," in Vendler, *Part of Nature*, 217.

47. David Lehman, "Elemental Bravery: The Unity of James Merrill's Poetry," in Lehman and Berger, eds., *James Merrill*, 307n.

48. Gardner, *Discovering Ourselves in Whitman*, 171.

49. De Certeau, *The Practice of Everyday Life*, 160.

50. Yeats, *A Vision*, 9. Hereafter cited in text.

51. Frye, *Anatomy of Criticism*, 5.

52. Wallace Stevens, "The Relations between Poetry and Painting," in Stevens, *The Necessary Angel*, 171.

53. R. P. Blackmur, "The Later Poetry of W. B. Yeats," in Blackmur, *Language as Gesture*, 81.

54. Wallace Stevens, "The Relations between Poetry and Painting," in Stevens, *The Necessary Angel*, 168.

55. James Merrill, "On Literary Tradition," in McClatchy, ed., *Recitative*, 9.

56. Helen Vendler, "James Merrill," in Vendler, *Part of Nature*, 97.

57. Sarton, *Journal of a Solitude*, 159.

58. Allen Ginsberg, "When the Mode of the Music Changes the Walls of the City Shake," in Allen and Tallman, eds., *The Poetics of the New American Poetry*, 327.

59. Dante, *Dante's Inferno*, 260. Susan Mitchell translates: "And so from bridge to bridge we went, talking / but not of things I mean to sing to all / the world; and talking brought us to the top" (*Dante's Inferno: Translations by 20 Contemporary Poets*, 96).

60. "Whitman's aesthetics . . . is a profound account of the common, and it imposes the requirement that the common be expanded until it fills out the real" (Philip Fisher, "Democratic Social Space: Whitman, Melville, and the Promise of American Transparency," in Fisher, ed., *The New American Studies*, 77).

61. Thom Gunn, "A Heroic Enterprise," *San Francisco Review of Books* (August 1979), in Polito, *A Reader's Guide*, 59.

62. Rilke, *The Selected Poetry*, 151.

63. Grossman, *Against Our Vanishing*, 70.

64. Rilke, *The Selected Poetry*, 155.

65. R. P. Blackmur, "The Later Poetry of W. B. Yeats," in Blackmur, *Language as Gesture*, 92.

66. Milton, *Paradise Lost*, in *Complete Poems and Major Prose*, 212.

67. Moffett, *James Merrill*, 171.

68. Guy Rotella, "Introduction," in Rotella, ed., *Critical Essays*, 12.

69. Helen Vendler, "James Merrill," in Vendler, *The Music of What Happens*, 351.

70. Drucilla Cornell, *The Philosophy of the Limit*, 13.

71. Lee Zimmerman, "Against Apocalypse: Politics and James Merrill's 'The Changing Light at Sandover,'" in Rotella, ed., *Critical Essays*, 187.

72. James Merrill, "An Interview with J. D. McClatchy," in McClatchy, ed., *Recitative*, 79.

Chapter 4. "This is what is possible"

1. Ammons, *Garbage*, 13.

2. The phrase is Jorie Graham's in "Some Notes on Silence," in Dow, ed., *19 New American Poets*, 415.

3. Rich, *An Atlas of the Difficult World*, 3. Hereafter cited in text as *ADW*. References to Rich's other books will be cited in the text as follows: *Snapshots of a Daughter-in-Law* as *SDL*; *Necessities of Life* as *NOL*; *Leaflets*; *The Will to Change* as *TWC*; *Diving into the Wreck* as *DITW*; *Poems: Selected and New (1950–1974)* as *PSN*; *The Dream of a Common Language* as *DCL*; *A Wild Patience Has Taken Me This Far* as *AWP*; *Your Native Land, Your Life* as *YNL*; *Time's Power* as *TP*; *Collected Early Poems 1950–1970* as *CEP*. Page references from *A Change of World* and *The Diamond Cutters* are taken from *Collected Early Poems*.

4. Jarrell, *Kipling, Auden and Co.*, 264.

5. Adrienne Rich, "When We Dead Awaken: Writing as Re-Vision," in Gelpi and Gelpi, eds., *Adrienne Rich's Poetry and Prose*, 171.

6. Ralph Waldo Emerson, "Self Reliance," in Whicher, ed., *Selections from Ralph Waldo Emerson*, 147.

7. Vendler, *Soul Says*, 215.

8. Wallace Stevens, "Anecdote of the Jar," in Stevens, *The Collected Poems*, 76.

9. Elizabeth Bishop, "Poem," in Bishop, *The Complete Poems*, 176.

10. Merrill, *The Changing Light at Sandover*, 107.

11. Adrienne Rich, "When We Dead Awaken: Writing as Re-Vision," in Gelpi and Gelpi, eds., *Adrienne Rich's Poetry and Prose*, 169, 171.

12. Ammons, *Tape for the Turn of the Year*, 144.

13. Jorie Graham, "Some Notes on Silence," in Dow, ed., *19 New American Poets*, 409.

14. Ralph Waldo Emerson, "Nature," in Whicher, ed., *Selections from Ralph Waldo Emerson*, 24.

15. Sylvia Plath, "Cut," in Plath, *Collected Poems*, 235.

16. Kalstone, *Five Temperaments*, 130.

17. Merrill, *The Changing Light at Sandover*, 110.

18. Audre Lorde, "Thaw," in Lorde, *The Marvelous Arithmetics of Distance*, 10.

19. James Merrill, "An Interview with Fred Bornhauser," in McClatchy, ed., *Recitative*, 59.

20. T. S. Eliot, *The Waste Land*, in Eliot, *The Complete Poems and Plays*, 48.

21. e. e. cummings, "may i feel said he," in cummings, *Poems 1923-1954*, 288.

22. Audre Lorde, "Poetry Is Not a Luxury," in Lorde, *Sister Outsider*, quoted as epigraph in Rich, *What Is Found There*.

23. Adrienne Rich, "Vesuvius at Home: The Power of Emily Dickinson," in Gelpi and Gelpi, eds., *Adrienne Rich's Poetry and Prose*, 179.

24. Adrienne Rich, "The Genesis of 'Yom Kippur 1984,'" Gelpi and Gelpi, eds., *Adrienne Rich's Poetry and Prose*, 254.

25. Jorie Graham, "To the Reader," in Graham, *The End of Beauty*, 23.

26. Jorie Graham, quoted in Thomas Gardner, *Regions of Unlikeness*.

27. Willard Spiegelman, "Driving to the Limits of the City of Words: The Poetry of Adrienne Rich," in Spiegelman, *The Didactic Muse*, 162.

28. A. R. Ammons, "Small Song," in Ammons, *Collected Poems*, 222.

29. Wallace Stevens, "Nuances of a Theme by Williams," in Stevens, *The Collected Poems*, 18.

30. H.D., "The Walls Do Not Fall," in H.D., *Trilogy*, 58.

31. Quoted in Gelpi and Gelpi, eds., *Adrienne Rich's Poetry and Prose*, 30.

32. See the discussion in Sword, *Engendering Inspiration*.

33. Merrill, *The Changing Light at Sandover*, 360.

34. Yenser, *The Consuming Myth*, 294.

35. Heschel, *The Prophets*, 9, 10.

36. Lowell, *The Dolphin*, 21.

37. Wallace Stevens, "Of Modern Poetry," in Stevens, *The Collected Poems*, 239-40.

38. Robert Lowell, "Our Afterlife II," in Lowell, *Day by Day*, 23.

39. Walt Whitman, "Starting from Paumanok," in Whitman, *Leaves of Grass*, 184.

40. Audre Lorde, "Echoes," in Lorde, *The Marvelous Arithmetics of Distance*, 7.

41. Kramer, *The Prophetic Tradition*, 25.

42. Couser, *American Autobiography*, 201.

43. Sword, *Engendering Inspiration*, 120.

44. Adrienne Rich, "The Genesis of 'Yom Kippur 1984,'" in Gelpi and Gelpi, eds., *Adrienne Rich's Poetry and Prose*, 255.

Conclusion

1. Louise Glück, "The Chicago Train," in Glück, *The First Four Books of Poems*, 5.

2. Louise Glück, "Thanksgiving," in Glück, *The First Four Books of Poems*, 9.

3. Louise Glück, "The Wound," in Glück, *The First Four Books of Poems*, 14.

4. Louise Glück, "World Breaking Apart," in Glück, *The First Four Books of Poems*, 145.

5. Louise Glück, "Grandmother in the Garden," in Glück, *The First Four Books of Poems*, 22.

6. Louise Glück, "Tango," in Glück, *The First Four Books of Poems*, 123.

7. Upton, *The Muse of Abandonment*, 136.

8. Louise Glück, "Education of the Poet," in Glück, *Proofs and Theories*, 5.

9. Louise Glück, "Portland, 1968," in Glück, *The First Four Books of Poems*, 128.

10. Vendler, *The Given and the Made*, 12.

11. Louise Glück, "The Untrustworthy Speaker," in Glück, *Ararat*, 34.

12. Louise Glück, "On T. S. Eliot," in Glück, *Proofs and Theories*, 19, 20.

13. Louise Glück, "Portrait," in Glück, *The First Four Books of Poems*, 122.

14. Jorie Graham, "The Geese," in Graham, *Hybrids of Plants and of Ghosts*, 38–39.

15. Wallace Stevens, "Sunday Morning," in Stevens, *The Collected Poems of Wallace Stevens*, 70.

16. Adrienne Rich, "Planetarium," in Rich, *The Will to Change*, 14.

17. Robert Lowell, "Mr. Edwards and the Spider," in Lowell, *Lord Weary's Castle*, 64–65.

18. Robert Lowell, "Skunk Hour," in Lowell, *Life Studies*, 90.

19. Wallace Stevens, "The Men That Are Falling," in Stevens, *The Collected Poems of Wallace Stevens*, 188.

20. Jorie Graham, "Self-Portrait as Apollo and Daphne," in Graham, *The End of Beauty*, 32.

21. Jorie Graham, "Still Life with Window and Fish," in Graham, *Erosion*, 32.

Bibliography

Allen, Donald, and Warren Taliman, eds. *The Poetics of the New American Poetry.* New York: Grove Press, 1973.

Alter, Robert. *The Art of Biblical Prophecy.* New York: Basic Books, 1985.

Altieri, Charles. *Enlarging the Temple: New Directions in American Poetry during the 1960s.* Lewisburg, Pa.: Bucknell University Press, 1979.

————. *Self and Sensibility in Contemporary American Poetry.* New York: Cambridge University Press, 1984.

Ammons, A. R. *Collected Poems 1951–1971.* New York: W. W. Norton and Co., 1972.

————. *Diversifications.* New York: W. W. Norton and Co., 1975.

————. *Garbage.* New York: W. W. Norton and Co., 1993.

————. *Lake Effect Country.* New York: W. W. Norton and Co., 1983.

————. *Northfield Poems.* Ithaca, N.Y.: Cornell University Press, 1966.

————. *Selected Longer Poems.* New York: W. W. Norton and Co., 1980.

————. *Sumerian Vistas: Poems.* New York: W. W. Norton and Co., 1987.

————. *Tape for the Turn of the Year.* New York: W. W. Norton and Co., 1965.

Ashbery, John. *Selected Poems.* New York: Viking Press, 1985.

————. *Self-Portrait in a Convex Mirror.* Harmondsworth: Penguin Books, 1976.

Auden, W. H. *The Collected Poems.* Ed. Edward Mendelson. New York: Vintage International, 1991.

Auerbach, Erich. *Mimesis: The Representation of Reality in Western Literature.* Princeton, N.J.: Princeton University Press, 1953.

Bakhtin, M. M. *Speech Genres and Other Late Essays.* Ed. Caryl Emerson and Michael Holquist. Austin: University of Texas Press, 1986.

Barthes, Roland. *Image—Music—Text.* New York: Hill and Wang, 1977.

Beckett, Samuel. *Waiting for Godot.* New York: Grove Weidenfeld, 1954.

Bedient, Calvin. "Books Considered." *New Republic,* June 5, 1976: 22–23.

Bell, Vereen. *Robert Lowell: Nihilist as Hero.* Cambridge, Mass.: Harvard University Press, 1983.

Bentley, G. E., ed. *Blake Records.* New York: Oxford University Press, 1969.

Berryman, John. *The Dream Songs.* New York: Farrar, Straus, and Giroux, 1969.

————. *The Freedom of the Poet.* New York: Farrar, Straus, and Giroux, 1976.

Bishop, Elizabeth. *The Complete Poems 1927–1979.* New York: Farrar, Straus, and Giroux, 1986.

————. *One Art: Elizabeth Bishop's Letters.* Ed. Robert Giroux. New York: Farrar, Straus, and Giroux, 1994.

Blackmur, R. P. *Language as Gesture: Essays in Poetry.* New York: Columbia University Press, 1952.

Blake, William. *The Complete Poetry and Prose of William Blake.* Ed. David V. Erdman. New York: Anchor Press, 1988.

Blanchot, Maurice. *The Space of Literature.* Trans. Ann Smock. Lincoln: University of Nebraska Press, 1982.

Blasing, Mutlu Konuk. *American Poetry: The Rhetoric of Its Forms.* New Haven, Conn.: Yale University Press, 1987.

Blodgett, Harold W., ed. *An 1855–56 Notebook toward the Second Edition of "Leaves of Grass."* Carbondale: University of Illinois Press, 1959.

Bloom, Harold. *Ruin the Sacred Truths: Poetry and Belief from the Bible to the Present.* Cambridge, Mass.: Harvard University Press, 1989.

————, ed. *Modern Critical Views: A. R. Ammons.* New York: Chelsea House Publishers, 1986.

————, ed. *Modern Critical Views: Elizabeth Bishop.* New York: Chelsea House Publishers, 1985.

————, ed. *Modern Critical Views: James Merrill.* New York: Chelsea House Publishers, 1985.

Bowering, George, and Robert Hogg. *Robert Duncan: An Interview, April 19, 1969.* A Beaver Kosmos Folio. Toronto: The Coach House Press, 1971.

Breslin, James E. B. *From Modern to Contemporary: American Poetry 1945–1965.* Cambridge, Mass.: Harvard University Press, 1983.

Bryson, Norman. *Looking at the Overlooked: Four Essays on Still Life Painting.* Cambridge, Mass.: Harvard University Press, 1990.

Buell, Lawrence. *Literary Transcendentalism: Style and Vision in the American Renaissance.* Ithaca, N.Y.: Cornell University Press, 1973.

Bunyan, John. *Grace Abounding to the Chief of Sinners.* New York: Everyman's Library, 1963.

————. *The Pilgrim's Progress.* New York: Oxford University Press, 1984.

Butler, Judith, and Joan W. Scott, eds. *Feminists Theorize the Political.* New York: Routledge, 1992.

Cavell, Stanley. *In Quest of the Ordinary: Lines of Skepticism and Romanticism.* Chicago: University of Chicago Press, 1988.

Cohn, Norman. *The Pursuit of the Millennium: Revolutionary Millenarians and Mystical Anarchists of the Middle Ages.* New York: Oxford University Press, 1957.

Cornell, Drucilla. *The Philosophy of the Limit.* New York: Routledge, Chapman and Hall, 1992.

Couser, G. Thomas. *American Autobiography: The Prophetic Mode.* Amherst: University of Massachusetts Press, 1979.

Crane, Hart. *The Complete Poems and Selected Letters.* Ed. Brom Weber. New York: Liveright, 1966.

cummings, e. e. *Poems 1923–1954*. New York: Harcourt Brace and World, 1968.
Dante. *Dante's Inferno*. Trans. John Sinclair. New York: Oxford University Press, 1977.
———. *Dante's Inferno: Translations by 20 Contemporary Poets*. Ed. Daniel Halpern. New York: Ecco Press, 1993.
Darsey, James. *The Prophetic Tradition and Radical Rhetoric in America*. New York: New York University Press, 1997.
de Certeau, Michel. *The Practice of Everyday Life*. Trans. Steven Rendall. Berkeley: University of California Press, 1984.
Derrida, Jacques. *Of Spirit: Derrida and the Question*. Trans. Geoffrey Bennington and Rachel Bowlby. Chicago: University of Chicago Press, 1989.
Des Pres, Terrence. *Praises and Dispraises: Poetry and Politics, the Twentieth Century*. New York: Viking Press, 1988.
Dickinson, Emily. *The Complete Poems of Emily Dickinson*. Ed. Thomas H. Johnson. Boston: Little, Brown, and Co., 1960.
Donoghue, Denis. "What the Ouija Board Said." *New York Times Book Review*, June 15, 1980: 11, 20.
Doreski, William. *The Modern Voice in American Poetry*. Gainesville: University Press of Florida, 1995.
Dow, Philip, ed. *19 New American Poets of the Golden Gate*. San Diego: Harcourt Brace Jovanovich, 1984.
Duncan, Robert. *Ground Work II: In the Dark*. New York: New Directions, 1987.
———. *Selected Poems*. Ed. Robert J. Bertholf. New York: New Directions, 1993.
———. *A Selected Prose*. Ed. Robert J. Bertholf. New York: New Directions, 1995.
Eliot, T. S. *The Complete Poems and Plays: 1909–1950*. New York: Harcourt Brace and World, 1952.
———. *Selected Prose of T. S. Eliot*. Ed. Frank Kermode. New York: Farrar, Straus, and Giroux, 1975.
Ellmann, Richard. *The Identity of Yeats*. New York: Oxford University Press, 1964.
Erdman, David V. *Blake, Prophet against Empire*. Princeton, N.J.: Princeton University Press, 1954.
Esterhammer, Angela. *Creating States: Studies in the Performative Language of John Milton and William Blake*. Toronto: University of Toronto Press, 1994.
Fisch, Harold. *Poetry with a Purpose: Biblical Poetics and Interpretation*. Bloomington: Indiana University Press, 1988.
Fisher, Philip, ed. *The New American Studies: Essays from Representations*. Berkeley: University of California Press, 1991.
Fletcher, Angus. *The Prophetic Moment: An Essay on Spenser*. Chicago: University of Chicago Press, 1971.
Friedman, Susan Stanford. *Psyche Reborn: The Emergence of H.D.* Bloomington: Indiana University Press, 1981.
Frost, Robert. *Collected Poems, Prose and Plays*. New York: Library of America, 1995.
Frye, Northrop. *Anatomy of Criticism*. Princeton, N.J.: Princeton University Press, 1957.

Gardner, Thomas. *Discovering Ourselves in Whitman: The Contemporary American Long Poem*. Urbana: University of Illinois Press, 1989.

———. *Regions of Unlikeness: Explaining Contemporary Poetry*. Lincoln: University of Nebraska Press, 1999.

Gelpi, Barbara Charlesworth, and Albert Gelpi, eds. *Adrienne Rich's Poetry and Prose*. New York: W. W. Norton and Co., 1993.

Ginsberg, Allen. *Collected Poems 1947–1980*. New York: Harper and Row, 1984.

Glück, Louise. *Ararat*. Hopewell, N.J.: Ecco Press, 1990.

———. *The First Four Books of Poems*. Hopewell, N.J.: Ecco Press, 1995.

———. *Proofs and Theories: Essays on Poetry*. Hopewell, N.J.: Ecco Press, 1994.

Graham, Jorie. *The End of Beauty*. New York: Ecco Press, 1987.

———. *Erosion*. Princeton, N.J.: Princeton University Press, 1983.

———. *Hybrids of Plants and of Ghosts*. Princeton, N.J.: Princeton University Press, 1980.

Grossman, Allen. *Against Our Vanishing: Winter Conversations with Allen Grossman on the Theory and Practice of Poetry*. Boston: Rowan Tree Press, 1981.

———. *The Bright Nails Scattered on the Ground*. New York: New Directions, 1986.

———. *The Long Schoolroom: Lessons in the Bitter Logic of the Poetic Principle*. Ann Arbor: University of Michigan Press, 1997.

———. *Of the Great House: A Book of Poems*. New York: New Directions, 1982.

———. *The Sighted Singer: Two Works on Poetry for Readers and Writers*. Baltimore, Md.: Johns Hopkins University Press, 1992.

———. *The Woman on the Bridge over the Chicago River*. New York: New Directions, 1979.

Hamilton, Ian. *Robert Lowell: A Biography*. New York: Random House, 1982.

Hardwick, Elizabeth. *Seduction and Betrayal: Women and Literature*. New York: Vintage Books, 1975.

Harmon, William. "The Metaphors and Metamorphoses of M." *Parnassus* 8 (1980): 29–41.

H.D. *Trilogy*. New York: New Directions, 1973.

Heaney, Seamus. *The Government of the Tongue: Selected Prose 1978–1987*. New York: Farrar, Straus, and Giroux, 1988.

———. *Station Island*. New York: Farrar, Straus, and Giroux, 1985.

Hertz, Neil. *The End of the Line: Essays on Psychoanalysis and the Sublime*. New York: Columbia University Press, 1985.

Heschel, Abraham. *The Prophets: An Introduction*. New York: Harper and Row, 1962.

Hill, Christopher. *Milton and the English Revolution*. Harmondsworth: Penguin Books, 1977.

———. *A Tinker and a Poor Man: John Bunyan and His Church, 1628–1688*. New York: Alfred A. Knopf, 1989.

Hill, Geoffrey. *New and Collected Poems 1952–1992*. Boston: Houghton Mifflin Co., 1994.

Hollander, John. *Spectral Emanations and Other Poems*. New York: Athenaeum Press, 1978.

Hopkins, James K. *A Woman to Deliver Her People: Joanna Southcott and English Millenarianism in an Era of Revolution*. Austin: University of Texas Press, 1982.

Hughes, Langston. *The Collected Poems of Langston Hughes.* Ed. Arnold Ramper-
     sad. New York: Alfred A. Knopf, 1994.
James, William. *The Varieties of Religious Experience.* New York: Modern Library,
     1999.
Jarrell, Randall. *The Complete Poems.* New York: Farrar, Straus, and Giroux, 1975.
————. *Kipling, Auden and Co.* New York: Farrar, Straus, and Giroux, 1962.
————. *Poetry and the Age.* New York: Vintage Books, 1959.
Jeffers, Robinson. *Selected Poems.* New York: Vintage Books, 1965.
Kalstone, David. *Becoming a Poet: Elizabeth Bishop with Marianne Moore and Rob-
     ert Lowell.* New York: Farrar, Straus, and Giroux, 1989.
————. *Five Temperaments.* New York: Oxford University Press, 1977.
Kaplan, Alice, and Kristin Ross, eds. *Yale French Studies* 73 (1987).
Kaplan, Justin. *Walt Whitman: A Life.* New York: Simon and Schuster, 1980.
Keats, John. *The Complete Poems.* Ed. John Barnard. Harmondsworth: Penguin
     Books, 1987.
Kerrigan, William. *The Prophetic Milton.* Charlottesville: University Press of Vir-
     ginia, 1974.
Koestenbaum, Wayne. "Logorrhea." *Southwest Review* (winter 1994): 102–7.
Kramer, Aaron. *The Prophetic Tradition in American Poetry 1835–1900.* Ruther-
     ford, N.J.: Fairleigh Dickinson Press, 1968.
Kugel, James, ed. *Poetry and Prophecy: The Beginnings of a Literary Tradition.*
     Ithaca, N.Y.: Cornell University Press, 1990.
Labrie, Ross. *James Merrill.* Boston: Twayne, 1982.
Laing, R. D. *Knots.* New York: Pantheon Books, 1970.
Langbauer, Laurie. *Novels of Everyday Life: The Series in English Fiction: 1850–
     1930.* Ithaca, N.Y.: Cornell University Press, 1999.
Larkin, Philip. *Collected Poems.* Ed. Anthony Thwaite. New York: Farrar, Straus,
     and Giroux, 1989.
————. *The Whitsun Weddings.* New York: Random House, 1964.
Lawrence, D. H. *The Complete Poems of D. H. Lawrence.* New York: Viking Press,
     1964.
Lefebvre, Henri. *Critique of Everyday Life.* Trans. John Moore. New York: Verso,
     1991.
Lehman, David, and Charles Berger, eds. *James Merrill: Essays in Criticism.*
     Ithaca, N.Y.: Cornell University Press, 1983.
Leithauser, Brad. *Hundreds of Fireflies.* New York: Alfred A. Knopf, 1982.
London, Michael, and Robert Boyers, eds. *Robert Lowell: A Portrait of the Artist in
     His Time.* New York: David Lewis Publishers, 1970.
Longenbach, James. *Modern Poetry after Modernism.* New York: Oxford Univer-
     sity Press, 1997.
Lorde, Audre. *The Marvelous Arithmetics of Distance: Poems 1987–1992.* New
     York: W. W. Norton and Co., 1993.
————. *Sister Outsider.* Freedom, Calif.: Crossing Press, 1984.
Lowell, Robert. *Collected Prose.* New York: Farrar, Straus, and Giroux, 1987.
————. *Day by Day.* New York: Farrar, Straus, and Giroux, 1977.
————. *The Dolphin.* New York: Farrar, Straus, and Giroux, 1973.
————. *For Lizzie and Harriet.* New York: Farrar, Straus, and Giroux, 1973.
————. *For the Union Dead.* New York: Union Press, 1972.

————. *History*. New York: Farrar, Straus, and Giroux, 1973.

————. *Imitations*. New York: Farrar, Straus, and Giroux, 1969.

————. *Life Studies* and *For the Union Dead*. New York: Farrar, Straus, and Giroux, 1972.

————. *Lord Weary's Castle* and *The Mills of the Kavanaughs*. New York: Harcourt Brace Jovanovice, 1978.

————. *Near the Ocean*. New York: Farrar, Straus, and Giroux, 1967.

————. *Notebook*. New York: Farrar, Straus, and Giroux, 1970.

————. *Selected Poems*. New York: Farrar, Straus, and Giroux, 1991.

Lyotard, Jean-François. *The Inhuman: Reflections on Time*. Trans. Geoffrey Bennington and Rachel Bowlby. Stanford, Calif.: Stanford University Press, 1988.

Mariani, Paul. *Lost Puritan: A Life of Robert Lowell*. New York: W. W. Norton and Co., 1994.

Marks, Herbert. "On Prophetic Stammering." *Yale Journal of Criticism* (fall 1987): 1–20.

Martin, Wendy. *An American Triptych: Anne Bradstreet, Emily Dickinson, Adrienne Rich*. Chapel Hill: University of North Carolina Press, 1984.

Martz, Louis. *Many Gods and Many Voices: The Role of the Prophet in English and American Modernism*. Columbia: University of Missouri Press, 1998.

McClatchy, J. D., ed. *Recitative: Prose by James Merrill*. San Francisco: North Point Press, 1986.

Merrill, James. *The Changing Light at Sandover: A Poem*. New York: Alfred A. Knopf, 1992.

————. *Collected Poems*. Eds. J. D. McClatchy and Stephen Yenser. New York: Alfred A. Knopf, 2001.

————. *A Different Person: A Memoir*. New York: Alfred A. Knopf, 1993.

Merrin, Jeredith. *An Enabling Humility: Marianne Moore, Elizabeth Bishop, and the Uses of Tradition*. New Brunswick, N.J.: Rutgers University Press, 1990.

Milton, John. *Complete Poems and Major Prose*. Ed. Merritt Y. Hughes. New York: Macmillan, 1957.

Moffett, Judith. *James Merrill: An Introduction to the Poetry*. New York: Columbia University Press, 1984.

Munk, Linda. *The Trivial Sublime: Theology and American Poetics*. New York: St. Martin's Press, 1992.

Nelson, Raymond. *Kenneth Patchen and American Mysticism*. Chapel Hill: University of North Carolina Press, 1984.

Norbrook, David. *Poetry and Politics in the English Renaissance*. London: Routledge and Kegan Paul, 1984.

O'Hara, Frank. *The Collected Poems of Frank O'Hara*. Ed. Donald Allen. New York: Alfred A. Knopf, 1971.

Oliver, Mary. *New and Selected Poems*. Boston: Beacon Press, 1992.

Parkinson, Thomas, ed. *Robert Lowell: A Collection of Critical Essays*. Englewood Cliffs, N.J.: Prentice-Hall, 1968.

Perloff, Marjorie. *Wittgenstein's Ladder: Poetic Language and the Strangeness of the Ordinary*. Chicago: University of Chicago Press, 1996.

Pinsky, Robert. *Poetry and the World*. New York: Ecco Press, 1988.

————. *The Situation of Poetry: Contemporary Poetry and Its Traditions*. Princeton, N.J.: Princeton University Press, 1976.

Plath, Sylvia. *Collected Poems*. New York: Harper and Row, 1992.

Poirier, Richard. *Poetry and Pragmatism*. Cambridge, Mass.: Harvard University Press, 1984.

Polito, Robert. *A Reader's Guide to James Merrill's "The Changing Light at Sandover."* Ann Arbor: University of Michigan Press, 1994.

Poss, Stanley. "'What Underlies These Odd / Inseminations by Psycho-Roulette.'" *Western Humanities Review* 30 (1976): 354–58.

Pound, Ezra. *The Cantos*. New York: New Directions, 1986.

————. *Selected Prose 1909–1965*. Ed. William Cookson. London: Faber and Faber, 1973.

Raban, Jonathan. *Robert Lowell's Poems: A Selection*. London: Faber and Faber, 1974.

Rich, Adrienne. *An Atlas of the Difficult World*. New York: W. W. Norton and Co., 1991.

————. *A Change of World*. New Haven, Conn.: Yale University Press, 1951.

————. *The Collected Early Poems*. New York: W. W. Norton and Co., 1993.

————. *The Diamond Cutters*. New York: Harper and Brothers Publishers, 1955.

————. *Diving into the Wreck*. New York: W. W. Norton and Co., 1973.

————. *The Dream of a Common Language*. New York: W. W. Norton and Co., 1978.

————. *Leaflets*. New York: W. W. Norton and Co., 1969.

————. *Necessities of Life*. New York: W. W. Norton and Co., 1966.

————. *Poems: Selected and New (1950–1974)*. New York: W. W. Norton and Co., 1975.

————. *Snapshots of a Daughter-in-Law*. New York: W. W. Norton and Co., 1963.

————. *Time's Power*. New York: W. W. Norton and Co., 1989.

————. *What Is Found There: Notebooks on Poetry and Politics*. New York: W. W. Norton and Co., 1993.

————. *A Wild Patience Has Taken Me This Far*. New York: W. W. Norton and Co., 1981.

————. *The Will to Change: Poems 1968–1970*. New York: W. W. Norton and Co., 1971.

————. *Your Native Land, Your Life*. New York: W. W. Norton and Co., 1986.

Rilke, Rainer Maria. *Duino Elegies*. Trans. J. B. Leishman and Stephen Spender. New York: W. W. Norton and Co., 1939.

————. *Duino Elegies*. Trans. Stephen Mitchell. New York: Vintage Books, 1984.

————. *Poetry of Rainer Maria Rilke*. Trans. M. D. Herter Norton. New York: W. W. Norton and Co., 1938.

————. *The Selected Poetry of Rainer Maria Rilke*. Trans. Stephen Mitchell. New York: Vintage Books, 1989.

Roethke, Theodore. *The Collected Poems*. New York: Doubleday Anchor, 1975.

Rossetti, Dante Gabriel. *The Poetical Works of Dante Gabriel Rossetti*. London: A. L. Burt Co., 1890.

Rotella, Guy, ed. *Critical Essays on James Merrill*. New York: G. K. Hall and Co., 1996.

Ruskin, John. *The Works of John Ruskin.* Ed. E. T. Cook and Alexander Wedder-burn. London: George Allen and Unwin, 1910.

Sarton, May. *Journal of a Solitude.* New York: W. W. Norton and Co., 1973.

Schor, Naomi. *Reading in Detail: Aesthetics and the Feminine.* New York: Rout-ledge, Chapman and Hall, 1989.

Scott, Nathan. *Visions of Presence in Modern American Poetry.* Baltimore, Md.: Johns Hopkins University Press, 1993.

Shetley, Vernon. *After the Death of Poetry: Poet and Audience in Contemporary America.* Durham, N.C.: Duke University Press, 1993.

Spiegelman, Willard. *The Didactic Muse: Scenes of Instruction in Contemporary American Poetry.* Princeton, N.J.: Princeton University Press, 1989.

Spivak, Gayatri Chakravorty. *In Other Worlds: Essays in Cultural Politics.* New York: Methuen, 1987.

————. *The Post-Colonial Critic: Interviews, Strategies, Dialogues.* New York: Routledge, Chapman and Hall, 1990.

Staples, Hugh. *Robert Lowell: The First Twenty Years.* London: Faber and Faber, 1962.

Stevens, Wallace. *The Collected Poems of Wallace Stevens.* New York: Alfred A. Knopf, 1976.

————. *The Necessary Angel: Essays on Reality and the Imagination.* New York: Vintage Books, 1951.

Stevenson, Anne. *Elizabeth Bishop.* New York: Twayne, 1966.

Stitt, Peter. "Knowledge, Belief, and Bubblegum." *Georgia Review* 33 (1979): 699–700, 704–7.

Swatos, William H., Jr., ed. *Gender and Religion.* New Brunswick, N.J.: Transac-tion Publishers, 1994.

Sword, Helen. *Engendering Inspiration: Visionary Strategies in Rilke, Lawrence and H.D.* Ann Arbor: University of Michigan Press, 1995.

————. "James Merrill, Sylvia Plath and the Poetics of Ouija." *American Liter-ature* 66, no. 3 (September 1994): 554–71.

Taithe, Bertrand, and Tim Thornton. *Prophecy: The Power of Inspired Language in History 1300–2000.* Gloucestershire: Sutton Publishing Limited, 1997.

Thomas, M. Wynn. *The Lunar Light of Whitman's Poetry.* Cambridge, Mass.: Har-vard University Press, 1987.

Thomas, R. S. *Selected Poems: 1946–1968.* Newcastle upon Tyne: Bloodaxe Books, 1986.

Torrey, Bradford, and Francis H. Hallen, eds. *The Journal of Henry D. Thoreau.* Vol. 3. Boston: Houghton Mifflin Co., 1906.

Trible, Phyllis. *God and the Rhetoric of Sexuality: Overtures to Biblical Theology.* Philadelphia: Fortress Press, 1978.

Upton, Lee. *The Muse of Abandonment: Origin, Identity, Mastery in Five American Poets.* Lewisburg, Pa.: Bucknell University Press, 1998.

Vendler, Helen. *The Given and the Made: Strategies of Poetic Redefinition.* Cam-bridge, Mass.: Harvard University Press, 1995.

————. *The Music of What Happens: Poems, Poets, Critics.* Cambridge, Mass.: Harvard University Press, 1988.

————. *Part of Nature, Part of Us: Modern American Poets.* Cambridge, Mass.: Harvard University Press, 1980.

————. *Soul Says: On Recent Poetry.* Cambridge, Mass.: Harvard University Press, 1995.

Von Hallberg, Robert. *American Poetry and Culture: 1945–1980.* Cambridge, Mass.: Harvard University Press, 1985.

Von Rad, Gerhard. *The Message of the Prophets.* New York: Harper and Row, 1967.

Waggoner, Hyatt. *American Visionary Poetry.* Baton Rouge: Louisiana State University Press, 1982.

Wagoner, David, ed. *Straw for the Fire: From the Notebooks of Theodore Roethke 1943–1963.* Garden City, N.Y.: Anchor Books, 1974.

Walker, Jeffrey. *Bardic Ethos and the American Epic Poem: Whitman, Pound, Crane, Williams, Olson.* Baton Rouge: Louisiana State University Press, 1989.

Warren, Robert Penn. *The Collected Poems of Robert Penn Warren.* Ed. John Burt. Baton Rouge: Louisiana State University Press, 1998.

Watkin, E. I. *Poets and Mystics.* London: Sheed and Ward, 1953.

Whicher, Stephen, ed. *Selections from Ralph Waldo Emerson.* Boston: Houghton Mifflin Co., 1957.

Whitman, Walt. *Leaves of Grass.* New York: Library of America, 1992.

Williams, William Carlos. *The Collected Poems 1909–1939.* Ed. A. Walton Litz and Christopher MacGowan. New York: New Directions, 1986.

————. *Selected Poems.* Ed. Charles Tomlinson. New York: New Directions, 1985.

Williamson, Alan. *Eloquence and Mere Life: Essays on the Art of Poetry.* Ann Arbor: University of Michigan Press, 1994.

————. *Pity the Monsters: The Political Vision of Robert Lowell.* New Haven, Conn.: Yale University Press, 1974.

Wittgenstein, Ludwig. *Philosophical Investigations.* Trans. G. E. M. Anscombe. Englewood Cliffs, N.J.: Prentice-Hall, 1958.

Wittreich, Joseph Anthony. *Visionary Poetics: Milton's Tradition and His Legacy.* San Marino, Calif.: Henry E. Huntington Library, 1979.

Wojcik, Jan, and Raymond-Jean Frontain. *Poetic Prophecy in Western Literature.* Rutherford, N.J.: Fairleigh Dickinson Press, 1984.

Wolff, Tobias. *The Night in Question.* New York: Vintage Contemporaries, 1996.

Wordsworth, William. *The Prose Works of William Wordsworth.* Vol. 1. Ed. W. J. B. Owen and Jane Worthington Smyser. Oxford: Clarendon Press, 1974.

————. *Selected Poems and Prefaces.* Ed. Jack Stillinger. Boston: Houghton Mifflin Co., 1965.

Yeats, William Butler. *A Vision.* New York: Collier Books, 1977.

Yenser, Stephen. *Circle to Circle: The Poetry of Robert Lowell.* Berkeley: University of California Press, 1975.

————. *The Consuming Myth: The Work of James Merrill.* Cambridge, Mass.: Harvard University Press, 1987.

Index

Abstraction, 38, 194–96; in Graham's works, 194–95, 244; readers and, 195; in Rich's works, 194–95
Aiken, Conrad, 124
Allegory, in Graham's works, 244–45
Altieri, Charles, 9, 43
Ammons, A. R., 12; accuracy as concern of, 100, 107–8, 110–11, 135–36; adjectives, restricted use of, 102–3; assignments and the everyday voice, 112–14; "Batsto," 109–10; "Bees Stopped," 106–8, 111; boredom and, 124; career of, 230–31; childhood in works of, 119–21; commencement in works of, 103–4, 106, 111, 127; compulsion and prophetic voice, 121–22; the concrete in works of, 131; constraints and freedom, 122–23; conversation in works of, 46, 124–26; "Coon Song," 123; correspondences and, 113–14; "Corsons Inlet," 125–28; countermotions in, 46, 99, 105–6, 124, 128, 137; delay and, 135–36; diction of, 126–27; directional chaos in works, 105–6; "Doxology," 115; "Driving Through," 104; "Essay on Poetics," 135; everyday voice, 111–14; false speech and, 200; formal experimentation, 111, 126, 128, 133–34; gaze and observation, 107, 110–11, 126; "Gravelly Run," 113–14; happiness and, 125–26; "Hardweed Path Going," 119–21; "He Held Radical Light," 128–31; the human in works of, 125–26; humility and, 111–12; "I Came Upon a Plateau," 104–15; "I Came in a Dark Woods Upon," 108; "Identity," 108; as interminable, 136–37; "Interval," 108; inventiveness of, 132–33; isolation or solitude in works of, 88, 89, 127–28; journal form used by, 111; juxtapositions in works, 122; landscape in works of, 101–3, 109–10, 118–19; length as limitation, 133–34; "Mansion," 117; motion as preoccupation of, 105–6; the ordinary in works of, 134; paralysis in works of, 105; place names, 109; pressure on language, 114–17, 120, 121–22; prophetic voice and, 34, 88, 89, 100–111, 117–19, 121–22, 127, 130–31, 133, 230; provisionality in works of, 126–27; "Rack," 101, 118; readers and, 115, 123, 128; Rich and, 207; "Ridge Farm," 112–13, 137; "Saliences," 128; "The Sap Is Gone Out of the Trees," 111, 121; scientific voice in works of, 46–47, 100, 106–7, 135–36; scope of project, 46–47; the

DATE D